PRAISE FOR

D0869075

"The funniest book I have read in a long time. This is a genuine good read."

—Harold Lederman, HBO Sports

"Not since Carl Hiassen's *Tourist Season* debut has there been a novel with such superb comic timing and laugh-out-loud lines."

—Ken Bruen, Shamus Award-winning author of *The Guards*

"An Everyman with a big heart and a wicked jab, Duffy Dombrowski may well be the new Spenser. I can't wait for Round Two."

—Marcus Sakey, author of *The Blade Itself*

"*On the Ropes* is sly, funny, irreverent, and one hell of a good time. Read it or be sorry you didn't. It's just that simple."

—Laurien Berenson, author of *Hounded to Death*

"It'll put you down for the count with laughter. Tom Schreck is a contender for funniest author working in the crime genre today."

—William Kent Krueger, author of *Thunder Bay*

"If you've ever despised your boss or secretly wanted to save the world, *On the Ropes* is a novel you'll devour."

—Steve Farhood, Showtime Boxing

"Duffy Dombrowski—a loose-cannon social worker and a boxer—has a lot more heart than is healthy for a guy. Give him an orphaned sidekick who hasn't been housebroken (literally), jam them into the middle of a sinister murder plot that packs a surprising wallop, and you've got a winning combination."

—Lee Charles Kelley, author of *Like a Dog With a Bone*

"One of my favorite writers…Can't wait for Duffy's next adventure."

—Nancy Claus, *Westchester Magazine*

"It won't take long to realize Duffy doesn't run to type…occasionally over the top, but warmhearted, tough, funny Duffy makes a promising debut."

—*Kirkus Reviews*

"Pure delight. The sharp-edged humor peppers you like a boxing master's jab, and the poignant undercurrent of theme delivers with the power of a left hook. Duffy Dombrowski is a major new contender in the world of private eye fiction."

—Michael A. Black, author of *A Killing Frost* and *A Final Judgment*

"Get ready to rumble with lovable losers, misguided misfits, and a disgustingly adorable dog."

—Michael "Let's Get Ready To Rumble" Buffer, the Voice of Champions

"This is one hell of a debut novel. *On the Ropes* is easily one of the best five books I've read this year."

—Jon Jordan, *Crimespree Magazine*

"If you like underdogs, colorful characters, a fighter who never quits and a canine with more bite and heart than Jake LaMotta—a unanimous winner."

—Teddy Atlas, ESPN Boxing Analyst

ON THE ROPES

BOOKS BY TOM SCHRECK

TOM SCHRECK

ON THE ROPES

DOWN&OUT
BOOKS

Down & Out Books
3959 Van Dyke Road, Suite 265
Lutz, FL 33558
DownAndOutBooks.com

The characters and events in this book are fictitious. Any similarity to real persons, living or dead, is coincidental and not intended by the author.

Cover design by Pixelstudio

ISBN: 1-64396-280-9
ISBN-13: 978-1-64396-280-1

For Sue, the Alpha and
Annette, the Matriarch
To Hound Farms and White Jaguars

What's the point of being Irish if you can't be stupid?
—Billy Conn

He can run but he can't hide.
—Joe Louis

I ain't got no dog-proof ass.
—Sonny Liston

1

"Hey Duff—did you hear what the Polack mom asked her pregnant daughter?" Sam from the business office said.

"Mornin', Sam," I said.

"Are you sure it's yours?" Sam laughed himself back to his cubicle.

With the last name Dombrowski, I've heard every imaginable Polack joke and people like Sam made sure I kept up-to-date. I hate the routines, but I especially wasn't in the mood on this particular Monday morning.

I am a caseworker at Jewish Unified Services in Crawford, a city in upstate New York, about fifty miles from New York City. Crawford is one of those northeastern cities that goes back to the time of the Revolutionary War. Years ago, it was a city with strong ethnic neighborhoods, the Irish, the Polish, the Jewish, the Italian, and the African American. Today, the neighborhoods are a shell of what they used to be, as most of the old families have participated in the white-flight to the suburbs. Much like a smaller version of New York City, the actual city confines are made up largely of poorer families of black and Latino extraction.

The other thing about Crawford that distinguishes it from other cities is the wind. Something about the valley formed by the Hudson and the Catskills causes it to be the windiest city in the country. I read something one time about Crawford being actually three times as windy as Chicago. The wind is a bizarre source of city pride—the city limit signs have this humanized cartoon of the wind, an old man with puffed-out cheeks, next to the "Welcome to Crawford," and McDonough High, my alma mater and the city's public high school, has the nickname "The Mighty Wind." To this day, opposing fans chant "Break the Wind" at football games.

I handle a caseload of about seventy-five clients at the clinic. They use our agency for everything from addiction counseling to parenting skills to anger management. Most of our clients live on welfare and whatever benefits they can get out of the government.

I'm not a Monday type of guy anyway, but this one was going to be an exceptional pain in the ass. I had a nine-thirty meeting with my boss, the clinical director, Claudia Michelin. Claudia is one of the educated, heartless bureaucrats that live to be in control of other people. She was well suited for the gig. She's the one who decides who gets thrown out of treatment for missing sessions or for not getting in line and doing everything she asks in just the right way. Claudia was not turning down offers from Victoria's Secret, either. She had hit her maximum density a long time ago, and I'm figuring she carried almost three hundred pounds on her considerable six-foot frame. In fact, I'm not sure if she was actually a blood relative, but she bore a striking resemblance to her namesake, the Michelin Man tire guy. She had one of those bushy, curly-haired perms that mercifully went out of style around the demise of Studio 54. The Michelin Woman had a scowl permanently affixed to her face, and she had this tendency to shift her eyes back and forth instead of looking right at you.

She also loves the control of being the boss to me and the other case managers here. Since she took over eighteen months ago, she's done everything she could to get me to quit or, preferably, to set up a future firing. Of course, I don't help myself with some of the things I try to get away with. For one, I despise paperwork and avoid it, procrastinate it, and—I'll tell you honestly—I lie about doing it. Michelin lives for it.

My extracurricular activities can sort of get in the way too. I'm a part-time professional fighter, the type that's known in the trade as a professional opponent. Promoters call me to fight up-and-coming prospects because they know I'll lose but not look horrible in the process. I split a lot of my local, small fights, but the money is in fighting the prospects that I don't have a chance of beating. As a heavyweight, I can make ten grand getting my ass kicked by some ex-Olympian on his way up looking for an easy win.

Unfortunately, I scammed some time off a month ago. I got Rudy, the doc who hangs out down at the gym, and who also happens to be my landlord, to get me a temporary disability for a condition known as fibromyalgia. It's a mostly improvable ailment of the joints that needs plenty of bed rest to get over. I was out of the office for three weeks with it, and it was all on the up and up because Rudy signed off on it.

The problem was, I was fighting on the undercard of a fight that was featured on ESPN. Not every bout on a fight card makes TV, usually only a main event and one or two of the better fights.

I'm almost never on TV. On this particular night, I was positioned in an off-TV fight scheduled to go on after the TV bouts went off. It's what's known as a "walkout" because that's exactly what all the fans are doing, but because there were three knockouts on the scheduled TV fights they moved my fight to the live telecast. There I was with my diagnosis of fibromyalgia fighting ten rounds on national television. At least I had the decency to get knocked out.

The Michelin Woman found no humor in this at all. Fortunately, because I had a doctor signing off on it, there was nothing she could do. What she could do was step up her Nazi-like review of my records, which were behind back to when Jimmy Carter was in office. I've already received "informal counseling" and "a verbal warning," which, strangely enough, I learned, comes in typed memo form. Today, I realized I was about to get the formal written warning, which is different from the written verbal warning, not by the fact that it is written, but rather by its content. In it was verbiage that amounted to saying my ass was grass and Claudia was the mower. It was an official documentation of the last straw.

I made my way to her office, dreading every step. Not because I feared getting written up—that's happened enough throughout my life—but because I would have to listen to Claudia go through her supervisory coaching. We both knew she hated my guts, but even in reprimanding me, she went by the book, encouraging me and telling me how much she needed me to improve. It was procedure for a supervisor to present disciplinary warnings in a positive coaching manner. It would feel better if she just called me a fuckin' asshole.

"Duffy, do you know why we're meeting today?" she asked.

"I'm guessing it's not to give me a raise," I said.

"This is not a time to get flip. I have some real concerns with your work. I want you to succeed here at Jewish Unified Services but I need you to keep your records up to regulations. It isn't fair to the clients," she said.

She always threw the part in about the clients and I hated it. My clients don't give a rat's ass about their files, unless it interferes with them getting benefits, and I always made sure that those reports were done. Even when I scammed disabilities to get out of work, I kept check of my caseload, calling the folks who really needed help and making sure they were all right— which was, by the way, against regulations.

"Claudia, can't we just get on with it?" I said, knowing it would piss her off because I wasn't scared and I was taking back some of her control.

"See, it's that type of attitude that is self-defeating to you. I need you to take a look at some of the issues that get in your way," she said.

This was the psychobabble that she employed that made her come off like a robot. The words were meaningless jargon and she hid behind them because she felt it gave her some sort of power. It was one of the reasons I liked hanging out at boxing gyms. If someone there didn't like you, they told you to fuck off and tried to take your head off. It was clear and unambiguous.

"Look, Claudia, do you have something for me to sign? I realize you would prefer it if I began to shake, soil myself, and weep out of fear, but I just don't have the energy this morning," I said.

"As a matter of fact, I do. This is a written warning. Today is August 16. If in four weeks your paperwork isn't caught up, you will be terminated," she said, sliding a formal-looking memo across the desk.

"Why don't you just can me now? There's no way I can get my files caught up in a month," I said.

"That's up to you, Duffy," she said.

I left the office realizing that in one month I'd be back in her office giving her the satisfaction of firing me. That was the worst part of it. I've been fired plenty of times; I just didn't want to give her the satisfaction. I should have figured today was going to suck. It's the anniversary of Elvis's death and every year something unlucky has happened on this date. I've been in car crashes, been knocked out three times, and even caught a case of crabs on August 16. Giving Michelin the pleasure of firing me would be worse than the crabs. The crabs I had were friendlier, easier to get along with, and, frankly, better looking.

It was the start of a great week.

2

I thought I'd take a look at the files Claudia was bitching about. I had just sat down when I realized I'd be in a much better frame of mind if I got some nutrition in me. Being a human service agency filled with overweight, issue-filled professionals, there were always large quantities of simple carbohydrated, fat-laden treats in arm's reach. I once thought that if you could somehow deep fry sugar and salt you could keep many social workers happy for a very long time.

This particular morning I was in luck. There was an in-service in the multipurpose room with an outside trainer on "Multicultural Nonverbal Communication." Technically, I was supposed to attend, but Trina the office manager always hooked me up with the attendance sign-in sheet just before she turned it in to Claudia. I figured being on the attendance sheet entitled me to a couple of donuts and a cup of coffee.

Just before the trainer started his exercise—breaking the room into discussion groups of threes to make nonverbal multicultural hand puppets—I slipped out of the multipurpose room and headed to my often little-purpose cubicle. Before I left, I waved to the trainer who clearly never quite disengaged from the sixties. He was bald on top of his head but maintained a brownish-gray ponytail. He had on army fatigues with lots of pockets and his gut hung over the top of them. The best part was his sandals with the separate loop for his fat and hairy big toe. Topping off the look was a toenail on the hairy big toe that looked like it was last trimmed right around the time Richie Havens left the stage at Woodstock.

I grabbed a stack of about ten files, took a sip of the lukewarm, brownish, cardboard-tasting coffee, and looked at the first file. I opened Eli Allison's chart and noticed that the last session note I charted was eight weeks ago. Eli is a fifty-one-year-old black guy who keeps getting arrested after he's had a couple of Olde Englishes, the potent malt liquor found in drug stores and gas stations in ghetto neighborhoods. With that added alcohol content, two forty-ounce bottles are equivalent to more than a six-pack of regular beer.

Eli's last arrest came six months ago when, after his customary two or three OEs, he asked the Pakistani owner of the Mobil station where he got the forties if he and his wife wanted to have some sort of three-way sexual Twister game. When Mr. Endou declined, Eli got so pissed he knocked over the Slurpee machine and took off all his clothes. The judge released him into counseling.

While I was trying to make up some notes for the four times I met with Eli in the last eight weeks, the phone rang. It was Mike Kelley, my cop friend.

"Duff, you better get over to Walanda's house," said Kelley. "We have to arrest her and she's losing it. Worse than I've ever seen her."

Walanda is a thirty-four-year-old crackhead with a dash of schizophrenia. She has a tendency to get loud and more than a bit wacky.

"Why are you arresting her?" I asked.

"Outstanding warrant for shoplifting. The DA is having one of his crackdowns. She'll probably have to do thirty days."

"She stole some hair extensions from the Dollarama, for cris-sakes."

"Duff, we can talk about it later," Kelley said. "Right now I could use some help."

Kelley was good people. He wasn't a bleeding heart, but if he could do his job just as easily by being decent, he did. He called me when he was involved in an arrest with someone on my caseload and he needed a calming influence. I filed Eli's and the rest of the unopened charts and headed to Walanda's house. She lived in Jefferson Hill, about two and a half miles from the office. It is the kind of neighborhood where you're better off not stopping when you hit a red light. I was in a hurry so I didn't plan on stopping anyway.

In the early part of the century, "The Hill," as it is known, was home to the city's blue-collar Irish and Polish. The city went through its own version of the Newark riots in the late sixties and the early seventies, suffering through the growing pains of the civil rights movement. Today there's only a handful of old Irish and Polish on The Hill, the ones too old, poor, or stubborn to leave.

My '76 Eldorado convertible's V-8 had plenty of power, but it was a tad temperamental. Just the same, to me there was no finer automobile in the world than this car. Burnt orange body, velour seats, and a deep-pile orange carpet, it was a little heaven here on earth. The eight-track player made it tough to get new music, but that didn't matter. I only listen to Elvis and while he was alive, so were eight-tracks.

The King was getting into his second chorus of hunka-hunkas when I came up on Walanda's house. It was a mess, as only ghetto houses paid for by welfare can be. The screen door on the porch was banging off the wall, three of her four front windows were broken, and there was a washing machine on what there was of a front lawn.

Walanda was rolling around with Kelley near the washer, screaming a slew of expletives that would've made Nixon blush. Kelley's uniform was covered in dirt and gravel and his hat had found its way to the middle of the street. At a less than solid two hundred thirty pounds, Walanda was no easy restraint, at least not at first. Her stamina wasn't the greatest, even when she was getting wacky, so she would tire before long.

I'd seen her go off before, but something was really getting to her this morning. She kept screaming something over and over, but it was hard to make out because of the wrestling match between her and Kelley.

"Mornin', Kel," I said. "What's new?" I was standing above the two of them, not sure how or if I should intervene.

"Thanks for the help, Duff," he said. "I don't know what I'd do without you."

Kelley and I had done this before, but on this particular morning it was going to take a little more than humor. Walanda was wound up.

"Duffy, my baby's gone," Walanda half screamed, half growled at me. "That Webster's got my baby, Duffy." I had no idea what she was talking about, but she kept screaming it over and over and over.

"Fuckin' Webster! Stop him!"

Kelley finally had her flipped over face down and was sitting on top of her ass, bending her arms to cuff her. I think fatigue had gotten the better of Walanda. Kelley's chest was heaving, his shirt was ripped, and he was covered with dust, gravel, and dirt.

Walanda was crying so hard it looked like she was going to choke. Her chest was heaving as she continued to cry, and she had bits of gravel from her front yard stuck to the tears on her cheeks. In the doorway to her house, a big, fat, long-eared, short-legged hound appeared. The hound saw what Kelley was trying to do and started to howl with his nose pointed to the sky. The howling was loud enough to hurt your ears.

"Al-lah-King, Al-lah-King, don't worry. Mommy's going to be all right." Walanda suddenly calmed herself for the sake of the dog. The dog, whatever his name was, stopped howling, started to whimper, and he waddled his fat self down the two steps of her porch and went over and licked the tears from Walanda's cheek.

"Duffy," Walanda said, "promise me something, right now." The craziness had left her voice and was replaced with a desperate but calculated take-care-of-business tone.

"Tell me what you need, babe," I said. Kelley had her up and heading toward the car.

"You got to find my stepdaughter Shondeneisha." Kelley was putting her in the car. "She's gone and I think the Webster got her."

I didn't have a whole lot of time to get details. I also couldn't ask much from Kelley. He had had a bad morning himself and he wasn't going to appreciate a lot of social work mumbo-jumbo.

"Duff, you can catch up on the finer points of these issues when Walanda gets situated. I've kind of had it for this morning," Kelley said.

"Gotcha," I said.

Walanda wasn't through yet. She started crying and yelling again.

"Take Allah-King while I'm away—promise me," Walanda was back to wailing. "He needs someone and there ain't no one else. You gotta, Duff—you gotta."

I had no time to think and I panicked.

"Don't worry—I'll take care of him," I heard come out of my mouth.

"Don't feed him no pork—he's Muslim," Walanda yelled as Kelley hit the siren and pulled out.

3

"Assalaamu alaikum," I said to my new best friend, Allah-King.

Assalaamu alaikum is the respectful way Muslims greet each other. I knew a couple of guys from boxing who were members of the Nation of Islam and I admired the discipline in their lives. I think the greeting means "peace be with you," or maybe that's what us Catholics say in response to whatever the priest says. I don't know if it mattered much at all to Allah-King. Judging from his appearance, he would have been more pleased with a greeting of "Salami and bacon."

He was sitting there whimpering, watching Kelley's patrol car disappear. Long after it was out of sight, he cocked his head in my direction as if to ask, "What next?" I've never had a dog, let alone a Muslim one, and I didn't know the first thing about having one. I wasn't really thrilled about having this fat stepdog to take care of for a month until Walanda got released, but I told her I'd take care of him, so I would.

"Let's go, Al." I made the decision to go with the shortened version of his name, not out of disrespect to his faith, but rather out of convenience. I headed toward the Eldorado, and a somewhat reluctant Al followed along. I opened the passenger-side door for Al to hop in, but he just sat there on the curb.

"C'mon boy, up you go," I said.

Not only did Al not move, but he also growled a little and had a look on his face like he resented being called "boy."

11

Suddenly, I felt a bit like a white devil. I leaned over and grabbed Al under his front paws and hefted him up.

Al probably weighed about eighty pounds, but it wasn't a neatly balanced eighty pounds, and his back legs hung down while I kind of flopped his front legs onto my front seat. The landing caused a rush of flatulence to escape out of Al's ass, which was perfectly positioned a mere eight inches from my face. Judging from the fragrance of his landing, I thought maybe Al's diet would be enhanced with some pork. We headed back toward my place when I realized I was going to need some dog supplies, so I changed directions and drove toward PetSmart. Al had his eyes closed and looked to be making his lifestyle adjustment by sleeping. A pool of slobber gunked up the velour on my front seat.

Walanda had been a client of mine on and off for five years. There was no doubt she was nuts and addicted. Of course, if I had her background I don't know if I could function as well as she, at least sometimes, did. She was sexually abused all through her childhood by her stepfather and several of his friends, got into prostitution at thirteen, and was addicted by fourteen. Her five kids by four different men were taken away from her six years ago because she was whoring and using, and she didn't have a chance at getting them back.

I had never heard of a stepdaughter, but she lived the kind of lifestyle where family was a broad term. The interesting thing about people like Walanda was that most people write them off because they don't ever seem to get better and because they just continue to do shit that gets them in trouble. Somehow, that qualifies people to devalue the Walandas of the world by calling them "hos" or "crack-heads." The reality is that these folks are flesh and blood, and from a very early age, the cards they were dealt weren't winning hands.

That's not to say that they have no responsibility for how their lives turn out, but it means you've got to do some thinking when you look at people and the places they have found for themselves in life. It would be simple to suggest that they should just pull themselves out of their miserable existence and better themselves. I tend to think that if your existence has been miserable enough, then you may not have what it takes to pull yourself out of it.

Unfortunately, it's much easier to devalue folks, and some people take great pride in looking down their noses at folks like Walanda. Giving them a label like "ho" or "crackhead" makes it easier to not see them as being human. Most people would much rather head to the mall, watch Survivor, and get in their SUV than give this shit any thought at all.

All of Walanda's men were abusive and at least two of them pimped her out on the street for their drugs. There was a brief period when she joined the Nation of Islam, and for eight months she was clean, sober, and working. I don't know if she ever even understood the principles of Islam, but the discipline and structure sure made a difference in her life. Then she found out her oldest son had been stabbed and killed in the boys' home he was in and that was it—Walanda went back to her old lifestyle.

She keeps about half of her appointments with me, which means I see her about twice a month. Most of the time we just shoot the shit, but that's an hour when she's not getting high or turning a trick. Sometimes in her sessions, she actually sets some decent goals for herself. Recently, she was talking about getting some training to be a nurse's aid. That was before the Dollarama arrest and lots of crack. I haven't seen her in a couple of weeks, which probably meant she was on a binge, getting into that ugly cycle of getting high and whoring around the clock. Walanda knew what happened when she got into the crack and though she could compartmentalize her behavior to a degree, it left scars on her psyche and, more importantly, her soul. Though often hard to recognize under the addiction and the craziness, Walanda cared about things and valued her family. It would be easy to say that she valued crack more, but that was an oversimplification of what was going on.

Al started to make a low humming noise and he shifted position. Anything he did seemed to require intense effort because of his belly. He stretched a bit, seemed to yawn, and then barfed into my carpeting. Once he got things out of his system, he shuffled about in the front seat until he was comfortable and then, when he was convinced he had found the exact right spot, he laid down and started a new puddle of drool on my front seat.

It was fun having a pet.

I got the essentials for Al, made sure he had a bowl of food and water, and headed back to the office. The Michelin Woman confronted me the second I walked in.

"Where have you been?" she asked.

"Home visit with Walanda—she got arrested and was having a tough time," I said.

"Considering our discussion this morning, Duffy, that's not a good use of time. You need to focus on your records."

"Yeah, I guess you're right. I wouldn't want the people on my caseload to get in the way of writing about them in their records," I said.

"Duffy, one of your issues is your inability to set appropriate boundaries. You don't let your clients feel the responsibility for their self-defeating behavior. They seek attention and you give it to them," she said.

"Gee whiz, boss. I never thought of it that way. Let me get after those records," I said.

Fortunately, Trina buzzed Michelin's phone, giving me a bit of a reprieve. As Claudia left to get the phone, I looked around the corner and gave Trina a thumbs-up and mouthed a "thank you." She winked at me and seemed to hold her eyes on mine for a second or two longer than she had to. It was summer and Trina's skin was smooth and tan and it contrasted nicely with the plain white collared shirt she wore. Her dark brown, almost black hair seemed to gather light and her teeth were flawless, as were most of her body parts.

I grabbed some records and headed back to the cubicle, ready to start on Eli's chart again. Monique, the caseworker whose cubicle was just across the small aisle made by the partitions, rolled back in her office chair.

"Why do you bait her like that?" Monique said. "It only makes it worse for you. Can't you just let it go?"

"If I can piss her off and not cave under her bullshit, I feel a little redeemed," I said.

"Talk about self defeating..." she said.

Monique was all right. She's a forty-two-year-old black lesbian with a cold veneer. She had her shit together and somehow was able to balance being good with her clients, getting her paperwork done, and keeping the Michelin Woman off her back. Monique tended to wear baggy clothes, often with an African print, which offset her almost midnight-black skin.

I liked and respected Monique and, though she often rolled her eyes at the things I did, I got the sense she respected me. She was for helping people, and she knew I was too. Even though I was Walanda's primary counselor, Monique had her in group and it was often the case that the client's group counselor would have different information on the clients. I filled her in about Walanda and her claims about her stepdaughter Shondeneisha and the whole Webster deal.

"In group, she used to talk all the time about Shony," she said. "She was the kid of one of the men she was involved with but didn't marry. For whatever reason, Walanda bonded with her, I think, as a reaction to the death of her son. That kid was her pride and joy."

"I wonder why she didn't bring it up in our sessions," I said.

"It's a motherhood thing, Duff," Monique said. "She talked about it with other women when the topic came up. She didn't talk a lot about it because it wasn't a problem for her. At least not until all this."

"I'm trying to remember if she ever mentioned the father," I said. "It's not easy keeping track of Walanda's men."

"You're right, you just described every single guy she was ever involved with."

"What about Webster—does that sound familiar in any way?" I asked.

"Webster?" she said. "That doesn't ring any bells. I don't remember any men with that name. You got me on that one."

"Yeah, me either."

Before Monique and I could do any more problem solving on Walanda's mysterious ramblings, Trina buzzed me to let me know the Abermans were here for their couple's session. The Abermans were one of the few Jewish clients we had, which was kind of ironic considering the name of the clinic.

Morris and Michelle had been married for seventeen years and they hated each other, which strangely enough seemed to be what bonded them. Their therapy sessions consisted of them bitching at each other, ignoring anything I said, and then leaving with absolutely no intention of changing anything at all about their lives.

I would like to say that the session with the Abermans would take my mind off Walanda, but it had just the opposite effect. Michelle was droning on about how Morris swam to the opposite side of the pool during adult swim at the Crawford Jewish Community Center and totally ignored her. I couldn't blame Morris—hell, if I had to swim with Michelle, I'd try to break the record for holding my breath underwater.

I know I'm not supposed to allow it to, but the lives of my clients get to me. Not the Abermans' chlorinated crisis—shit, that was all their own doing. Walanda never had a chance, and all psychobabble bullshit aside, what was there in her life to be hopeful about?

I stewed while the Abermans bickered. Morris had moved on to the pressing issue of Michelle's refusal to attend Morris's college debate team reunion. I decided we didn't have enough time to tackle such an emotionally challenging issue this week and I politely ushered the lovely couple out.

Right after the Abermans, I had an appointment with Michael Osborne.

"Mikey," as he preferred to be called, was a flaming gay guy who hung around Jefferson Park taking hits of poppers and engaging in anonymous sex with the crowd of gay men who frequented the park. There was also fairly consistent traffic of straight men that seemed to gravitate to the park to play an anonymous game of kielbasa hockey with guys like Mikey. Mikey spent a lot of time in women's clothing and some of what he talked about in sessions was the idea of getting the series of operations to get transgendered. He wasn't terribly committed to it, so it was never really pursued. Mikey favored leather skirts and they were usually of a color not found in nature like electric pink or purple, but it worked for Mikey—that is, if you liked a really hairy calf coming up from a stiletto pump.

Mikey got into treatment because he was forever getting arrested for his park activities and he always had some drugs on him. My concern for Mikey was that he was either undiagnosed with HIV or he was bound to catch it very soon. The goal of treatment was to get him out of the park and out from behind the bushes. His lifestyle excited him and he was addicted to all of it, not just the drugs or the sex—it was all of it together.

Mikey always made his sessions and he usually was fun to talk with. He played the flamer role to the max and with it came a terrific sarcastic sense of humor. Several times when he talked about how his family disowned him or his lifelong failure to sustain any kind of normal relationship he'd break down and sob. He cried so hard one day I hugged him and he shook and cried until he seemed exhausted. When he was done, he broke our hug by goosing me and then winking at me.

That was kind of a microcosm of who Mikey was. There were layers of hurt that he would get to and touch, but as soon as he could muster the strength, he would gather it and assume his role. It was the shell he'd retreat into to feel safe.

Mikey didn't show for his session, which was very unusual for him. That would've given me time to get after some more notes, but I just wasn't in the mood. That meant that for the day my bookkeeping took a few steps forward and a few more steps back, but I didn't care. Honestly, it made me feel a bit uneasy, but not uneasy enough to stick around writing.

4

I got home just after six; I was exhausted and had picked up a cup of coffee on my way home. I live in a 1968, twenty-seven-foot Airstream Overlander trailer on some land out on Route 9R that belongs to Doctor Rudy. There's nothing on 9R in either direction from my place, it is just a series of stretches of land east of the industrial section of Crawford. The area's environmentalists insist that the fields on 9R are polluted from SGG Industries, a multinational corporation that used to be headquartered in Crawford. SGG made those hockey-puck-shaped disinfectant things that go in urinals and other plastics up until the mid-seventies when they moved to Bolivia. For twenty-five years, their sewage emptied into Cramer's Creek, which runs about two hundred fifty yards from my trailer. I've lived on 9R for the last six years, and I still don't glow in the dark and I haven't grown a third ear in the middle of my back or anything. My environmentalist social worker friends insist something like that is coming real soon.

Airstreams are those shiny, silver, bullet-shaped trailers you still occasionally see on the highway, usually attached to pickup trucks and driven by senior citizens. My Airstream is named "The Moody Blue" after the last song Elvis had a hit with, at least while he was alive. Mine hadn't been pulled behind a senior citizen in a long time. Rudy's uncle died and left him the Airstream in his will and Rudy, a wealthy doctor, didn't have much use for it.

The thing is a marvel of efficiency. Everything you could imagine is in it and most of it is bolted to the floor. I've actually built an addition onto it so both the living room and the bedroom would be bigger. I also stuffed an air conditioner into one of the small windows, though I had to plug a lot of insulation around it and use about three rolls of duct tape to jerry-rig the thing in there. Around the middle of August every year, in the middle of a heat spell, it usually falls out.

I was curious to see how my new Muslim brother had spent the day in his new digs. As I approached the door to the Blue, I listened and heard nothing, which I took as a good sign. I came in the door, flicked on the light, and there was Al, spiritedly chewing on the foam rubber that made up the inside of my couch cushions. The reason he was chewing on the foam rubber was because he had already chewed through the velour cover, which was now shredded and on the ground underneath him.

Al had eaten about a quarter of the way through the foam rubber when my entrance got his attention. He cocked his head at me, took a dramatic pause, and sprang to his feet. Sprang may be a bit of an overstatement, considering his legs are about three and a half inches long and his belly only allowed for about a half inch of ground clearance.

Seeing me, he clearly got excited, started barking his baritone, and sprinted to meet me at the door. When Al got within three feet of me, the excitement got the better of him and he hurled himself like some sort of long-eared, heat-seeking missile in my direction. I watched in amazement as this overweight canine went airborne and transformed himself into a black, brown, and white fur-covered projectile.

My amazement quickly changed into horror when Al's front paws, which, by the way, looked liked he bought them used off a mastiff, came crashing in full flight on my nuts. My knees buckled, the coffee in my hand blew across my face and chest, and I fell back on my ass, hitting the back of my head against the door. As I tried to reach over to console and comfort my poor nuts, Al headbutted me as he walked the remaining length of my torso to lick my face.

Ahh…it was good to be home.

I forgot about the coffee and figured it was time to forget about this day being productive in any way. I went to the fridge and cracked open an ice-cold Schlitz. Al followed on my heels wherever I went throughout the Blue and it got on my nerves. I sat down on the good side of my couch, took a hit of the Schlitz, and hit the button on my message machine. There were a few messages for me.

The first was from Smitty, who ran the gym inside the old Crawford YMCA. Anyone could use the boxing gym in the Y, but there was sort of a Darwinian law at work that kept the place from getting too crowded. Fighters are generally suspicious people, and it takes awhile to warm up to them. Most people who think it would be neat fun to learn how to box usually rethink it after someone punches them in the head. People come and people go and there's no point in making friends with guys until they earn their stripes.

Smitty acted as my default manager. A promoter from Kentucky had a fight offer for me as a main event on a card he was having in Lexington. Kentucky is famous for lousy boxing and lousy pay, and though it would be cool to be in a main event and actually have a chance to win, I didn't feel like driving all that way for what would probably amount to seven hundred bucks in my pocket. With gas, tolls, motels along the way, and all the little expenses that get taken up with travel, the two-thousand-dollar purse would be gone in no time. It's the sort of stuff that Oscar de la Hoya doesn't have to spend a lot of time thinking about. I wanted to think about it before I made any decisions.

The second call was from Lisa, the woman I had been dating. We'd been seeing each other for about seven months, and for about the last three weeks she'd been acting weird. There were nights when she seemed pretty normal, happy to be with me, and, frankly, interested in the things that people who date are interested in, namely sex. Then there'd be times when she was distant and seemed to take everything I said as an offense. Though I would never say it out loud in front of her or, for that matter, anyone else carrying two X chromosomes, I might think it was PMS. Actually, if it wasn't PMS, it could be "the time right before" or "right after" or any of a number of those coded expressions women use to explain why they're being weird. The way I had it figured, women could excuse their mood and behavior about twenty-seven out of every thirty days in the month if they tried hard enough.

This seemed more than that. I've stayed unmarried but have had enough relationships of varying lengths to recognize the signs. It hasn't been a particularly pretty love history for me— my relationships usually follow the same arc. First, the woman gets charmed with the fact that she's met an adult male who is physically fit and able to speak using words with more than one syllable. During this phase, sex occurs freely and often and googly eyes are made during tender moments in which the woman usually voices her joy of just spending time with me.

That phase, which can last from several hours to almost a month, but seldom more than that, is replaced with the second phase. In the second phase, the object of my affection begins to exhibit tendencies that make me believe that she may not be quite as enamored as I thought she might be. This stage manifests itself in symptomatology such as a tendency to find fault in my hobbies, especially my devotion to boxing, a dislike for my choice of restaurants, and then, most telling, the postponement of any coital activity.

My reaction, which has been tested over more trials than I care to admit, is to deny that such symptomatology exists. Then I try to convince myself that the said object of my affection is just going through a phase.

The third and usually final phase is when my partner returns to the psychotic diagnosis that she somehow had been able to mask during our brief love affair. The psychosis can manifest itself in schizophrenic thinking, rage disorders, or complex paranoia. During this time all sexual activity ceases and the relationship ultimately implodes, followed by the request of the now psychotic partner that the two of us remain friends.

Lisa had begun to enter the second phase or was indeed battling an extended period of pre-, active-, or post-menstrual difficulty. On one of our evenings out having drinks after attending the movies, I made the mistake of asking her if she was "puffy," my special code for menstrual-cycle-induced dysphoria. That may have been my first mistake, but it certainly wasn't going to be my last.

"Duffy," Lisa had addressed me with the tone you might reserve for someone who farted at a tea party, "I'm not sure you're ready for intimacy at all."

"I thought I was pretty ready last Saturday night, if I do say so myself," I said with an exaggerated wink and a loving punch to her upper arm.

"Uh…that's exactly what I'm talking about," Lisa rolled her eyes, hunched her shoulders, and sipped her Chardonnay while turning away from me.

It was one of those unanswerable digs that a woman throws out when she wants to righteously make a statement. The fact that the statement makes no sense is beside the point. The point is, I'm an asshole, unfit for the righteous pursuit of intimacy, who has the nerve to want to have fun and enjoy sex once in a while.

She hasn't returned my phone calls since that date and I'm not sure what happened. I'd like to say that it doesn't bother me and try to pull off the flip "can't live with 'em, can't live without 'em" deal, but I can't. I like Lisa, I respect her, and I think we could go someplace. I don't get what I did wrong or what I need to do to make it better. The way she's been acting, it could be something she just snaps out of, but something inside made me doubt it.

Anyway, her message was a simple "Duffy, please call me." It had a weird feeling to it, and I wasn't sure I wanted to. I have always talked to Trina at work about my various relationships, and right from the start she didn't approve of Lisa. Trina made it clear that I put up with way too much goofy shit with Lisa. In fact, Trina almost always thought that the women I got involved with were way too needy and that I should choose more carefully. That always sounded good, but when it came to dating women, it's not like they do a full disclosure when you first meet them. When I first meet them they're always attractive, interesting, and engaging, and it usually takes time before the psychotic behavior starts. Then I'm left with trying to figure out if their wackiness is an aberration or if they really are funny-farm certifiable. Inevitably they should be getting their mail delivered to One Funny Farm Circle, Wack-job, USA.

The third call was from Walanda. She was using one of her two weekly calls to contact me from jail. She was not doing well.

"Duffy, get me out of here, they're goin' kill me. He has people in here…they're goin' kill me. Duffy, you gotta get me out of here!" She was holding back tears and half shouting in that weird way that people sometimes do on the phone when they're trying to control the volume of their yells.

Al whimpered when he heard Walanda's voice.

Before she hung up, she paused and, as an afterthought, said, "Remember, don't give Allah-King no pork."

No doubt Walanda felt she was in trouble—the difficult thing was trying to get a handle on whether it was real or brought on by withdrawal from the lack of psychotropics, both legal and illicit, in her system. Whether or not the danger was real or imagined, her anxiety certainly was authentic. One thing I've learned over the years of working with people like Walanda is that reality has very little to do with emotion. Right or wrong, true or false—Walanda was hurting and hurting bad.

Her short-legged, overgrown sausage continued to whimper

for a few minutes after the phone call. After a minute or two the whimpering must've exhausted him, because he laid down on his back with all four paws pointing straight up and went to sleep.

Even though Walanda was nuts, it didn't necessarily mean she was imagining the danger. Still, she was coming off crack and who knows what else and probably wasn't taking her antipsychotic medication. It would be a few days before the jail doctor would see her and prescribe her Haldol, and then a few days after that the medication would work again. The stress of being taken out of her environment, losing Al, the situation with her stepdaughter—real or imagined—and being in jail were all sufficient to put her over the edge.

Just the same, I called Kelley to see if he could help. He wasn't in, but I knew where I could find him. I put Al's new leash on him and we headed for AJ's. AJ's is a grill on the West Side, in the middle of the city's industrial section. It was a speakeasy during prohibition, and I think that was the last time that any of the AJs had put a dime into the place. The bar has been passed down three generations to its current proprietor, the one and only Andrew Jursczak III. The place reeked of stale beer, cigar smoke, and the poor hygiene of the people who frequented the place. Kelley hung out there a lot when he was off duty.

AJ's is a dive, which is why I like it. I parked right in front of the entrance, told Al I'd be back, and headed in. As I closed my door and walked around the car, I could hear Al's protest. I did my best to ignore him, that is, if you can ignore the baritone woofing of a hound fixated on getting your attention.

The place is long and thin with a bar capable of holding maybe eighteen patrons, and there are a half-dozen tables set close to the wall that no one ever sits in. The walls feature old-time beer signs, not because AJ III thought they were trendy, but because AJ's grandfather got them for free in the forties.

The regulars, or the Fearsome Foursome as I called them, were present. There was TC, a lifetime state worker, sipping a draft of Genny with a back of B&B. TC's view of the world consisted of figuring the best way to expend the least amount of effort in life and maximize the greatest amount of pleasure. There was Jerry Number One, a contractor, drinking a draft of Bud. Jerry Number One told the filthiest and least funny jokes that you never wanted to hear. Next to him was Jerry Number Two, who didn't work and took one too many acid trips, drinking his signature Cosmopolitan. Lastly, there was Rocco, a retired construction worker and a WWII vet with a scotch on the rocks in front of him. He had spent the war in Okinawa and often referred to the hand-to-hand combat he learned from the "Japs." Age hadn't mellowed Rocco, and at seventy-five he still hated everything and everybody, mostly because things were perfect in his day and now they completely sucked. The Foursome sat in the four seats directly behind the stick, in the same order from left to right every night.

Kelley was sitting to the left of TC with a seat in between the two of them, turned in the opposite direction toward the TV, half paying attention to the Yankee game. AJ always had the Yanks on with the TV sound turned down and a radio turned on to catch the play-by-play. I took the stool between him and TC. AJ opened a bottle of Schlitz and slid it in front of me without me asking. They kept Schlitz at AJ's just for me.

"What's up, Duff?" Kelley said.

"Ahh, you know," I said. "Still in the business of saving lives."

"God bless you, man," Kelley said.

Kelley was the kind of guy that didn't make a lot of small talk and, though he was good guy, you kind of got the message when he wanted to get a few beers in him and zone out while watching a game on the TV. Just the same, I needed his help tonight.

"Can I ask you something?" I said.

"You just did," Kelley said.

"Seriously…," I said.

"Go ahead," Kelley said.

"Walanda left a message on my machine," I said. "She was hysterical about somebody trying to kill her in jail."

"Yeah?" he said. Kelley took a pull off his Coors Light and watched Jeter lead off the inning with a single between third and short.

"Well, should I be worried?" I said. "Do you think she's just being nuts?"

Kelley put his beer down and swung his stool partially around.

"Look, Duff, you and me have different relationships with these people." Kelley took a sip from his bottle and wiped his mouth with the back of his hand. "I don't want to see anyone get hurt, so don't get me wrong, but I can't spend a lot of time playing these things out in my head. That's for you guys. She's in jail because she broke the law, and I helped get her there. The long and the short of it is, jail is often a dangerous place and Walanda is crazy. Just because she's crazy doesn't mean she's not in danger."

"I think I got ya," I said.

"Regardless of whether she's in danger or not, there ain't nothing you can do about it," Kelley said.

I decided to leave it alone. I bought Kel his next round and let him get lost in the game. Meanwhile, the Foursome were locked in a heated debate about the important subject of why we have daylight-savings time.

"It's because the farmers need the sunlight," said Jerry Number One.

"Tell me one thing," said Rocco. "How the hell does turning the clocks back give them more sunlight?"

"It's simple," said Jerry Number One. "It's because they get sunlight earlier in the day instead of having to wait."

"Why don't they just get up earlier?" asked Jerry Number Two.

"They do," said TC.

As fascinated as I was with the topic, I decided to get going and headed out the front door toward the Eldorado. From the front of AJ's, I could see Al sitting up on the passenger seat happily chewing on one of my eight-tracks. It was the soundtrack to Paradise, Hawaiian Style, which was going to be hard to replace.

5

"Hey Duff—how can you tell when a Polack's been using your computer?" Sam said. I did my best to ignore him.

"There's Wite-Out all over your screen!" Sam laughed.

"Mornin' Sam," I said.

I was trying to catch up on my notes, which was mostly the equivalent to dabbling in fiction. Notes are supposed to be written in D-A-P format, which stands for Data, Assessment, and Plan. The idea is to make each session with a client sound strategic and planned so that if a third party, like an insurance company, picked up your files they could understand the direction your client's life was going. Unfortunately, the lives of most people, let alone the people who find themselves in need of our services, rarely work out in neat, organized ways.

Take, for example, the session I did with Eli when he came back to treatment following the unfortunate Slurpee machine/public nudity incident. In our session behind closed doors, this is actually how it went:

> Eli: "I was so trashed that the towel-headed woman looked like Diana Ross to me. Somehow I convinced myself that Mr. Endou was Barry Gordy and I know Mr. Motown gotta be into some kink."
>
> Me: "But Eli—they don't look even slightly

black, they work in a Mobil station, and she had on one of those Pakistani outfits. Besides all that, they said 'no.'"

Eli: "To me it was just one of Diana's funky outfits and I thought she was playing hard to get."

Me: "Whatever, Eli—it's pretty clear you ought to lay off the Olde English."

Eli: "Fuck yeah—nothin' but fuckin' trouble."

In my notes, that session appears:

> D: Client discussed self-defeating behavior patterns related to alcohol use involving poor relationship boundaries.
> A: Client struggles with personal relationships and uses alcohol to facilitate social interactions.
> P: Client to identify alternative means of making social contact without alcohol.

Notes like this make it seem like Eli is chock full of insight and I am the ultimate conduit to him seeking enlightenment. It's not easy being a professional in the business of saving lives.

I had seventy-five records with a ton of these notes, a few treatment plans, and treatment plan updates to do. It was boring and, as far as I was concerned, it didn't really serve a whole lot of purpose, except for the anal retentive of the world. Unfortunately, my boss was captain of the all-anal all-star team. My guess was the Michelin Woman's sphincter was so tight it would be easier for a camel to pass through the eye of a needle than it would be for a raisin to pass through the entire length of her digestive tract. My apologies to the biblical scholars of the world; I sure wish I didn't think in such visual terms.

With the crazy phone call I got last night, I thought it would be a good idea to call and set up a session with Walanda in jail. The red tape that you had to go through to set up an in-jail appointment was a nightmare, and it would take two days to get an approved time. I called to get the ball rolling and was told Thursday afternoon about two p.m. would work. There was no point in trying to call her—I wouldn't reach her, but if I did and she accepted, that would take up one of her two weekly phone calls. I had learned over the years that it was proper jailhouse etiquette to let the inmates call you, and even though Walanda had left a message for me, I should still wait for her to call me again. On Thursday I'd see her and it wouldn't count against her phone calls.

I got through five or six records and I just couldn't do it anymore. I know that's what gets me in trouble, but I can't bring myself to do shit that doesn't matter. The threat of getting in trouble will only motivate me so much and fortunately, I had afternoon sessions. I'd rather spend time talking to the clients than writing about them.

One o'clock was Martha Stewart—not the one you're thinking of. This Martha Stewart was a stack of flapjacks over three hundred pounds and had a history of (surprise!) compulsive behavior. The compulsive behavior included not only eating, but also obsessive sexual activity. In fact, I don't know if I've ever met anyone who had more sex with more people than Martha. Her issue, she told me, is that she just never felt fulfilled. She kept a running classified in the adult section of MetroCrawford, the local alternative magazine, letting the folks who were so inclined know that she was a BBW searching for fulfillment. Apparently, there was no shortage of men willing to lend a big, beautiful woman a hand when it came to her pursuit of fulfillment.

At two p.m., I had a session with Clogger McGraw. Clogger got his nickname from an unfortunate bathroom incident at a crowded party. Suffice it to say, Clogger conspicuously interrupted the natural flow of things at this gigantic house bash and was forever stuck with this incredibly visual moniker. Clog at one time was a talented navy pilot who spent his days landing

F-something-or-others on aircraft carriers. Unfortunately, this activity was the most fun for the Clog-man when he was stoned out of his mind. Amazingly, Clogger made it out of the service with an honorable discharge. The real trouble began when he flew his single engine plane upside down under a Thruway overpass.

Never a detail man, Clogger did it a quarter of a mile from a state police barracks. After the stunt, he noticed he was dangerously low on fuel and landed the plane in the right-hand lane of I-87, just south of the New Paltz exit. Clogs still had a joint going when a trooper pulled his plane over, and they got off on the wrong foot when Clogger refused to turn down the Dead on his custom plane stereo. When the trooper tried to give him a Breathalyzer, Clogger took an exaggerated inhalation on it and thanked the officer for the bong hit. He was laughing so hard when the trooper handcuffed him that he strained an abdominal muscle.

Clogger was a trip, but he rarely showed up for sessions. He recently got his wings back on a provisional basis and he was making his money flying a plane that pulled a message behind it. Most recently he was advertising a car dealership by flying the plane past Yankee Stadium during their big weekend home stands. The Clogmeister had even developed his own following. After a few games of making the pass in his little single engine, he got bored, and boredom often led to trouble for Clog. In this case, it seemed to be harmless or at least mostly harmless.

Instead of just flying by with the sign, Clogger started to do a series of acrobatic rolls through the sky. He planned it so it would occur at the end of the bottom of the fifth inning. It got to be a favorite with the crowd and Steinbrenner, ever the businessman, even got an exemption for Clogger to fly closer to the stadium. Pretty soon after that, the Yankee radio announcers also got into the act. Now, at the end of the fifth, they went to a commercial late so John Sterling, the announcer famous for saying, "Yankees win, thhhhhhhhhhhe Yankees win!" at the end of games could announce Clogger. He would announce Clog's arrival and then after Clog did his roll, Sterling would say, "Clogger cannnnnnns it!" It got so popular that Steinbrenner had Sterling do it over the PA, in addition to the live radio broadcast. It was pure Clogger. Being a big Yankees fan myself, I had always wanted to see the Stadium from Clogger's view and the Clogster agreed to let me be his copilot someday. I made him promise to stay off the Thruway on the way home.

After Clogger came Larry Kingston, who was chronically depressed and incredibly boring to talk to. During Larry's sessions I usually pretended to jot notes down on what he said and instead wrote out what I needed at the grocery store.

The very last session of the day was with Emmanuel "Froggy" Bramble. Froggy was another gay guy who hung out in the park and lived pretty much the same life as Mikey. Froggy didn't have any desire to go the transgendered route, but he was flamboyantly feminine. He accentuated a lisp as if playing to the stereotype and he often said he had no desire to change his lifestyle.

His numerous arrests for park activity and low-level drug possessions forced him into treatment. Like Mikey, he was fun to talk to but he did very little therapeutic "work" in our sessions—what-ever that is. Froggy was originally from Jamaica and he had very dark skin and wore his hair in neat cornrows. At six-two and a well-muscled two hundred fifteen pounds, he didn't really fit the body type of your basic, central-casting flamer.

He was about ten minutes late, which is actually early by our clinic's standards. Froggy was wearing knee-length black spandex pants and a white mesh shirt. He kept his wraparound mirrored sunglasses on.

"Hello Mr. Duffy," Froggy said.

"Hey Froggy," I said. "Tell me what's been going on."

"Oh, you know, just doing my thing."

"That's what I'm afraid of. You're talking about your nocturnal park rendezvous?"

"You say it so nice," Froggy said, exaggerating his lisp.

"C'mon, Frog, you know it's not safe."

"That doesn't seem to bother the steady stream of upstanding businessmen who come visit us," he said. "'Course when I get through with them, they're all upstanding."

"Yeah, but—"

"This week we had a Crawford city council member, a prominent tax attorney, and my new favorite—that TV doctor," Froggy rolled his eyes like someone who just finished a superb flaming baked Alaska for dessert. "That man gives as good as he gets—just like he says, 'body and spirit,'" Froggy said.

"Look, Frog, let's talk about drugs…"

"He's so cute in his white coat and to think, a TV celebrity, doing me the favors."

"Frog—the drugs?" I said.

And so it went. Froggy wanted to get off bragging about his sex life and I wanted to talk about anything else. Part of it was because it was a little gross, but mostly because it didn't help Froggy focus on doing anything to better himself. It was an uphill battle, but toward the end of the hour Froggy halfheartedly agreed to at least look at his addictive tendency.

Such is a day in the business of saving lives. It was a full day and I had had enough. I needed to do something physical and get my heart racing, so I headed to the gym to hopefully get some sparring in. My own rule is to get a sparring session in at least every two weeks if I have no fight scheduled. If I'm training for a specific bout, then I spar three times a week. As a professional opponent, it behooves me to stay in shape in case a decent payday, short-notice fight comes up. There was the possibility of that fight in Kentucky, but I didn't think I wanted to take it. After that, you just never know when the phone is going to ring.

Smitty was watching a couple of teenage featherweights in

the ring. The cool thing about Smitty was he gave everyone the same attention regardless of ability or potential. The determining factor about whether Smitty took time to coach you was whether you sparred with heart. If you avoided fighting, if you got in the ring and pussied it, or if you made a ton of excuses about sparring, then Smitty had little use for you. He wouldn't be mean; he just wouldn't take you seriously.

Fighting was a spiritual thing to him. He believed it was an important thing in life to face what you're scared of and keep on keeping on despite your fears. We met when I was a teenager and I was doing karate. The Y has a karate class and some of the guys from the class come in during the boxing sessions to work out or to add boxing to their skills. I thought I was a badass as a kid because I had a black belt until I decided to box with another kid who had a few amateur fights. The kid punched me in the stomach and I threw up. The next day I asked Smitty if he would train me and I never went back to karate. Real fighting, I've learned, involves being hit and dealing with it and in karate classes there just isn't enough real hitting.

If you looked at Smitty, you'd think he was the quintessential, old-time, gym-rat boxing trainer. He was in his sixties, black, and still all wiry muscle with a close-cropped head of gray hair. He favored Dickies, flannel shirts, and work boots as his fashion statement. Smitty devoted his life to boxing, which made his central casting role authentic, but it was far from all he was. Smitty got out of Korea and with the GI Bill went to Dartmouth where he got a degree in American literature. He reads voraciously and continues to teach literacy courses in the state prison sixty miles away three times a week for nothing. Smitty is independently wealthy, though you'd never guess it from looking at him. He never said how he happened to make his fortune and he never flaunted it, living in one of the city's old brownstones and driving an Olds Ninety-Eight from the late eighties.

I loosened up and Smitty came over to work me through the

mitts. In mitt work, the trainer calls out punch combinations and you have to respond with the right punches. It drills proper technique and reaction time. The way Smitty did it, it worked your defense too, because if he saw you drop your guard, he'd crack you in the face with a mitt.

"Turn the hip over on your hook," Smitty said. "That's where your power comes from."

I threw four or five more hooks in a row, none of which pleased Smitty.

"Do you want to hit like a bitch your whole life?" he growled. "Throw the hip into the hook!" he said.

This has been going on since I was a teenager. I didn't have much power in my punches and I knew it. Power in boxing comes less from muscle strength and more from the subtle shifting of body weight. Some fighters naturally have the knack of shifting their body weight just right so they maximize their power. If you don't have it, you can have success by being crafty in the ring and by hitting the other guy more than he hits you. Without the shifting of body weight, it's tough to get one-punch knockout power.

"Smitty—I'm trying," I said. "I've been fuckin' trying since I was fourteen."

"Let it happen, Duff. Let your hip out, then snap it in at the right moment. It's just like givin' it to a chick," Smitty said.

He's used that analogy every day I've been in the gym since I was fourteen. Maybe if Lisa let me throw it to her once in a while it would mean something to me. Smitty finally changed up from the hooks and had me working some other combinations and moving. Moving and being crafty was my game, and it's what keeps me in boxing. I get knocked out, but I rarely take beatings, because I know how to move. That's why I can beat the local guys and the nobodies and can't beat guys with one-punch power.

"You're good for today, Duff," Smitty said. "I ain't got nobody for you to spar."

"I was hoping to get some work in the ring. Ain't nobody around?" I said.

"Nobody for you, Duff. If you really want to, do some bag work," Smitty said. "You got to let me know about the deal in Kentucky."

"I don't want to go down there unless they come up with more money."

"I'll see what I can do," Smitty said. He was no Don King, but he knew how to work small-time promoters and squeeze the most money out of them.

I did a few rounds on the bag, once again pursuing the elusive right hook. As a lefty, I hooked off my right hand, and no matter how I broke it down, I couldn't get the snap Smitty was looking for. I guess I was destined to hit like a bitch.

I finished up and was undoing the wraps on my hands and absentmindedly watching a couple of teenagers in the ring when I saw Kelley come in the front door. He occasionally dropped by the gym to hit the bags. He didn't have any gear with him and he was still in uniform.

"Hey Kel," I said. "Dropping by to watch the next heavyweight champ do some work? Hate to bum you out, but I'm finished for the day."

"Duff, I got some bad news."

"What's up?"

"Walanda was murdered this afternoon."

6

I showered and headed home, staring at the lines in the road, the sky, the street signs—anything that kept me from thinking. I felt guilty; I felt negligent and incredibly sad because I liked Walanda. She asked me for help and she asked me to protect her and now she was dead. I dismissed her fear and shrugged it off as the rantings of a crazy crackhead, which was the exact type of disrespect that Walanda hated so much. I felt like shit.

Walanda was a fuck-up, there's no doubt about that, but she tried. It wasn't long ago that she told me about her plans to go get training to become a certified nurse's aid. That may not sound like a whole lot, but in Walanda's world of multigenerational welfare and crime, it was huge. Sure, she was an addict, she was a prostitute, but she also cared about her kids, including this stepkid I never even heard of. For all her faults, Walanda never quit trying and though it wasn't obvious to many people, I knew she was doing what she could to be better. When you come down to it, that's about all you could ever ask of anyone.

I got to the Moody Blue and prepped myself for Al's assault. Sure enough, as soon as I put the key in the lock I heard his paws hit the floor, move across the carpet, scratch across the tile, and then bounce off the inside of the door. I opened the door and he sprung up, again hitting me in the nuts, but at least this time I was prepared. Besides, Al, low-riding pain in the ass that he was, deserved a little slack today. I don't know shit about animal psychology and my Muslim brother didn't seem to be all that emotionally complex, but the guy did just lose his mom.

I cracked open a Schlitz and sat down on the good side of the sofa. Apparently, Al had a busy and productive day, because the remainder of the foam rubber that he started on yesterday was chewed up and spit out on the floor in front of the couch. I didn't have the energy to get furious right now. I slumped into the couch, threw on the TV, and took another pull off the Schlitz. The local news was on, but they wouldn't be reporting on a jail incident because the jail was pretty good at keeping stuff like that out of the media and even if it did get out, the press had a tendency not to care when people like Walanda got killed. Just another dead crack ho.

The thought of not taking Walanda's phone call ate at me. When the fourth Schlitz gave way to the fifth, sixth, seventh, and, I think, eighth, it didn't get any better. I was drunk, but the beer didn't touch the feeling in my gut. I knew it wouldn't, but I didn't know what else to do.

Kelley told me it looked like it was just a battle over jailhouse dominance. Someone, or a couple of someones, caved in the side of her head with a mop wringer. She was found outside the chapel by one of the corrections officers and, to no one's surprise, no inmate saw anything or knew anything. Kelley said that one of the COs told him that it might've been over cigarettes—either Walanda stole somebody's or somebody stole hers. It's the sort of thing that happens inside jails and prisons and I believe it happens so much because wherever people are, they have to struggle over power. More cigarettes means more power, just like more money means more power, or more stock shares means more power.

Just the same, the fact that she had called me, scared for her life, didn't sit right with me. Still, it wouldn't be much of a reach to figure the two events were mutually exclusive. After all, it's not uncommon to feel in danger in jail, especially when you're schizophrenic and addicted to crack. It's also not terribly unusual to be assaulted in jail. The two could've just happened. All her yelling and carrying on about "Webster" made no sense. There wouldn't be much of an investigation. Walanda had no family around, she was a crack ho who didn't vote, and she was a criminal. The DA wouldn't exactly be overwhelmed with pressure to solve this one. That wasn't right and I wasn't sure what to do about it. Right now, I was getting bombed, so there wasn't a whole lot I could do about anything. Going to bed made the most sense to me.

The next morning came a whole lot sooner than I expected. Having gotten Schlitzed the night before, I didn't anticipate rising and shining. I also didn't anticipate my Muslim brother, Allah-King, barking incessantly at the foot of my bed at 5:04 a.m. For reasons probably only revealed to Muhammad, the short-legged pain in the ass wouldn't shut up. I yelled at him, I threw pillows at him, I tried to throw the contents of the half-empty Schlitz on the nightstand at him—none of it mattered. He was a barking machine.

I sat up in bed and got one of those waves of wishy-washiness that comes with an overindulgence in that product that made Milwaukee famous. Trying to think of anything to stop the racket, I stepped out of bed to get the long-eared beast some food so he'd shut up. I was slightly dizzy when I got out of bed and when I stepped toward Al, my bare foot splatted into something slippery, sending my vastly hungover body to the hard tile. I had a good idea of what it was without looking, but, like a bad car wreck, I couldn't not look. Sure as shit, it was between my toes and because of the fall, all over my foot.

All through this, Al never stopped with the racket, though I swear to God, I thought I heard him laughing through the barking. I hopped to the bathroom to stick my shit-foot under the shower-head, and for some reason the sight of me hopping threatened Al. He growled and jumped at me, again striking me in the nuts and sending me sprawling, shit-foot and all, into the bathroom wall. I now had a streak of dog shit throughout my house, poo between the toes, and a bump on my hungover head from the second of two falls in the last forty-five seconds. This is not what I consider nursing a hangover.

I cleaned my foot, mopped the floor, fed the beast, and took a shower. I couldn't bear the thought of going to the office, but I had to. The Michelin Woman was gunning for me and any unexplained absences would surely do me in. Walanda's death would be a big administrative deal not because ol' yellow teeth cared about Walanda's loss of life, but because she would have to oversee the filling out of forms that would have to be filed with the state. On top of that, an incident such as this would undoubtedly mean an emergency meeting of the board.

The board was comprised of the biggest group of phonies and opportunists I'd ever met. They got on the board because it was politically correct for them. For some, it meant a tax deduction, for others, help with the Jewish vote, and for others, business connections with other board members. They'd come in their suits and ties and say a bunch of crap like they gave a shit about the people we served and then leave in their BMWs and go about their business.

The one exception was Hymie Zuckerman. Hymie was the eighty-seven-year-old benefactor who put up the original money for the agency. He was an old Brooklyn Jew who made his fortune in the dry cleaning business. It seemed to me he cared about helping people and giving back and didn't care about kissing ass and political opportunity. He had enough money to air condition hell and he knew it, and he also knew that was the reason these other business people joined the board. Being friends with Hymie meant instant business connections and that's why they were sucking up to him. He didn't care about people manipulating him if it helped the agency and therefore, in his mind, helped the greater good.

I also liked Hymie because he liked me. He was a fight fan, knew the game inside and out, and loved to talk about it. A lot of people don't know that Jews, along with the Irish, dominated boxing in the twenties. Throughout its history, boxing has been dominated by whatever minority was experiencing the most oppression or prejudice at the time. It probably has to do with being hungry, tough, and angry. When a minority group rises in the social order, they usually drop out of boxing dominance. It helps explain why there aren't a hell of a lot of WASPs with fine pedigrees in the game, which is another reason I like boxing. As far as I am concerned, golf and WASPs deserve each other.

As a fighter and a student of boxing history, I'd kibbutz with Hymie about the fighters of his era, especially the greatest Jewish fighter of all time, Benny Leonard, a lightweight who remains one of the best pound-for-pound fighters ever.

Hymie also got a kick out of an Irish Catholic Polish guy like me mixing some Yiddish into our conversations. I'd greet him with a big "Shalom aleichem," making sure I rolled the "ch" as much as I could. I'd also give him an "Abi gezunt," a Yiddish expression that meant something like, "Go with good health." Hymie loved it and would come over and pinch my cheek and say something like, "Do you hear this goy? Can you believe him? He could sell gefilte fish in Brooklyn!"

Claudia hated the fact that Hymie liked me, partly because she hated me and partly because he had little use for her. Hymie knew about helping people and he knew about administrators. He knew Claudia was a blowhard administrator and he saw her as a necessary evil. His dislike for her probably wasn't enough to ever save my job if it came down to it, but she sure sensed he didn't like her.

Despite my respect for Hymie, having the rest of the board in was a pain in the ass. Claudia had recently formed a subcommittee board group to oversee quality assurance. It was a perfect vehicle for her to point out to the board my poor paperwork and how it put the agency at regulatory risk. She was laying further groundwork to can me and this subcommittee would utilize the power of the board to justify my firing. The place would be so much better if she only put a similar amount of effort into actually doing something for the clients.

Regardless of the bullshit, regardless of my hangover, and regardless of Al's objections to the contrary, it was time to go to work. I grabbed a stack of files to start to work and, as luck would have it, opened up the Abermans' chart. The only thing in all of life that could possibly approach doing a couple's session with the Abermans on the boredom meter was having to write notes about it. I was trying to think how to write the psychobabble term for chronic nag when the phone rang.

"Duff, it's Rudy." In addition to being my landlord and coconspirator when it came to bullshit disabilities, Rudy also made rounds at Crawford Medical Center, which everyone called CMC.

"What's up, Rude?" I asked.

"I wanted to give you a heads-up," Rudy's voice was all business, which wasn't like him. "You're Mikey the gay guy's caseworker, aren't you?"

"Is he in detox again?" The way these guys went in and out of the hospital made me crazy.

"No, Duff." Rudy got quiet. "Somebody worked him over pretty good. He's in ICU."

"Worked him over?"

"Somebody beat him to within inches of death. He's not conscious," Rudy said.

"Holy shit…"

"Yeah, I know," Rudy exhaled hard. "He doesn't have anybody, does he?"

"No, the family deserted him a long time ago."

"Look, Duff, with the way things are here, it would be nice if someone showed Mikey some attention."

"What are you talking about?"

"The administrator here, Broseph, is a real bastard. With someone like Mikey with no insurance or crummy Medicaid, the hospital is likely to lose a ton of money. He's been all over my ass to discharge guys no matter what shape they're in."

"You just said Mikey was in rough shape," I said.

"It doesn't matter." Rudy raised his voice just a little. "That's what I'm trying to tell you. The last time I kept a guy like Mikey longer than Broseph wanted me to, he wrote me up—I'm on thin ice here. He hates anyone with bad insurance."

"That's fucked, Rudy," I said. "I'll be right up."

I started to put the files away and felt myself slam the cabinet drawer hard enough that it got Trina's attention.

"Hey—are you all right?" Trina asked.

"No," I said.

I'm not a big believer in peace and love and all that shit, but I don't understand it when people cause harm to someone who isn't even bothering them. Every now and then some assholes go into Jefferson Park with the idea of "rolling fags." Fuckin' cowards hurt people for no other reason than because they hate gay people. Another fuckin' way of labeling people so that they have no value, only this shit is another step into evil. The fact that once a guy got the shit beat out of him his health depended on which insurance plan he signed up for was beyond ludicrous. This Broseph asshole sounded like a real charmer.

I was getting ready to leave when the phone rang again. It was Dr. Gabbibb. Dr. Gabbibb was a piece of work. He's Indian, five foot two, and very dark. It's very difficult to understand him, and because he's so fucking arrogant, he refuses to repeat himself. He also has some sort of Tourette's-like affliction, so when he's talking, he'll suddenly blurt, "DAT, DAT, DAT, DAT, DAT, shit." After each one of those episodes, he'll say, "excuse me," like he just had a tickle in his throat or something. I had to talk to him frequently because the detox sent us lots of cases and the conversations would go something like this:

"Allo, Doofy? Dees is Doctor Gabbibb at the datox."

"Yes, doctor," I'd say.

"I dave un clynt to send at you for treatment now," Gabbibb would say.

"Excuse me, doctor," I'd say.

"DAT, DAT, DAT, DAT, shit! Excuse me," he'd say and hang up.

I just got in the habit of agreeing to whatever he said and then calling his secretary to find out what was up.

Gabbibb worked a ton of hours because he was a research oncologist in addition to his duties as the detox medical director. Technically he may have been very good, but his social skills and bedside manner were the worst. I don't know if it was a cultural thing or what, but I never met a more condescending man in my life. The hospital gave him whatever he wanted because he headed the cancer research at the medical school. I guess if you can cure cancer, people will put up with a lot of shit.

I was hoping I could keep Gabbibb's phone conversation short and uneventful.

"Doofy? Dis homosexual patient in here is on your responsibility caseload?"

"What?" I said.

"DAT, DAT, DAT, DAT, shit…excuse me." The doctor was going on his roll.

"I'm on my way up there, doctor," I said, hoping to get off the phone quickly.

"No rush, Doofy. Dees man is not worth time," he said and hung up.

It was probably a good thing he hung up, because I was about to go off and I don't know how many DATs he had in him.

They let me in to see Mikey for fifteen minutes in ICU. His head was swollen to twice its normal size, he had a tube taped to his nose, his face was mostly purple from the bruising, and he had five different sets of stitches. He was surrounded by computerized machines with little red and green lights and something that checked his heart rate.

I felt cold and sick to my stomach, and though I couldn't quite identify what it smelled like, I hated the hospital smell. Mikey was unconscious and when I touched his hand there was absolutely no response. I'm not really a religious guy, but I didn't know what else to do, so I said a quick prayer. I said, "Hang in there, Mikey" out loud and felt foolish, but I had heard somewhere that it was good to try to speak to people in comas.

I went through the sliding doors of the ICU and there was Gabbibb with his stethoscope around his neck and a clipboard in his hand.

"Doofy." Gabbibb's big brown eyes grew wide. "Don't tell me you were here visiting dee homosexual."

"His name is Michael Osborne," I said.

"I know dat," Gabbibb said. He didn't get it. "Shouldn't you be catching up on dose files?"

I shook my head and started to walk away. I got about ten feet and I couldn't help myself.

"Hey, Gabbibb," I shouted.

He turned and looked down his nose and over his glasses at me.

"Go fuck yourself."

I turned back around and headed out. All the way down the hallway I could hear it.

"DAT, DAT, DAT, DAT, shit…excuse me…DAT, DAT, DAT…"

The next set of sliding doors closed and the rest of the DATs faded into the rest of the hospital sounds.

I wound my way through the hospital corridors, looking for Rudy's office. I'd been there a bunch of times but I can never find it easily. After a couple of wrong turns, I found him. Through the window I saw him at his computer with his belly causing maximum stress to the elastic waistline of his trousers and beads of sweat gathering on his forehead. The man was always sweating.

I let myself in and Rudy didn't even look up from his computer.

"Hey, Rude, I—"

"Hang on." His face cringed and he pounded a few more keys. "Sorry, Duff. I'm trying to get caught up."

"Lot of that going around," I said.

"What's up?"

"Is Mikey going to make it?" I asked.

"Duff," Rude exhaled heavily. "I ain't going to bullshit you. It doesn't look good. He might even be better off if he didn't."

"Are the cops involved?"

"Some detective talked to me in the ER. He didn't seem all that energetic." Rudy lifted his glasses off his nose and rested them on top of his balding head.

"I'm guessing the cops aren't going to sweat the assault of a guy who spent his life in the bushes of Jefferson Park."

"Probably not," Rudy added. He was about to say something else when his beeper went off. "It's the ER, I gotta run."

I got out of the way. Rudy ran past me, and with the weight he carried, there was likely to be a second code blue if he continued to run. He disappeared down the stairs and I headed to the elevator.

I was walking through the ER to get to the parking lot, and there was some sort of crisis going on. Rudy was yelling, they had that cart with the paddles, and they were working over someone on the floor. Whatever it was, it wasn't good.

They started to move the guy onto a gurney and a nurse was holding a clear bag that was connected to a tube that was running to the guy on the table. They had an oxygen mask on him, and I could see that Rudy had blood splattered all down the front of his white shirt and tie. I heard something yelled about surgery and they ran the gurney down the hall.

Rudy wiped the sweat from his brow and picked up the phone on the triage desk. He hung up angrily and barked orders at the nurses. He took a deep breath and looked up and saw me.

"Duffy," he was breathing hard. "That was another one of your guys. That was Eli."

7

It had been a hell of a twenty-four hours. I had drunk myself to sleep last night with Walanda's death on my mind. There was also the question of what, if anything, I could do to find Shony. Then Mikey, then Eli—getting hit in the nads by Al and stepping barefoot in shit was the highlight of the day. The karma or whatever drives the world was getting really fucked up. I mean, these folks weren't exactly on top of things before this shit storm blew into them. I just didn't get it.

I got to the Moody Blue and cracked open a Schlitz. I hit the answering machine and there were a couple of messages. The first was Smitty again, and he had news that the promoter in Kentucky had sweetened the purse to seven grand. He also found out more about the opponent and that he was fifteen and zero with fifteen knockouts, all coming in three rounds or less. Smitty said the guy was being groomed for a title shot, and from the videos he'd seen, the guy could really swat.

The second was from Lisa. She was forcing back tears and I could tell it wasn't going to be good news.

"Duffy, I've been thinking." She sniffed through the tears. "I hate to do this on the phone, but I just can't bring myself to do it in person."

I think I knew how this was going to go.

"I haven't told you, but I've been seeing a therapist. She thinks that now isn't the right time for me to be in a relationship. She also thinks that you're an archetype of my relationship with my father and that I'm recreating dysfunctional patterns," she said.

Maybe I didn't know how this was going to go. This was thicker bullshit than even I was used to from women.

"The fact of the matter is that though you and I had fun together and seemed to care for each other, it wasn't on a deep enough plane. My therapist says I need more intimacy and that's impossible with a man like you…"

Oh geez…

"I also have begun to explore myself, and my therapist thinks that I may have a better chance of exploring intimacy with other women."

I definitely didn't know how this was going to go.

"So I'm going to explore some lifestyle changes…I'm glad I got this out. My therapist says it's important for me to be assertive and direct. Please don't call me, Duff, not for a while. I need time to think. Then maybe we could work on being friends."

I'm so glad she was assertive enough to call my machine and let me know about her lesbianism. I've lost a lot of relationships, but never have they cooked up the lesbian card to bail. Ah, the satisfaction of another relationship milestone.

As for the being friends thing, that was my absolute favorite. Somehow women felt that that absolved them from the guilt of ripping out your heart and treating it like a pig that was slated for sausagedom. Then they can keep you around like some emotional tampon that they can insert once a month when they're lonely and whoever they were most recently fucking dumps them.

Not that I'm bitter or anything.

I called Smitty to find out about the fight. Smitty stayed up most of the night reading, so I never worried about waking him. He was never what you'd call chatty, but on the phone he was even less so. He picked up on the first ring.

"Yeah…" That was his usual greeting.

"You know, you really ought to work on being more engaging."

"You want to fight or not? The fight is this Saturday. That gives you three days," Smitty said.

"Yeah, that's all right. I kind of feel like fighting," I said.

"Duffy, this boy is no joke." Smitty's voice was serious. "He can hit and you'll have to be sharp."

"I'm always sharp, Smitty—you know that."

"I ain't playin', Duff," he said.

Smitty gave me the particulars about the opponent, the travel schedule, and the other logistical stuff I needed to know about the fight. The guy I was fighting was named Tommy Roy Suggs. We were going to fly Friday after work, which was good considering how things in the office had been going. It probably wasn't going to be a great time to ask for a day off. The fact that they raised my purse and were allowing us to fly meant they really wanted their boy and me to get it on. I was looking forward to fighting and the cash would be nice too.

I was in decent shape, not great shape, but decent enough to fight. In my line of work as a short-notice fighter, I can't afford to ever get out of shape. Matchmakers liked me because I would take the fights when they needed somebody in a hurry and no one else was saying yes. It was something I accepted, but I never actually got used to it. Managing my emotions over the next three days would be hell.

Fighters get scared; they just don't talk about it or focus on it. You really can't and stay sane. For me, the anxiety will come out in other ways, usually manifesting itself in irritability and short temperedness. With the way things had been going, I didn't think anyone would notice me get any crankier. There were some advantages to distracting myself over a pending fight, what with work being such a shit sandwich lately.

With three days left before the fight, there was really nothing physical left to do that would prepare me for it. The best thing I could do would be to watch some tape of the guy and get myself as mentally prepared as possible. The seven grand would be nice—getting hit by some hotshot who could punch wouldn't. Getting hit by someone who could throw hard was on the list of things I thought about while I wasn't sleeping that night.

It was that, getting dumped by my assertive, potential-lesbian ex-girlfriend, but most of all, it was about Mikey and Eli.

"Hey Duff—didya hear about the Polish Olympic hockey team tragedy?" It was Sam.

"The team drowned during spring training," he said.

I heard him laughing to himself all the way back to his cubicle. I had gotten almost no sleep the night before, and I was really on edge. There were so many things eating at me that I had difficulty thinking, so I had bigger things to worry about than Sam. For starters, there was a New York State Client Death Form on my desk and two Incident Report forms with a yellow sticky from the Michelin Woman attached to the top one. It read:

Duffy—This needs to be completed and on my desk by the end of the day. Claudia.

She was a real joy. A client is dead and two close to it, and her concern is getting the state their fuckin' forms. I wasn't in any kind of mood for her bullshit today. The only redeeming thing going on today was that she'd be distracted by the board members. She likes to impress them, so she'd have on her newest polyester stretch pants and she'd be obsessed with making a good presentation for the day.

I saw Monique coming back to her cubicle with a cup of coffee in her special coffee cup with the Nefertiti head on it.

"Duff, I'm so sorry to hear about Walanda, Mikey, and Eli," she said. "You must be hurtin'. If there's anything I can do, please let me know."

"Thanks 'Nique, I truly appreciate it," I said.

She meant it. Monique and I weren't exactly close, but we respected each other and I think we had a mutual understanding about each other. It's hard to explain, but I think people can tell when you really respect them and when you're just trying to make an impression.

The various board members were filing in and I had yet to see Hymie. L. T. Espidera, the guy who owned six car dealerships in Crawford, came in, making his usual loud and obnoxious entrance. He epitomized the type of board member I despised. I was convinced that his entire motivation for being on the board was to get on Hymie's good side so that eventually Hymie would sell him his dry cleaning headquarters. That shop happened to take up prime real estate on Main Avenue in the heart of the city. If Espidera had that piece of land, he would have not only the majority of car dealerships in town, he would also have them all in ideal locations.

Espidera liked people to call him "LT" because he thought it sounded macho. He was a late thirty-something guy who kept in what I call "gym shape," meaning his body looked good but you could tell that if you hit him in the gut he would puke for a month. Just to piss him off, I always called him by his given name, Lawrence. "Hi Lawrence," I said. "How are the Hondas moving?" "Fantastic, Duff, couldn't be better," he said. "Hey Duff—getting any Ws in the ol' squared circle?" It was a dig because I knew he knew my record.

"Oh yeah—didn't you hear?" I said. "I knocked out Mike Tyson. First, I bit him, then I knocked him out."

Espidera shot me with his thumb and forefinger. He winked at me and ran his fingers through his mulletted, jet-black hair. His skin was a ridiculous tanning-hut brown.

Claudia came out of her office, hearing a board member and not wanting to miss an opportunity to suck up.

"Good morning, LT," she said. "Thanks for coming in on such short notice."

"No problemo, Claud," LT shot back.

"Duffy, did LT tell you about the new committee?" Claudia said. It startled me because she never acknowledged my presence when board members were in. It was as if being just a lowly staff member in the presence of greatness made me unworthy.

"I don't know what you're talking about, Claudia," I said.

"LT is going to be the board representative on our Quality Assurance Ad Hoc Committee. The committee will oversee things like record-keeping and risk management. After we have our emergency meeting, we'll invite you in for the first of what will be bi-monthly meetings."

Now her talking to me made sense. It was another opportunity to stick the whole paperwork thing to me, only this time, with the added strength of throwing in a board member. It was just an extra special treat that Espidera was going to be involved.

Recently, Espidera donated an old piece of property that at one time had been an old hotel. It was in disrepair and way out in the middle of nowhere, and several agencies had gotten together to convert it into a women's shelter. The plan was to make the old hotel a halfway house for addicted women and their children. I was convinced that Espidera donated it for the tax break. Also, because of its location, it had no marketable value.

Next in was Dr. Gabbibb. I was figuring he was going to come right over and chew me out with a series of DAT, DAT, DATs, but he surprised me.

"Good morning, Doofy," he flashed me a big toothy smile. He had on a Jason Giambi jersey today. "Notar feeleends I hepe?" He extended his hand.

This was pretty bizarre for the most arrogant man I ever met.

"Sure, Doc," I said.

"Doofy—you dar dinto du Yankees, no?"

"What's that, Doc?" I asked.

"DAT, DAT, DAT, DAT, shit…excuse me," he yelled.

"Oh yeah—sure, I love the Yanks."

"Ere's two teeckits I can't use," he said.

I loved the Yanks and the tickets were for the September 11 game against the Mariners, right behind the dugout, but I just couldn't. I didn't know what his motive was, and I didn't want to be indebted to him.

"I can't, Doc, I'm going to be away then," I said.

"DAT, DAT shit," he said. He couldn't have been too upset because he only let out two DATs.

Finally, he turned his attention to Claudia, who was anxious to talk about her committee. Claudia kept on about how the new committee was going to ensure that our paperwork was always in compliance. It was crystal clear that she was trying to get a reaction from me in front of the board members. Before I could respond to Claudia's bait about the new committee, I heard Hymie's entrance.

"Where's that goy friend of mine?" Hymie said. "The one who should be wearing the Star of David on his trunks, he's a Jew in harp's clothing!"

"Hymie!" I got up to greet my buddy. "Shalom aleichem! My friend," I said.

"You hear this schmeckel?" he said. "He's not foolin' me—he's not a Jew—but I love 'im." He pinched my cheek.

I smiled and looked down at the four gray hairs and multiple liver spots that made up his scalp. He was about five foot six, with glasses and two Miracle-Ears turned up to maximum. He had on his tan Sansabelts and white shoes.

"Hey Hymie—shalom," LT said.

"Oh, hello, Lawrence," Hymie said.

He also turned and greeted Claudia, and soon after that they went in the boardroom to talk privately about Walanda's death and to wait on the rest of the board. They'd probably also talk about my written warning. Hymie wouldn't be pleased, but he wouldn't stand in the way of what had to be done because he knew that type of influence wasn't right. I understood that, and I wouldn't ask him for anything different.

After the board met privately for about forty-five minutes, they called Monique and me into the boardroom to introduce us to the quality assurance process. Besides Claudia, Hymie, and Espidera, the committee was made up of Mrs. Sheila Silver, a board member and retired social worker; Rhonda Bowerman, the executive director of the Eagle Heights Jewish Unified Services, which was about forty-five miles away; and Gabbibb.

Sheila Silver was a goof. She had an MSW degree and passed her certification, so she was a certified social worker, but as far as I could tell, she had never worked a day in her life. She was in her early fifties, with jet-black hair, overplucked eyebrows, and every possible type of plastic surgery you could imagine. She weighed about one hundred fifteen pounds and talked incessantly about losing weight, dieting, and exercise, though she always had an injury of some sort that kept her from actually doing much other than hiring a personal trainer. She was always coming from or going to her therapist, her hairdresser, her ob/gyn, or the manicurist.

Sheila was married to an ophthalmologist who was the first guy in Crawford to do laser surgery. They were set financially, but you couldn't pay me enough to deal with Sheila. Don't get me wrong, she wasn't mean, she was just incredibly self-absorbed. The type of person that never wanted to offend you, not because she didn't want to hurt your feelings, but rather because she didn't want anything to bother her conscience. Sheila knew social work theory and kept abreast of current events, but she had never actually gotten her hands dirty working with real people.

Bowerman did the same job as Claudia at our sister agency. The Eagle Heights clinic operated in much the same way as ours with the exception that many of their clients came from more rural areas. Eagle Heights is a couple of towns away from Kingsville, where the new halfway house was going to be, and is about a forty-five minute drive from Crawford. There are dairy farms and cornfields, but there's also some of that unwashed small-town feel to the area. Lots of broken-down cars and large, rusted appliances in big backyards that lead out to sections of woods where kids go to drink, get high, and feel each other up. Many of these people lived on public assistance just like the clientele at the Crawford clinic, and they had a lot of the same issues. The difference was that somehow they had an attitude that they were above people who lived in the ghettos. I could never figure out if it was a notion of racial superiority or the fact that their forefathers, however scummy they were, lived on the same land for generations. Just the same, between our two clinics you could cast the Jerry Springer show and still have enough characters for half a year of Montel.

Bringing Bowerman in was supposed to give the committee an element of an impartial, unbiased view. I highly doubted that had any chance of occurring because Claudia wouldn't risk it. Bower-man and Claudia were acquaintances, if not friends, and they were both part of that sorority of angry, unattractive female social workers. Bowerman was a tall, mean-looking woman who resembled Katherine Harris, that scary-looking woman who was counting or not counting, I forget which, Al Gore's hanging chads. Bowerman looked like Harris's less attractive older sister with frizzy dishwater-brown hair, cut in a misshapen bob. I didn't know her well and only met her a couple of times, but it was enough to draw the conclusion that I didn't like her.

I was the last one to make it into the conference room for the meeting. Monique sat with a chair between her and Espidera. Monique, without saying anything, could show more disdain for a person than most people could by spitting. The thing was, Monique never did anything to put herself in a compromised position. I also believe spending her life as a member of three minority groups gave her the capacity to read people and to some extent know how to protect herself. Some people in the same position get aggressive, some get subservient, but Monique got quiet and thoughtful. She exuded confidence, and at five feet four inches and no more than one hundred thirty pounds, she gave off an air of being, if necessary, very dangerous.

The only chair left meant I got to sit next to my best friend, LT.

"Hey Duff," he said. "What's happening?" He threw a few

shadow boxing combinations, trying to impress me. They were poorly thrown.

"Good morning, everyone," Claudia was getting the meeting started. "Thank you for coming. The purpose of this committee is for us, as an agency, to examine where we are at risk in regard to regulatory standards."

She was at the head of the table and fortunately, I was four seats away from her, which meant I could doodle and have it look like I was taking notes.

Claudia cleared her throat.

"The New York State Office of Alcoholism and Substance Abuse clearly states."

I figured she was good for twenty minutes before anyone else got a chance to speak. If I could occasionally look up, make eye contact, and nod, she wouldn't have any idea what I was thinking about or writing down. During these types of meetings, I usually take the time to write my all-time list of boxing's best pound-for-pound fighters. By the way, Willie Pep gets my number one spot and Ali isn't even in the top five. I've also tried to relive every sexual episode I've ever had, but that never got me through more than a few minutes. Sometimes, I simply resorted to my Salvador Dali-type pencil drawings. Hippopotamuses were my favorite.

Claudia was going strong.

"The essential feature of the new regulations is the importance of the quarterly treatment plan updates, which must be signed by the client, the primary counselor, and the supervisor on or before the seventh visit for those in nonintensive programs, the third visit for those in intensive programs, and on the second visit for those in day treatment..."

That was as interesting as it got. I was on to my fifth hippo and I just couldn't get the ears the way I liked them. The trick was to make the ears ridiculously tiny against the round fat of the hippo's body. The perfectionism of my art often tortured me.

I looked up to give one of my nods to show that I was paying attention and Claudia was in mid-sentence."…which is the biggest challenge we face here and now. It is what will define our agency and ultimately lead to our success or failure. Duffy, can you give our board members and Rhonda three examples of how we've already begun to address this issue?"

"Uh…of course, Claudia. Uh…before I do that though, I would like to point out that we, as an agency, uh, excel in the face of challenge, and to quote Vince Lombardi, 'Winning isn't everything, it's the only thing.'"

"Thank you, Duffy." She glared at me. "But please give us three examples." She knew I wasn't paying attention and now she wanted to embarrass me.

"Yes, uh, well first and foremost, it is something that both Monique and I have incorporated into our daily work here. It's something that she thought of, and I don't feel right taking the credit for it. Monique, go ahead."

She didn't blink, God bless her.

"Thanks, Duffy, but you're being modest. The three things we've incorporated that exemplify what Claudia is speaking of are one: peer review of all records; two: monthly self-audits of treatment plans; and three: corrective action within forty-eight hours when outliers occur. It has made a big difference."

"It sure has!" I chimed in.

Claudia barely hid her rage, but she didn't want to lose her cool in front of the outsiders. Monique saved my ass perfectly. The list of people I owed favors to was getting longer.

Mercifully, the meeting only went on for another half an hour. I never did get the hippo like I wanted, but the important thing with art is progress. After the meeting, I made sure I finished the death reporting form and put it in the Michelin Woman's mailbox.

The rest of the day I spent catching up on records because I didn't have any sessions scheduled, which I was grateful for. Walanda's murder had me feeling less than therapeutic.

I spent the early evening at the gym listening to Smitty tell me how I threw the hook like a bitch. He drilled me on the footwork to stay away from Suggs's power. The plan was for me to jab him and keep moving to my right so he couldn't reach me with his right hand. The problem with that was he could also throw a wicked left hook and I'd be moving directly into that.

The thing with fight strategies was that they always looked good on paper, but when you're standing in front of someone set on taking your head off, it didn't always seem as easy. Smitty's strategy was the right one, though, and I planned on following it as closely as I could.

After the workout, we sat in Smitty's office and watched tape of the guy on Smitty's old TV console. Suggs was a huge and ripped white guy with a shaved head and a Fu Manchu beard. There was no doubt this guy could fight. The guys who fight in the South and Midwest circuit fight shitty competition, but it doesn't mean they all suck. Suggs was knocking everyone out and doing it quickly. Sure, a lot of them were tomato cans, but he was making them unconscious. My movement was going to be the key.

I finished up at the gym and headed home. Once again, Al gave me his customary greeting at the door, but this time I was ready. I intercepted his paws and moved gracefully to my left, deflecting his testicle-seeking charge. Already, I was emphasizing movement.

It had been a productive day for Al. In between couch gnawing sessions, he busied himself by making a mess with every single newspaper and periodical he could find in the Blue. He got halfway through the second cushion on my couch. I now had one half of a cushion to sit and unwind on at the end of the day. I couldn't tell if I was imagining it or not, but Al's early-morning activity that made its way between my toes seemed to linger in the air like some evil potpourri that you'd find in a very special ring of hell.

I didn't feel at all like straightening the place up or, for that matter, deodorizing it, so I headed to AJ's. I was hoping to find

Kelley to see what he could tell me about Walanda and jail. I took Al with me in an attempt to minimize the damage to my home. For whatever reason, he seemed to be easier on the Eldorado, that is, if you consider barf in velour easier. Come to think of it, the barf from his last ride had formed somewhat crunchy concentric circles on the passenger seat. Perhaps I could find some mystic palm reader to tell me what the circles could tell me about my future. Suffice it to say, the Eldorado was no longer what I'd describe as "daisy fresh."

I left Al sleeping on the front seat with his head on the center armrest. I slid the eight-tracks under the seats so he'd be less tempted and headed into the bar. The Fearsome Foursome were all in their places and so was Kelley, in his usual slot, one seat removed. The Foursome were already deep into it.

"The guy who played Sergeant Schultz was a Nazi in real life," Rocco said. "I saw it on the E! True Hollywood Story"

"I never heard that. I know that the Hogan guy got killed by Colonel Klink after he filmed the two of them having gay sex," said TC.

"That's not true, is it?" Jerry Number Two seemed genuinely disturbed by the revelation.

"No, it's not true," said Jerry Number One. "It was the French guy he was having sex with. His name was Pepe Le Pew."

AJ had the Yanks on TV with the sound down and a radio going. The Foursome were about to move on to their next topic when AJ shushed them.

"Fellas," AJ said. "It's the bottom of the fifth."

The talking ceased and AJ turned up the radio as everyone set their eyes on the TV. John Sterling had the call.

"Well, here it is. The end of five and you know what that means. It's time to flush out the Clogger—and here he is, right on time, the pride of the real Windy City, Crawford, New York...Clogger McGraw!"

The Yankee Stadium crowd was on its feet like it always was waiting for the Clog to do his thing. Sterling waited, giving the

Clogster an exaggerated pause, and then did it.

"aaaaaand Clogger cannnnnns it!"

The bar roared right along with the crowd at the stadium. It was great to see a local guy make good.

I took the seat next to Kelley, and AJ opened a Schlitz for me. I asked him to back everybody up. The Yanks were beating Tampa Bay eleven to nothing and it wasn't much of a game, so I figured Kelley was approachable. At least he was as approachable as he got.

"What's up, Kel?" I said.

"Hey Duff," he said. "Thanks for the drink."

That was pretty talkative for Kelley. I decided to take a chance.

"You mind if I pick your brain about Walanda?"

"Go ahead, Duff, but I got to tell you, I don't know a whole hell of a lot."

"Did anything ever come of the Webster stuff she mentioned?" "Not that I heard of. Walanda has said a lot of shit to the both of us over the years," he took a sip of his Coors Light. "I wouldn't put a lot into it, Duff. Who knows what she meant."

"How's the investigation going on her murder?" I asked.

"Duff, I'm a beat cop," he put his bottle on the bar with some force. "I don't decide what the department does. They'll send someone over and ask some questions. The COs will keep their eyes open, and it might eventually come out who did it. But to be honest, it isn't a big deal at the station."

"Does that feel right to you?" I said. It came out more confrontational than I wanted it to.

"Duff, this is all day, every day for me," he turned to look at me. "The answer is no, it doesn't feel right, but keep it in perspective. Walanda has no family to speak of looking for answers. She didn't have a lot going on that was positive, and— let's be honest—the society as whole probably won't miss her. I don't like the way that sounds, but it's true."

Kelley was, of course, right. He wasn't being a jerk about it; he was being pragmatic in the reality he has to deal with every day of his life.

"Did anything about her stepdaughter turn up?" I asked.

"Not that I heard of but, Duff, that girl could have gone thirty different places and still be with family," he said.

"Would you think I was crazy if I looked into this whole deal a little bit?"

"Looked into?"

"You know," I said. "Tried to get some answers."

Kel shot me a look that was part disbelief, part disdain.

"What are you, fuckin' 'Duffy for Hire, Private Eye' all of a sudden?"

"No—nothing like that. I just want to look into it a little bit."

"Look, Duff, I know you're a tough guy," he said. "I know you can take a punch, but you don't know anything about being a cop." "Cop?" I said. "Who said anything about being a cop?"

"Duff—don't mess around with this. It's not a good idea."

"I'll be fine—I'm just going to get enough answers to settle my mind. I feel I owe her."

He rolled his eyes, clearly not approving my plan, but as was his way, he didn't say I shouldn't or couldn't. He did go back to watching the TV. The way Kelley reacted, I didn't dare get into Mikey and Eli; it just wasn't the right time. I finished the Schlitz and headed to the door. The Foursome had dropped the Hogan's Heroes debate and had moved on to Green Acres.

"You know," TC said, "they all wound up eating Arnold Ziffel in the last episode."

"You mean they were cannibals?" said Jerry Number Two.

"What are you—an idiot?" Rocco said. "Arnold was a pig!"

"That's not very nice," Jerry Number Two said. "And it's no reason to perform a cannibalization."

Though I tended to agree with Jerry Number Two, it was late and I headed home.

8

I got through work on Friday, met Smitty at the gym, and headed to the airport. Al was staying in the Moody Blue for the weekend and Jerry Number Two and Trina both agreed to check in on him. Between the two of them, they would stop by three times a day to record what damage he had done to my worldly possessions.

In the car on the way over, Smitty talked nonstop about strategy and attitude. It was what he did building up to fight time, and sometimes I wondered if it was his way of dealing with his own butterflies. Smitty's whole life was regimented; he did the same things every day in the same ways. It made him a good trainer because he drilled you on the same stuff over and over and over.

Repetition is important in boxing. You might bring your guard back to the side of your head ninety-nine times out of a hundred, but the one time you don't, you're liable to get knocked unconscious. Smitty's tendency to go over things a lot helped in the ring, but it tended to make you crazy when he was a travel companion.

In some ways, Smitty's strategy repetition was a relief because it prevented me from thinking about Walanda, Shondeneisha, Mikey, Eli, Lisa, or about getting fired from my job. Just the same, even if everything wasn't on my mind persistently, the uneasy feelings along with the fight jitters were there. There was something incredibly fucked up about people putting hurt on other people for stupid reasons. That may sound strange coming from a guy whose main hobby is punching other men in the face, but it's the way I feel. There was a certain meanness in this world and I didn't like it when it got to people I cared about.

We were booked into a Ramada Inn, but there was only enough time to leave our bags because there was some sort of press conference to promote the bout that we were required to attend. Usually, the fights I'm in don't warrant press conferences, but Suggs was a big deal in Lexington. The ballroom at the Crowne Plaza down the street from the Ramada was set up for the press, and I was supposed to be there by nine o'clock. It was a quarter after nine when Smitty and I found our way there.

The place was all lit up and there were about ten reporters, some local TV, and a whole group of Suggs's fans. Suggs was there, standing on his chair, leading some sort of cheer when we walked in. As Smitty and I made our way to the podium, I noticed Suggs had about fifteen guys with him as an entourage. Just about all of them sported acid-washed jeans and mullets. Welcome to Kentucky.

Suggs abruptly ended his cheer and gave an exaggerated look in our direction. He raised one eyebrow and smiled crookedly.

"Looky, looky here…" The crowd hung on everything the guy said. "It's two-thirds of an Oreo cookie."

The crowd and the mullets laughed hard as Suggs paused. The guy worked the room well—that is, if you were a fan of pro wrestling.

"Hey boy—you teach the Polack everything he know?" Suggs pointed at Smitty. "You gonna use the monkey defense?"

This got another big laugh. This whole thing caught me off guard, not because of the fact that he was talking trash—that came with the game—but this was getting ugly. I was expecting a few people and some reporters and the same stupid but harmless questions that always seemed to get asked before fights. I wasn't ready for this festival of idiocy.

"And you, boy, which was it with you?" he pointed at me and paused again for dramatic affect. "Was your mommy the drunk and your daddy the Polack, or was it the other way around?"

The crowd roared, the entourage hooted and hollered, and Suggs stood there with his hands on his hips in mock confusion. I didn't hear all of it because I was busy flying out of my chair and knocking over the podium. Smitty was holding me back and a couple of the mullet-heads stepped forward toward me. I pushed three of them back and one fell to the ground. Through the confusion I heard one of them say, "Get the nigger."

I swung around and grabbed the back of the mullet of the guy who was heading toward Smitty. The guy's feet went out from under him and he fell to the ground. Somebody else pushed me from behind and then I saw somebody spit at Smitty.

I wheeled again but Smitty grabbed me and pulled me toward the door. I fought it for a while, but over the years doing what Smitty said came as second nature to me. He walked me out of the room like an angry mother walks a kindergartener who she had just caught misbehaving. The security cops had intervened between the mob and us, so there wasn't anything left for us to do anyway. Smitty pushed me into the elevator and hit the button for the lobby. When it started to move he pulled the emergency stop button.

"What the hell is a matter with you?" He stared at me like I had done something terrible. "All these years, and this is how you act." "Smit—"

"Shut up. You know better," he said. "That fool wanted a circus and you gave it to him."

"He was way the fuck out of line, Smitty, and you know it." Now I was getting pissed off.

"That's not the point. The point is the damn fight is tomorrow night." Smitty raised his voice even more. "That's what's important." "I'm fuckin' sick of people like him—I ain't taking it any more," I yelled right back at him.

Smitty stared at me, thought for a second, and let out some air. "Settle down, settle down." Smitty's voice went soft. "It's over, you need to get your head back into the fight and clear your mind." Smitty was talking to me like I was a child, and he put a hand on my shoulder.

"Now we're going to our rooms, and let's get our rest," he said. He hit the elevator button, and just as quickly as it erupted, the anger subsided. We hit the lobby and headed out to the street for the walk back to the Ramada. We hadn't walked a block when Smitty started in again with the fight strategy.

"Son, don't fight this guy. It's all about movement." Smitty was consoling now, almost hypnotizing.

"Yeah, Smitty, I know, I know," I said.

Back at the Ramada, we went to our separate rooms and settled in for the night. Actually, settled wasn't the right word. Like the night before most fights, I got very little sleep and whatever sleep I got was shitty, the kind where you sort of cruise over real sleep. This was the worst part about fights. There was nothing to do but sit around and get edgy the night before and most of the day of the fight.

I walked around the town the next day, mostly trying to avoid Smitty a bit because he was getting on my nerves with all his repetition about moving and using the jab. Walking the streets and spending a lot of time on my legs wasn't a good idea because I was going to need them for the fight, but sitting around was making me nuts.

I thought about calling Rudy to check in on Eli and Mikey. I thought about calling Lisa and decided against it. I almost called Trina to see if she could tip me off about Claudia's plans to fire me. Then I thought about Kelley, and I wanted to call him about Walanda and Shony. The more I walked, the more shit got to me.

It had been a hell of a week and now tonight I was facing this fuckin' asshole who was probably going to knock me out.

Honestly, the guy was stronger, hit harder, and was younger than me. I could probably take him into the later rounds, absorb a lot of punishment, and lose a decision. I just couldn't stomach looking across the ring and seeing that asshole grinning and exalting himself.

I got back to my room to rest for a couple of hours before I had to leave for the fight. I sat on my bed, and as I looked down at my hands, I noticed they were curled up into tight fists. My right knee wouldn't stay still, and I got up and paced the room. This was more than the usual pre-fight bullshit—this was something else. My breathing was hard and my palms were coated in sweat.

Whatever this was, it needed to be exorcised and I knew how. It was going to mean something I'd never done before but knew how to do. I might not be a top-ten fighter, but I've spent years in inner-city gyms paying the tuition of this game. I knew boxing in and out, and that included the underbelly of what was sometimes a cruel and unforgiving game. Suggs had the strength, he had the talent, but he hadn't paid for his tuition like I had. He was brought along, managed, and taken care of, and he didn't know about the respect that was due to another fighter.

I've seen and known some fighters who the average guy on the street would think were the biggest assholes in the world. A lot of those guys understood the gym and understood the code fighters lived by, and I respected them. Maybe they wouldn't be getting citizen-of-the-year awards, but around gyms they had integrity. Suggs pissed on that integrity, he pissed on me and a man like Smitty, a man who should be revered in this. He also hated people for the sake of hate, and I decided then and there that he had to be taught a lesson—Duffy Dombrowski, judge, jury, and executioner.

When Smitty came to my room, I stared straight ahead with nothing but a scowl. I'm usually loose before a bout, cracking wise and making jokes, but this was different and Smitty didn't like it at all.

"Boy, where's your head at?" Smitty said.

"I'm good, Smitty, let's get there," I said.

"Son," Smitty almost begged. "It's about the movement, remember?"

"Uh-huh," I said.

We waited for the preliminaries, and with two fights to go before the bout, Smitty wrapped my hands. He kept looking up at me with a worried expression on his face. He was concerned, even baffled, because after fifteen years together he'd never seen me like this. When it was time to go, I stared straight ahead and when they announced me, I walked out instead of jogging with my usual bouncing and trotting.

I had on my custom-made trunks, which blended the Irish, Polish, and American flags together. Usually, I come out to Elvis's opening, the Space Odyssey theme, but tonight I changed it to Elvis's song "Trouble." The King was screaming a challenge about whether another man had the guts to look me right in my eye, and I knew that this guy was about to get the trouble he seemed so eager to find.

The crowd booed and heckled, but it sounded like it was detached from me. Soon after I made it into the ring, the crowd erupted as Suggs made his entrance to some goofy country song about kickin' ass. He was thumping his chest and acting like he was coming to a coronation rather than a fight. He danced past me when he entered the ring.

"You're getting hurt, you nigger-lovin' Mick Polack," he said.

I stared straight ahead, just barely shuffling my legs to stay loose. When the ref called us together for the final instructions, I stared right through Suggs. He said some bullshit that I didn't hear. I just looked through his eyes. I could taste it.

The bell rang, and I came out in my southpaw stance. I studied the ref's movement, noticed he was inexperienced, and right from the opening bell I could see he was easy to get out of position. Suggs threw a hook that I partially blocked and partially took on the side of the head. He could hit and it wobbled me.

The crowd cheered like Suggs was the second coming of Joe Louis and Ali mixed together, and I decided to do what I had to do sooner rather than later. The tuition I spent in gyms for years paid for a lot, and not all of it on the square. Tonight, it didn't matter. Tonight was about something else.

I moved to my right, making sure the ref was behind my left shoulder. I gave Suggs a stutter step to get him on his heels and then I threw my right jab as hard as I could. The jab is the best thing I throw, but tonight I gave it something extra. In the split second before it was to land on Suggs's face, I snapped my right hand down counterclockwise and I stretched my thumb out as far as I could. My thumb landed solidly into Suggs's eye and I felt his eyeball give slightly and then bounce against the back of the bony orbital. It was thrown perfectly.

Suggs gasped and then grabbed his eye, temporarily blinded while I threw a wicked body shot into his left side. That made him drop his guard, which was exactly what I wanted. Then, I stepped closer to him and threw an uppercut with my left, except I deliberately made my fist miss his chin and instead connected with my elbow. My elbow came directly in contact with his jawbone and it made a sick crackly sound. His knees crumpled and he went through the ropes.

As Suggs lay on the ring apron going in and out of consciousness, I called to him.

"Hey, asshole—nis govia and top of the mornin' to you!" I figured he liked my heritage so much I wished him good health in Polish and good luck in Irish.

Then I spit on him.

The crowd and the ref hadn't picked up the thumb and the elbow, but they did catch me spitting on him, and that's when the bedlam started. Beer cups started to fly, Suggs's corner started to yell at me and Smitty, and the crowd, which was made up of a bunch of toothless Deliverance extras, were getting nuts. There were about two thousand fans there and not a single one for me. It was definitely time to go.

Smitty grabbed me and we ran straight out the exit for the car, getting pelted with beer and popcorn and everything else on the way out. Whatever we had in the locker room wasn't worth going back for. We started the car and hit the gas and got out of there as fast as we could. We got back to the Ramada, packed whatever shit we had, and got back in the car. Smitty drove us about twenty miles to a nameless motor inn where no one could find us, checking all the way to make sure no one was following us.

It wasn't until we had checked in to the new motel that we had a chance to say anything to each other. We checked in to separate rooms and for the longest time I just stared into the mirror looking at myself like I was going to find some sense in what had happened. I feared Smitty wouldn't want anything to do with me, that I violated everything he held dear, and that I was going to lose him and, more importantly, his respect, forever. I needed Smitty; he'd been my anchor since I was a zit-faced teen, and the thought of losing his respect made me feel sick. I couldn't take that now, not with everything else swirling.

I wasn't real confident about my mental state. I mean, I knew what I just did and I did it on purpose. I'm glad I did it, but that worried me. Something...something to do with the mess of Walanda's lost life, the potential of her stepdaughter losing hers, and the bullshit cruelty Mikey and Eli were suffering was eating at me. Maybe it was that existential angst bullshit about the cold cruel world, or maybe that thinking was just a convenient way of categorizing it to cover up the fact that I let Walanda down. She asked for help and I didn't give it.

Then there was Mikey and Eli, and even with all my day-in and day-out touchy-feely social work bullshit, they were in hospital beds. Hey, they may be in excruciating pain, inches from death, but they can identify their feelings.

Fuck me.

I didn't know what to do. I stared into the mirror for I don't know how long and lost track of time.

A knock at the door brought me out of it. A quick look at the clock told me I had been in this motel for an hour and a half. I carefully cracked the door with the chain still on. It was Smitty. I let him in.

"I don't know about you, Duff," he cracked a smile, "but I need a beer."

"Where'd you find the Schlitz?" I said.

"Right across the street there's a beer distributor," he said, pulling two cans out of the twelver.

He opened his, handed me one, and toasted me.

"You know what Billy Conn said when they asked him why he went for the knockout when he had Louis beat through twelve rounds?" Smitty asked.

"No."

"What's the point of being Irish if you can't be stupid?"

"I'll drink to that," I said.

Smitty took a pull off of the Schlitz and let his body fall into the chair by the window. "You know you'll get suspended," he said matter-of-factly.

"New York won't find out, Smitty." I figured fighting in Kentucky kept me off the radar.

"Son, it made the news."

"Aw shit…" I said.

"Duffy, can I tell you something, straight up?" Smitty sat up in his chair and looked me in the eye.

"Sure, Smitty."

"That was one hell of an impressive piece of work you did tonight," Smitty said. Then he started to laugh so hard the Schlitz came out of his nose.

We laughed most of the night.

9

Smitty and I were back up in Crawford by Sunday afternoon. The incident didn't make the local papers but some of the boxing websites were making a big deal about it. Suggs was an up-and-comer, so for hardcore fight fans it meant something. If it had been just me fighting another professional opponent, it probably would've stayed off the radar. It was only a matter of time until the New York Athletic Commission caught wind of it, and once they did, I'd probably have to answer for my actions. If I had known I would've got in trouble, it wouldn't have meant not doing it—I'm glad I did it. Besides, the state I was in at the time wasn't exactly my right mind. Geez, I was starting to make the same excuses my clients did.

What I hadn't counted on was my purse being held up. If you flagrantly foul your opponent, the promoter can get away without paying you. Now that might have entered into my thought process—maybe. Seven grand is a lot of money to me. I just should've broken his jaw without spitting on him was all.

Being home brought back all the things that were on my mind before I left for the fight. One of the reasons I love fighting is that it interrupts what you're thinking about. You really can't think of anything else while you're fighting. The process of fighting jumbles up the usual pattern of what I obsess on so when I'm done boxing I have a fresher point of view.

I got to thinking of what Kelley had warned me about in

Walanda's case. Though I wasn't about to apply for a PI license, "Duffy for Hire" had kind of a nice ring to it. Spenser for Hire was a retired fighter and his girlfriend had a dog, though it was one of those yuppie pointer dogs. It certainly wasn't a kick-you-in-the-nuts, unmistakably masculine hound like Al.

I really didn't have any plans to do the whole private eye thing, but I did want to find out what I could so maybe I could sleep better at night. The first thing I wanted to do was to check things out at the county jail.

I had a quasi-legitimate reason for going to the jail. We get quite a few referrals from the jail's counseling programs. I've had a standing offer from the caseworker to come sit in on her group. Her name was Jane Wishburn and she was a tough-as-nails recovering heroin addict who had seen it all and been through most of it in her forty-something years. Jane was wiry thin and had long prematurely gray hair. Her face showed the mileage, but in a way that made you respect her. She was attractive in that way but certainly didn't have what you'd call classic good looks.

Jane's therapy style wasn't complicated. She once told me that when you do a session with an addict all you really need to know is one word and the word was "bullshit." No matter what an addict says, just say "bullshit" when they're through and 99 percent of the time you'll be on target. Jane didn't get bogged down in a lot of touchy-feely stuff. Considering the population of people she worked with, avoiding the touchy-feely was probably a pretty good strategy.

I showed up at the jail half an hour before the group started. I had checked with Jane and she told me it was no problem to sit in. On the way in, I emptied my pockets, took off my shoes and let the disinterested guard wave the wand over me. They checked out my five dollar bill, my sixty-one cents, my paper clip, and my wadded-up Wal-Mart receipt and waved me in.

Jane met me just outside the entrance and we walked through a series of very large metal doors to her office. She had a desk in a small classroom-type area and there were hardback chairs aligned in a circle waiting for the inmates. Jane's desk was made from a dark metal and it had nothing but a cardboard blotter on it. Next to the wall there was a set of shelves with what looked like old and tattered self-help books.

Another disinterested guard escorted eight women into the room. They all wore green Dickies and white, orange, or black T-shirts. Some had on the jail-issued Keds or black work boots, while others had on their own Nikes or Reeboks. Most of the women had that rode-hard-and-put-away-wet look to them. This wasn't the crowd that fussed over exfoliating and moisturizing at night and toning in the morning.

Going to group was semi-optional, meaning they didn't have to go, but if they did, it would help take off a third of the time they had to do. That's what Jane had to work with, but she was good at putting the tough ones through their paces. The inmates may not turn around when they leave, but they definitely leave with a different level of insight than when they came in. I've heard some women describe the experience as taking the fun out of getting high.

The women in this group were almost exclusively into crack and alcohol. The weird thing about addiction is that when you say that someone's using crack and alcohol, the alcohol gets mentioned as an afterthought. The fact is, alcohol was there before the crack, often is there after they stop the crack, and all by itself it causes a world of problems.

This is the group Walanda was in before she was murdered. There was a good chance that at least some of the women in this group were in the group with her and would know something about what happened. The group happened to be made up of women between the ages of seventeen and forty. The seventeen-year-old was Sherrie, a Latina who could have passed easily for fourteen. The thirty-two-year-old was Marcie, a white woman with summer teeth—you know, some were here, some were there—who had been in and out of county jail since she was Sherrie's age. There was Katherine, Rebecca, and

Rosie, three black women in their twenties, who were big and loud and intimidating. The remaining three women were the creepiest. They were Lori, Stephanie, and Melissa, and they were tough white women who looked to be in their late thirties. They all wore black T-shirts to go with their Dickies.

The three in black stayed to themselves and spoke to each other in the kind of way that was designed to exclude the others. They exuded evil, not that the rest of the crew would have been mistaken for charm school graduates.

"We have Duffy Dombrowski from Jewish Unified Services with us today," Jane said. "Many of you will be referred there after you get out." That was the extent of my introduction. The group looked underwhelmed.

"All right—who wants to get started today?" Jane said.

Sherrie had that deer-in-the-headlights look to her. Clearly, this was her first time in and she was scared to death. Jane picked up on it.

"Sherrie," Jane said. "You look like you better talk. What's going on?"

"I...I...oh God!" Sherrie burst into tears and dropped her face into her hands.

The three in black giggled and threw each other mocking looks. Jane's concentration was with Sherrie.

"Start talkin' girl. That's what this is for."

"I can't take this." Sherrie sniffled back the tears. "Michael made me steal for him. If I didn't, he beat me—I can't stand this—I don't know what to do."

"Waaa..." Lori mocked Sherrie to her two friends. "Poor baby."

Jane's attention left Sherrie and her eyes were like daggers at the three of them.

"Lori—you got something to say?" Jane's stare would melt steel. "You got your life together so well you think you can mess with someone else? Let me see...the last I remembered your three kids, by three different men, if I might add, have all been taken away. This is your fourth trip inside and you're still on crack. I guess when you've got your life so together you can make fun of others."

Lori tried to flash a look that said "Whatever," but she didn't pull it off. The other two losers looked down into their laps.

Jane went back to Sherrie.

"What did you try to do to help yourself?" Jane said. "Was getting high helping? Did it make you more or less powerful?"

"I needed it." Sherrie bowed her head. "I was so messed up because of him. I needed to get high."

"Bulllllllshit," Jane said. Having seen her work before, I knew it was coming. "You got high because you were an addict, period," Jane said.

Sherrie's head hung down in shame. Jane was tough, but this is what Sherrie needed. She was about to be released, and Jane's goal was to keep it real for her. I also knew Jane well enough to know that she would make sure to address the abusive boyfriend issue before she left. It was important, right now, for her to blow away any denial about the addiction Sherrie still harbored. Despite the horrendous circumstances that some people face, getting high remains a choice. Sometimes a likely choice, but in Jane's mind it never stopped being a choice. In her world, she was right. Jane believed that no matter what your circumstances were, you had to get the addiction under control before you could do anything else.

Jane moved on to Stephanie, another one of the in-black trio. She was a slightly younger version of Lori. She was thin and pale with long, dirty blonde hair and a disproportionately large chest, the kind that just had to be fake. She tried to look disinterested when Jane called on her.

"Stephanie, the last time you said it was no big deal to have your eleven-year-old daughter taken away." Jane's eyes locked on her. "You were supposed to do some thinking on that."

"So?" Stephanie said.

"Don't give me that 'so' bullshit. Did you?" Jane said.

"Yeah, I did."

"Well?"

"Well, I think it's none of your fucking business, bitch," Stephanie said.

"Excuse me?" Jane said, but not with surprise or concern in her voice. The "excuse me" was her way of making it clear that that kind of talk was not permitted.

"Whatever…" Stephanie said.

"Don't give me that 'whatever' bullshit, girl." Jane didn't raise her voice. "You don't have to be here and don't count on scoring any jailhouse kiss-ass points for showin' up and being like this."

Stephanie raised her right hand slowly and very dramatically extended her middle finger. As she did, I noticed a small indigo mark, some sort of tattoo in the loose piece of skin between her thumb and forefinger.

"Fuck you, bitch," she said.

"Fuck me?" Jane smiled. "I don't think so—guard, get these three out of my face."

The disinterested CO stepped in the threshold of the door, stick in hand, and silently motioned to the trio to move. They did, but not before Lori and Melissa took the time to flip off Jane. They all had the identical mark in the same spot on their hand.

Jane was not ruffled; this is what she did, day in and day out. She saw it as a mission, and she was one of the few who did human service work in the jail who lasted more than a month. It was important to her. Without missing a beat, she moved on to Katherine.

"Katherine, talk to me," Jane said.

The group went on another half hour in a much calmer fashion. Katherine talked about making things different this time and really following through with NA. The rest of the group sort of cheered her on. Jane didn't do any more confrontation with the rest of the group, choosing to let the group end on a positive note with some hope for the remaining members.

While they were lining up, waiting for their escort, she called Sherrie aside, put an arm around her, and told her to come see her in the morning. Jane was an expert at gaining respect. Sherrie knew she was rough, but she also knew she cared deeply for her—enough to be hard. It's what made the difference and what allowed Jane to connect when others never had a chance. Sherrie caught up with the others and Jane and I were alone.

"Well, Duff," she said. "Wha'dya think?"

"It's a pleasure to watch you work, Jane," I said.

"Yeah right, Duff. Stop the bullshit."

"What?"

"You're here to find out about Walanda," Jane said, not asking but stating.

"It's that obvious?"

"Hell yeah," she smiled. "You've been taking my referrals for three years and this is the first time you come by? C'mon, man."

"Jane—I'm trying to get a sense of what happened to her, that's all."

"Duff, in this place, who knows?" She put a hand on my shoulder. "We both know Walanda was a little nuts and a lot aggressive. That's a bad combination in here."

"You got any ideas?"

"Nah…though I don't trust those three I threw out."

"What's their deal?" I said.

"They've been in for six weeks. All three were busted for a liquor store holdup. They hang together all the time in here, watching each other's back," Jane said.

"Gang stuff? They all seemed to have some tattoo on their hand." "Not real gang shit," Jane took a seat behind her desk. "They're from out in the boonies, near Forrest Point, outside of Eagle Heights—not exactly the South Bronx."

"What's the tattoo?"

"Got me." She put her feet up on her desk. "It looks like some sort of cross hatching pattern, like tic-tac-toe. Over the years I've stopped paying attention to colors, earrings, belt buckles, and tattoos. I don't want to treat anyone different because of some goofy accoutrement," Jane said.

"Gotcha."

"Hey Duff, you could do me a favor. I'm going to send you Sherrie tomorrow for follow-up. Will you take her on your caseload? I think she'd work good with you."

"Sure. How bad is it at home?" I said.

"Bad. Douchebag boyfriend is some sort of macho shithead who gets off on the whole power thing." Jane put her feet back on the floor and picked up Sherrie's file. "She gets high and makes being under his control easy."

"I'll make sure she gets on my caseload, and I'll see her tomorrow," I said. "Hey, if you hear anything about Walanda, give me call, okay?"

"I will, but I doubt I'll hear anything in here, Duff."

I headed back to the office not sure if I learned anything. My gut told me that the three women Jane threw out of group knew something or did something, but that was only natural because they acted so evil in the group. Jail was full of evil people and not all of them necessarily had something to do with Walanda's death.

Not necessarily, anyway.

10

Jail just plain sucks. The handful of times my job brought me there I always felt like it gave me a hangover. Part of it was that it was such an obvious failure as a system for the people incarcerated and part of it was some of the pure evil that lurked in there. I'm not naive enough to believe we don't need jails or that jails should be philosophical retreats where everyone gets hugged all day. People like Jane seemed to have the right mixture of common sense and the desire to help the problem. She didn't spend time trying to figure it out. She kept her world and her goals small and focused. I guess it's what the twelve-steppers call "Keeping it Simple."

I headed to AJ's to drink Schlitz and think deep thoughts. If Kelley was there, I figured I wouldn't bring up anything deeper than the Yankees' middle-relief issues. The Fearsome ones were in and tonight's intellectual foray was on the subject of popular music.

"He had his stomach pumped," Rocco was saying. "It's a known fact."

"Hold it," Jerry Number One said. "Rod Stewart or Elton John?"

"I always heard it was Rod Stewart," TC said.

"Nah," Jerry Number Two said. "It was Elton John—haven't you ever seen the hats that guy wore?"

"What the hell does that have to do with getting his stomach pumped?" TC said.

"A man's haberdashery says a lot about him," Jerry Number Two said.

"What does that say about Sinatra?" said Jerry Number One.

"Be very careful," Rocco warned. "This conversation is over."

Everyone knew you just didn't disrespect the Chairman of the Board in Rocco's presence. There were very few things held as absolutes at AJ's, but holding Sinatra in the proper regard was one of them. Never mind the general theme of the conversation, you just didn't disrespect Frank.

The stuff I love with the brown-and-white label was slid in front of me. Kelley wasn't around, which was good because even if I was tempted, I couldn't bug him for details on Walanda, Shony, Mikey, or Eli. Tonight it was just me, the Foursome, and the Yanks on the tube. Tonight, Mussina was pitching and Alex Rodriguez was in the middle of twelve-game hitting streak. A-Rod was making about twenty-five million a year and I was trying to figure what his weekly paycheck looked like. Even without the Schlitz that was tough to do, but after slamming three on an empty stomach, my desire to figure it out slipped away. I did wonder if he had to go to the business office and see a guy like Sam who wouldn't give him a check until he got told a Polish joke—or in Rodriguez's case a Mexican joke, or was it a Dominican joke? Ahh—fuck it.

Matsui had just bounded into a double play when I heard Rudy come in. Rudy wasn't a regular-regular, but he came in often enough to have earned his AJ's stripes, which meant his balls were up for being busted like anyone else's.

"Hey, it's the good doctor," Rocco announced.

"Hey Rude," Jerry Number One said. "My prostate's been acting up again. Wanna give it a look?"

"Tell you what, Jer," Rudy said. "You're a big enough asshole—why don'tya squat on a mirror and do it yourself?" he said.

That got a few laughs, but its edge was a little sharp for

Rudy. I tapped the bar in front of me once to alert AJ that I wanted to buy Rudy's drink. Rudy looked like he needed one, and I heard him order a Hennessy with specific instructions for AJ not to bruise the ice.

I slid off my stool and headed down to the one on Rudy's right, away from the Foursome. Rudy had beads of sweat on his forehead and great big rings of sweat under his arms. The man was stressed out.

"Rude," I asked, "you all right?"

"Fuck, yeah," Rudy exhaled heavily and took a serious sip of the brandy. "That fuckin' prick Gabbibb…"

"What's up with him?" I asked. "Or is it just his usual bullshit?"

"That fuckin' asshole is Broseph's suck-up. They're both on my ass because of my charts being behind. Gabbibb blows off any of my recommendations, and he's so fuckin' arrogant I want to rip his throat out."

"So it is his usual shit," I said.

"Yeah, I guess," Rudy said. "There's no doubt Gabbibb's a fuckin' genius, but where's the rule that he has to be a fuckin' asshole to go with it? Besides all that, I get the sense I'm being set up." Rudy got quiet and stared at his drink.

He ran his fat, stubby fingers through his thin hair and drank his cognac. He vented like this frequently, and I was glad to listen. The man had done me more than a few favors over the years.

"Is that all that's getting you? You usually don't let the DAT man rile you like this," I said.

"No, there's something else." Rudy looked down into his Hennessy and ran his stubby index finger around the rocks glass. "The hospital administrator, Dr. Broseph, is going to take away my privileges."

"Privileges? What's that mean, you won't be able to golf at the club or something?"

"Nah, Duff." Rudy looked up but not at me. He stared

mindlessly into the mirror on AJ's back wall. "Privileges are what allow you to practice in the hospital. Without privileges you don't work." "You're saying you're getting canned?"

"Pretty much."

"How can they can a doctor? Who's going to take care of your patients?" I said.

"That's the problem, Duff. Broseph says my average length of stay is three days over the average and that's unacceptable." "Average length of stay?"

"How long each patient of mine is in the hospital."

"What does that have to do with anything?"

Rudy threw down his entire drink and motioned to AJ for another.

"The way it works now, the insurance companies pay the hospital by the ailment. The longer a patient stays in the hospital, the less money the hospital makes," Rudy said.

"What if the patient isn't ready to go home?"

"Too bad—they send them home and have a nurse visit once a day. Except I won't go for it and I've defied his orders to discharge patients."

"And now it's going to cost you your job?"

"Yep." Rudy finished the second Hennessy. "It's even worse for your guys. They all have Medicaid, which pays shit, so they are always getting run out. Sometimes they find reasons to refuse them admission, which is, by the way, against the law," Rudy said.

"That's bullshit. I can't believe you'd get fired for taking care of people."

"Yeah, Broseph ordered me to send home an eighty-three-year-old woman two days after her hip replacement operation even though she lived alone. He said she'd be fine because we assigned her homecare."

"He can do that?"

"You better believe he can. The guy takes in half a million a year, more if the hospital finishes in the black. He's got a mansion outside of town with two Mercedes and a Porsche. He treats people like shit."

"Can't you sue him or bring him to some board or something?" "Ahh, fuck it, Duff, it doesn't work that way. Everything he does is wrapped up in all this hospitalese that makes it sound like he's loving and caring. Look, let me change the subject."

"Sure, please," I said.

"I got some mixed news on one of your guys," he said. Rudy's tone had changed. He was speaking as a doctor again, not an AJ's rummy.

"Mixed?" I said.

"Mikey came out of the coma, and he looks like he'll make it," he said.

"What's the but, Rude?" I said.

"They found cancer in him," Rudy exhaled hard. "He's got pancreatic cancer pretty bad. They're going to have to go after it aggressively."

"Fuck…what the fuck kind of luck is that?" I said to no one in particular.

"No kind of luck at all," Rudy said back.

Rudy explained to me the type of therapy Mikey would be up against. It involved radiation to get the cancer but it would also mean a brutal toll on Mikey's body. Mikey was obsessed with his appearance, and losing his coif, his tan, and his body weight would be devastating for him emotionally. There wasn't a choice, but this was going to be an incredibly hard row for Mikey to hoe.

It also meant that Mikey, Rudy, and me would be dealing with Gabbibb all the time. Cancer-wise, there wasn't a better man in the country. Human-wise, I would rather get jabbed in the eye with a sharp stick than have to deal with him. I guess if the guy could keep you alive when the grim reaper paid a visit, I shouldn't care what kind of asshole he was.

There was something else on my mind.

"Rudy?" He was busy ordering a double order of wings from AJ, so I waited for just a second.

"What's up, Duff?"

"Mikey say anything about who beat him?" I said.

"He was kind of in and out, but he kept talking about some bald bastard. You know how Mikey talks," Rudy paused trying to remember Mikey's words. With a bad imitation of Mikey, Rudy continued.

"'That bald biker bastard...' was what he kept saying, but he was pretty close to delirium."

"Couple more Schlitzes and I'll be pretty close to delirium myself," I said.

Rudy's wings were delivered and I didn't want to disturb him or witness the carnage that was involved when a stressed-out Rudy sublimated his emotions on twenty-four innocent chicken wings. Instead, I went back to my original spot and watched the Yankees middle relief blow their lead.

I lost count of the Schlitzes and figured it was time to check in on Al, so I began to head for the door. The Foursome had a new focus as I was leaving.

"Yeah, the pilots got in big trouble," Rocco said.

"What?" TC wasn't buying it. "You're telling me that the Navy pilots were deliberately flying over groups of penguins just so they'd tip over as they flew by?"

"I'm one hundred percent serious," Rocco said.

"Isn't it dangerous for jets to tip over like that?" Jerry Number Two said.

"God, you did too many drugs, Jer," Rocco said. "Not the planes, the penguins. They would look up and tip over while they watched the jets fly by."

"How'd they get back up?" Jerry Number One asked.

"The Seals helped them," Rocco said.

"I wonder if their whiskers tickled the penguins' backs?" Jerry Number Two asked.

"You asshole," Rocco said. "The Navy Seals."

"I wonder how they keep the sailor caps on...?" I heard Jerry Number Two say as the door closed behind me. I headed home and didn't even try to sort out the day, there was just too much. The Schlitz evened it out a little for me and I let Elvis take me home.

The ride to the Moody Blue isn't a long one, but between the industrial section of Crawford at night and the deserted area where I live there isn't much traffic. It probably wasn't anything, but a block or two after I left AJ's, I noticed a Crown Victoria was behind me. It was silver and it was pretty new, and whoever it was stayed behind me all the way home. When I pulled onto the gravel in front of my house, the Crown Vic just kept going. It was probably nothing.

The next day, I was in the office waiting for Clogger McGraw to show up for his 9:00 a.m. session. At about 9:35, the Clogster knocked on my door.

"Yo, Duff, what's up?" Clog was wearing a Hawaiian-style shirt with little airplanes all over it.

"Clog, you're a little late, man," I said.

"I am? Shit, sorry man," he said without a clue about his tardiness.

We got a little into the session and it was tough to focus Clog on any real sobriety-related issues. He was so thrilled with the Yankee Stadium gig that it was hard to get him to talk about anything else.

"It's a rush, man," Clogger said, wide-eyed. "The crowd cheering, the announcer, the rolls...the whole thing, man. I'm lovin' it," he said.

I couldn't really find anything wrong with Clogger's new gig, though I wasn't convinced he wasn't doing the whole deal stoned.

He was happy, he was working, and he didn't seem to be hurting anyone.

"Oh yeah, Dr. Gabbibb is giving me some work too," he said. "Gabbibb is buying a sign for you to pull?" I asked.

"No, man, he's having me use my plane to deliver shit to Staten Island on the same nights I do the Yanks."

"What kind of shit does Gabbibb need delivered?"

"Electronics shit, Duff." Clogger scratched the side of his head. "You know, CD players, pagers, cell phones. He has two cousins who are always doing business together. The one guy Enad runs an electronics type store in Staten Island. The other guy, Tunad, has a convenience store twenty miles from here in East Dunham. I pick up some shit from them and deliver it back and forth. Each run gets me an extra fifty. Gabbibb even gave me a free cell phone."

"Not a bad gig," I said.

"Sweet, man," Clogger said.

Clogger and I talked halfheartedly about some of his relationship issues. Clogger had a strong preference for Asian women and he had dated or lived with a string of them. The current one, Foon, barely spoke English, but she was a great cook and lived her entire life to please the Clogman. We kicked around the idea that intimacy might be limited by their ability to understand each other, but Clogger disagreed and really believed the fact that it was ideal that Foon and he could barely exchange pleasantries. There wasn't much to argue about and Foon not only was great in the kitchen and around the house, but she was also quite accomplished in the bedroom. Clogger speculated that before leaving Thailand, Foon may have had some professional experience in the art of pleasing men, but that was not at all an issue for him. She had shown him her tests from the health department and that was all the man needed for domestic bliss.

I finished up with Clogger and wrote a note in his file and got ready for my next session. Sherrie was due out of jail last night, and she was supposed to come in this morning. Trina buzzed me right at ten thirty, and I went to greet her in the waiting room and saw that she was wearing a Knicks cap, pulled down over her eyes. When I said hello and went to shake her hand, I saw why. She had two black eyes and her lips were swollen and split.

"Sherrie," I said. "Tell me what happened."

"What the fuck you think happened?" Tears ran down her face, but she kept a hard look on her face. "Michael beat the shit out of me, like always."

"Why?" I said.

"Why—that's what he does. He said it was for leaving him alone while I was in jail."

"Did you call the police?"

"C'mon, Duffy, what are they going to do?" She sat back in her chair. "He will just beat me worse after they leave."

"Why do you stay with him?" I said.

"Cause he'll beat me if I leave. I went to a shelter one time and when I went for cigarettes he was there. He took me home and fractured my cheek."

"I'm going to set you up in a safe house. There's one in—"

"Fuck that—don't even try." Sherrie held up a hand. "The last one I was at, some lesbian women kept coming on to me and all my shit got ripped off."

"You need to be safe," I said. "What can you do?"

"If I try to give him what he wants and not piss him off, sometimes that works."

"What pisses him off?"

"Everything," she said.

It went on like this for the next hour. I learned that Michael was Michael Calabreso and that he'd made his living dealing hot merchandise, usually DVD players, car stereos, and boom boxes, though he'd hustle anything. He liked to drink and he hung out at a dance club called Cinderella's.

Supposedly, I should have written up an incident report and alerted the Michelin Woman. Practically speaking, that was going to be a waste of time, and I would lose any trust I had built with Sherrie. Claudia would go by the book, make me refer her to the shelter and call the police. Sherrie would refuse,

Michael would find out about the police, make up some story, and not get arrested. Then, Sherrie would get the beating of her life. Letting her go was risky, but it was less risky than following the goofy social work protocol. Despite the wacky dysfunction of it all, women like Sherrie knew how to survive—at least for a while.

I made her promise to call me if she needed any help. I also made her promise to get to an NA meeting and to try to get some phone numbers there so she'd have some support. It seemed like the best thing to do—the best thing, given a whole range of choices that really sucked.

This was the shit about the job that made me nuts. When Eli gets drunk and gets naked at the gas station, I can deal with that. If Martha wants to eat or fuck herself happy, I can live with that. I can even listen to the Abermans bitch at each other or Larry drone on about how his life sucks. I could sleep well on those nights. I couldn't sleep well thinking about Sherrie.

At seventeen, she wasn't old enough to know better. Her mother's boyfriends beat her mom, so this craziness seemed normal. Michael was a guy with money, a city tough guy with city respect and to someone like Sherrie, that was status. It was a whirlpool of dysfunction and all the social work bullshit in the world wasn't going to stop that seventeen-year-old girl from taking a beating.

I stopped off at the Blue to take Al for a walk and to go through the mail. There was a very official envelope from the Department of State/Athletic Commission and I got a sick feeling. I opened it up and read the first line.

"Due to inappropriate actions in clear violation of the boxing regulations set forth by the Association of Boxing Commissions and the New York State Athletic Commission, you are hereby indefinitely suspended from boxing as a professional anywhere in the United States."

That's just swell, I thought. I figured this was coming, but it still sent me into a bit of a shock. The term "indefinitely" didn't sit well, and at the very least this was going to involve appeals and hearings and a bunch of other bullshit. On top of that, I'm sure I would have to feign remorse and as politically correct as things have gotten, I wouldn't be surprised if I got sent to some sort of anger management course.

Me and the low-riding Muslim went for a walk to get some air and to give me a chance to think a bit. There comes a time, I believe, when enough shit has happened that thinking becomes worthless. Sometimes I prefer to act than to think, and though over the course of my life that philosophy has gotten me into trouble, it still seemed like the right thing to do. Pondering is the way of the social worker, and I think I'm wired to act differently, even if it too often winds up a tad self-defeating. It's as if the waiting is so uncomfortable that action, even if it brings about negative consequences, is preferable.

Al sniffed his way up Route 9R and back and seemed to be somewhat mellowing to his new digs. He jumped back up on what was left of the couch he had mostly eaten and put his head down and closed his eyes while I hit the messages. I had begun to learn that good, long walks calmed my brother down a bit, and it was long stretches alone that tended to freak him out.

The first message was from Smitty. As my manager, he had gotten a similar letter, and he was anxious to start a strategy to get my boxing license back. I wasn't terribly interested in thinking about that tonight. The second one was from Lisa, and I felt my gut tighten when I heard her voice.

"Duff…uh…it's me." She sniffed back tears. "Um…I'm afraid I made a mistake…uh…I know this isn't fair, but I'd really like to see you. Can you call me?" she said.

That was just swell too. I was dying to see her, but inside I knew what was happening. I'd go see her, she'd cry and hug me and probably want to go to bed, where she'd ravage me. Trust me, I wasn't above that, but within seventy-two hours she'd get weird again and become distant and cold. As much as I wanted to go over there, especially with the type of week I'd been having, I didn't want to sign up for pain on the delayed-payment schedule. Still, I could use the company.

The third call was from Rudy.

"Look, Duff," he exhaled heavily into the receiver. "I hate to keep piling on with the bad news, but I figured you'd want to know. During tests on Eli they found a cancerous mass in his lung. Gabbibb wants to go after it aggressively just like Mikey's. Call me if you want some more information. I'm sorry."

What the fuck was going on? You couldn't make this shit up. This felt like God had some sort of Job-like vendetta, and trust me, I didn't have Job's faith. My brains were fried, and I decided against even thinking about Lisa, or dealing with the suspension or anything else. I felt like drinking.

My usual routine would've been to hit the gym and work everything out physically, but I just didn't want to get involved with Smitty yet. I had a pain in my chest from where the stress had tightened me all up. I looked down at my hands and they were balled up into fists like they were before the Suggs fight. I couldn't think straight and I could feel my heart race. AJ's seemed like a good choice.

The beauty of AJ's was that whether it was early or late, it didn't matter. The Foursome would be there before I got there and after I left, and there was a good chance that Kelley would be there early.

"You know, if she won't use birth control," Rocco said, "just get her to douche with Coca-Cola after sex."

"She gets grossed out by the thought of me in a rubber," Jerry Number One said. "But she's going to warm up to the idea of sticking a Coke bottle up there? That makes a lot of sense."

"Talk about 'the pause that refreshes'!" TC chimed in.

"I once got high drinking five Cokes and taking a half a bottle of aspirin," Jerry Number Two added, sipping his Cosmo and looking nostalgic for the old days.

"Did that work?" Rocco asked.

"Hell yeah," Jerry Number Two said.

"C'mon!" TC said. "Really?"

"Sure," Jerry Number Two said. "Though I guess I had done quite a bit of acid that day, before the Coke."

I wasn't in a good mood and I ordered a sidecar of bourbon to accompany my Schlitz. Kelley was there and picked up on the bourbon.

"Uh-oh," he said. "That's not a good sign."

"Shitty day, Kel," I said.

"Yeah?"

I told him about it, and the more I spoke, the more pissed off I got. The thing is, if you talk about this shit in the office with all the social-work types, everybody has a clinical name for the bullshit. Instead of being an asshole, a guy has "poor impulse control." Instead of a poor kid getting beat, you have a woman with "boundary issues." It made me nuts.

The crowd at AJ's didn't burden themselves with political correctness.

"Duff," Kelley said. "These people live like this and it sucks, but that's the way it is and that's how it's always going to be. Let it go and help when you can."

"Yeah, sure. You're right." I didn't feel like hearing it. Right or wrong, it made me crazy knowing there was a good chance Sherrie was going to take a beating tonight. The fact that that was the way of the world didn't help. It didn't help even a little. I ran this through my head while the Schlitzes kept going down, one after the other.

"Look, I'm outta here for tonight," I finally said to everyone and threw some cash on the bar. "I'll catch ya later."

I wasn't drunk, but I wasn't sober either. I thought it might be a good idea to take a ride past Cinderella's and eyeball Calabreso. I wasn't dressed to impress the Cinderella's crowd, but that didn't bother me too much. The Eldorado's V-8 hummed and I threw in the original Elvis as Recorded at Madison Square Garden from '72. The eight-track was queued on "Suspicious Minds," the live version of which always got me pumped. Along the way, the vision of Sherrie being full of fear every moment, the physical pain she must've experienced, and the corresponding humiliation she'd feel played over and over in my mind. I could feel my hands tighten around the steering wheel 'til my knuckles were white.

Cinderella's was very dark with lots of mirrors, chrome, and neon. The speakers blasted that obnoxious bass that went along with today's house music. It was only ten thirty, pretty early by club standards, but there were twenty or so people around. The barmaid had on a belly shirt that showed the piercing in her navel. She wore those tight, form-fitting black pants that young women wear today, and she filled them out very well. Her long, straight blonde hair came midway down her back. She was hot and she knew it, which made her an awful bartender.

I sat without a drink for a full five minutes while the belly shirt checked her hair, smoothed the fabric covering her ass, and checked the nails. She approached me without saying anything and just lifted her head and eyebrows slightly in what I gathered was a substitute for asking me if I wanted a drink.

"Jim Beam on the rocks."

She served it without a smile, took the ten that I'd thrown on the bar and I got two dollars change. I loved these places. I could still feel the blood pumping through me, but I contained it and hid it the best I could.

A few sips in, I got talkative with Belly Shirt.

"Hey, where can I get a DVD player around here?" I said. "Know anyone who gets them?"

Belly Shirt went to the other end of the bar, motioned to a guy talking in a circle of women, and sent him over. She said something to him and he nodded. He took a sip of his Jagermeister and came over. He had three gold chains around his neck and he wore one of those tight, black silk T-shirts along with black pants. His hair was greased back and he had a big head with a prominent nose and dark eyes. He was a weight lifter and he wore the T-shirt to show off the biceps and chest.

"You lookin' for somethin'?" Calabreso said.

"Yeah," I said. "I was hoping to get some DVD players."

"Some?"

"As many as you got," I looked him straight in the eyes. "Can we deal?"

"What you want with a lot of 'em?"

"What's this?" I said. "What do you care?"

"Just curious." He sipped his drink and broke the eye contact. "You got money on you?"

"Yep."

"Follow me."

We walked out of the front of the club and around the corner. His white Lexus SUV gleamed in the moonlight. He had custom gold trim all over the obnoxious thing. He walked ahead of me with an arrogant street swagger that I'm sure he had honed over the course of his life.

Calabreso was my height, about six foot one, and he was ripped from the weights. He put the key in the back of the car and lifted the door. There were boxes neatly stacked with all sorts of electronic stuff, like DVD players and boom boxes, all the way up to the front seat. It was like a rolling RadioShack.

He looked at me closely.

"You're the fighter, ain't you?"

"Yeah."

"I recognized the old-school flattop. You're not real big for heavy-weight—what you go, about two ten?"

"Yeah, just about."

"I got a question for you," he said with a half smile. "How come you keep fighting even though you hardly ever win?"

The thing people don't understand about boxing is that it's a whole lot harder to do then it looks. The pitty-pat you see on TV is actually guys getting punched in the face really hard. Assholes like Calabreso who thought they were tough didn't have any respect for it. He figured I was a bum.

"I like it, I guess," I said.

"Well," he laughed, "maybe you could get a collection of your losses on DVD and watch 'em over and over before you go to bed every night."

"Or maybe I could get a one-hundred-fifteen-pound girlfriend," I said, "and beat the shit out of her to make me feel like a man."

"Hey, fuck you, asshole." A prominent vein in his neck throbbed. "Mind your business or you're bound to get hurt."

Calabreso straightened up and took a step toward me with his chest out and his eyes glaring. It probably scared the hell out of street guys, but stepping forward was a bad idea.

I threw a good straight jab with my right hand and it landed squarely on his nose. Fighters know the sound; it's not a big "whack" like you hear in the movies. It's more of a low, muffled crack, like when you crack your knuckles really good. The best part is, it really fuckin' hurts and it makes your eyes tear up so you can't see.

Instinctively, I followed the jab with a left cross, smashing both his hands and his nose this time. You can't spend twenty years boxing and not let the cross follow the jab. The punches were automatic, like they couldn't not come.

Calabreso writhed, moaning like a guy who hadn't been hit before. I dropped a wicked body shot into his solar plexus. He let out a loud groan, grabbed his stomach, and fell, doubled over on the pavement. His face was covered in blood and he was rolling around on the pavement with one hand on his midsection and the other over his nose. That was probably enough, but then I remembered Sherrie—and a flash of the helplessness and fear she must have felt ran through me.

That was it.

"I wouldn't mind this on a DVD, asshole," I said, grabbing him by the neck and slamming his head into his gold-colored bumper. His big head made the sound of a pumpkin getting smashed and he fell backward behind the SUV. He was on his back; his face was a burgundy mess.

"Please, please…," he said, in what the great philosopher Mike Tyson once called "womanly noises."

"Fuck you," I heard myself say, and I slammed him face first into the bumper again. He fell backwards onto the pavement.

"You know what, asshole?" I knelt with one knee on his chest and grabbed him by his silk T-shirt. "They're gonna know inside that you beat a little girl. This is what your life is going to be like for the next few years."

I took his cell phone out of his pocket. He was bleeding all over my jeans, my hands were covered with his blood, and he was gagging every now and then from the bleeding. I called AJ's.

"AJ," I said, "put Kel on." Calabreso didn't move under the pressure of my knee. Kelley picked up the phone.

"Kel?" I said. "I need you to arrest somebody for me."

"What?"

"I happened across what I think is some stolen merchandise." Calabreso groaned a little under my knee. "I'm on Allen, that alley around the corner from Cinderella's. Oh, and the guy got banged up a little."

"Duffy—are you fuckin' nuts?"

"Kel—I think I'm going to get going," I said. "I probably don't want to be around here much longer. Can you do something official for me?"

I hung up. Calabreso was unconscious and wasn't going anyplace for a while, but I didn't want to take any chances. I hoisted him up fireman-style and loaded him into the driver's seat behind the wheel. There was a roll of duct tape on the floor, so I taped his hands to the steering wheel and figured it was time to go. I closed the door to the back of his car and headed to the Eldorado. A set of parked headlights had appeared a couple hundred yards down the street. I didn't know who or what it was, and I didn't figure it was in my best interest to hang around and find out.

I gunned the Eldorado and headed to the Moody Blue as fast

as I could. I turned up the eight-track just as Elvis was finishing up the glory hallelujahs in "The Battle Hymn of the Republic." It was the last part of a song he did called the "American Trilogy."

We sang it together all the way home.

11

I was almost to the Moody Blue, with lots of adrenaline pumping through my veins, when I realized Al had been in there alone since I left for AJ's. That meant that he was alone for the last seven or so hours.

I heard him start to howl and scratch the door as soon as I took the first step up the stairs to the front door. I opened the door and before I got it a quarter open, Al was through the door, jumping up on me, jumping off of me, spinning around, and then repeating this whole circuslike act. I inched my way into the trailer, and it looked like a clip from either the Discovery Channel's feature on hurricane damage or Animal Planet's special on neglected dogs living in squalor.

The house was littered with papers, the curtains were down off the windows, crushed Schlitz cans were strewn about the house and Al had chewed the fabric off two kitchen chairs. Apparently, after finishing off the sofa cushions he was bored. The place didn't smell great, either, and I'll spare the fine details, but let's just say Al clearly has no need for added dietary fiber. But I would need to flip my mattress over and change the sheets.

I fed Al and took him for a walk down Route 9R. He needed the walk, and I needed to unwind a bit. I took a Schlitz along with me, though I was going to need a lot more than one to settle down. Al was happy to be out and got busy sniffing every foot of land we covered on our walk, stopping to give extra attention to any vertical object stuck into the ground.

I didn't feel completely okay with what had just happened. I was okay with the first three punches because he had them coming for a couple of reasons. One reason was the abuse he'd been giving Sherrie and another reason was I had to hit him to subdue him, so he could be arrested. The last reason had more to do with street shit. I didn't like him mocking my ability to fight and spreading his nose all over his face was something he was asking for by disrespecting me. Different jungles have different rules and he violated one of his own jungle's rules. If you're going to sell wolf tickets you have to be prepared for someone to cash one in once in a while.

Smashing his head into the bumper was an act of rage. I didn't have to do it to protect myself or to make sure the cops would get him or even to make the point that he shouldn't hit a young girl like Sherrie. It left him unconscious and maybe seriously hurt, and that was more than the situation called for. Maybe it was the bourbon, maybe it was Sherrie, or maybe I was getting my shit off from my own frustration. It didn't feel completely right.

It probably is inconsistent with good social work practice as well, but I cared less about that. If I had followed protocol, Sherrie would have taken another beating and a lot of other useless bullshit would've gone on, not to help anyone, but to cover a lot of administrative ass. Of course, smashing someone's head into a bumper probably isn't the most acceptable therapeutic intervention for couples that aren't getting along.

It also wasn't fair to Kelley, who had to go clean up the situation. Clearly, he would have to face questions about how he knew about the situation and how he got tipped off. Kelley could finesse his way around all of that, but that wasn't the point. He shouldn't have to do that because his social-work friend wanted to play Robin Hood. I owed Kelley more than a drink.

Al finished sniffing and leaving his own biological calling card along Route 9R, and we headed to the Moody Blue. It wasn't until that point that I realized my right hand had swollen up. Later, when I washed my hands I noticed I had scraped the skin on my first two knuckles. They were so covered in Calabreso's blood that I just figured the blood wasn't mine. I drank another Schlitz and sprayed as much lemon-scented deodorizer around the trailer as I could. Despite the fact that I just made my living space smell like lemony dog shit, I fell asleep hard with Al next to me.

The next day Sam greeted me before I even made it to my cubicle.

"Hey Duff," he said. "Didya hear about the Polack who wore a condom on each ear?"

"Mornin', Sam."

"He didn't want to get hearing aids."

Sam moved on, and I sat at my desk to go through my mail, e-mail, and interoffice stuff. Monique poked her head into my cubicle on her way back from getting coffee.

"Did you read the paper this morning?" she said.

"Nah."

"Sherrie's boyfriend was busted on stolen merchandise, but not before he took a pretty good beating."

"No shit?" I said.

"Couldn't have happened to a nicer guy, huh?"

"Ain't that the truth." I tried not to give it my full concentration. "When are you seeing her again?" Monique asked. "It will be interesting to see how she handles it."

"I'm supposed to see her this afternoon."

"Sometimes women in abusive relationships have bizarre reactions to this sort of thing."

Monique knew a lot about the dynamics of abuse. I wasn't one hundred percent sure, but I believe she had some personal experience with it. I knew she tended to get most of the clients with that kind of background on her caseload. She was comfortable with their issues, and I don't think she got drunk and drove around town looking to beat up their boyfriends.

I got the office paper and went through the local section. On the second page there was a story about Calabreso's arrest.

Off-Duty Cop Comes Across Stolen Merchandise

Off-duty Crawford Police Officer Michael Kelley came across a suspicious vehicle last night and made an arrest for stolen property estimated at over twenty thousand dollars. Charged with possession of stolen property was twenty-four-year-old Michael Calabreso. Calabreso is likely to face additional charges. It appeared as if a deal for the stolen property had gone wrong as Calabreso had been found unconscious and taped to his own steering wheel.

"The alert actions of Officer Kelley have resulted in the recovery of stolen property and the apprehension of one of the city's kingpins in contraband and stolen merchandise," said Crawford's Police department spokesperson, Randy Weiser.

Calabreso is recovering and is listed in stable condition at Good Samaritan Hospital.

That was a relief. I was glad Calabreso wasn't going to be crippled or brain dead. I was also relieved to read that it didn't look like Kelley was going to be in any trouble. The fact that he was being made out as a hero wouldn't please him, and he'd still be plenty pissed, but at least he wasn't facing any problems on the job.

I headed to the medical center to see Eli and Mikey and to talk to Rudy. The Michelin Woman wouldn't approve, but I could say I was doing a session within the hospital or I was providing support or some shit. In reality, I wanted to get a handle on what to expect in terms of a prognosis for each of the guys and visit with them. Neither of them had any family and the people they hung out with were the type of friends whose lives centered around drugs and tricking. Those peer groups had a silent code that when you're gone—gone being in jail, in the hospital, or dead—you're gone. Taking into consideration the dangers of that type of lifestyle, it was a necessary mindset.

I got Mikey's and Eli's room numbers and they were both on the seventh floor, which I figured was the cancer floor. Like most people, I felt squirrelly in hospitals, but I tried not to let it get to me. Mikey's room was all the way at the end of the wing, and when I got there, the door was closed. There was a warning on the door.

WARNING! No visitors—Radioactive treatment in process.

I definitely needed to talk to Rudy.

I checked the number for Eli's room and it was right across the hall from Mikey's. It had the same sign.

I skipped the elevator and ran down the steps to Rudy's office. As always, he was sweating in front of his monitor and he had jelly-donut stains on the front of his lab coat.

"Rude—what the fuck is up with this radioactive shit?"

"What happened to 'Good morning'?" He didn't look at me and kept typing. "Hang on, just a second."

He finished up typing with his two fat index fingers and looked up.

"That's how you treat cancer aggressively. They're being treated with something called cesium. It's very powerful," Rudy said.

"How come no visitors?" I asked.

"This shit is no joke—if you're around someone who's radioactive, you can be exposed to harmful levels."

"So they're in there alone?"

"Yeah, pretty much. Of course they get their cheery visits from Dr. DAT and a few of his international med students," Rudy said. "Gee whiz, now I feel a whole lot better."

"Yeah, I know, they're all kind of a Hindu candy striper

detail." I was back to the office around lunchtime. It seemed bizarre to me that two guys would get beat up in the same park at roughly the same time, require pretty similar medical treatment, and then both be diagnosed with advanced cancer even though they hadn't complained about anything before. I never quite made it to medical school but, just the same, my instincts told me something wasn't the way it should be.

Trina buzzed me to let me know that my twelve thirty was here. That was Sherrie, and I could feel the nervousness spread throughout my body as I hung up the phone. I went out to the lobby to greet her.

"Good afternoon, Sherrie."

"Hi Duffy."

Sherrie still carried the bruises but her head wasn't buried under a hat, nor was she trying to hide. We went back to the conference room.

"Did you see the paper?" Sherrie asked.

"Yup—how are you doing with all of that?"

"I'm okay. I'm a little worried about him, but between jail and what we talked about yesterday, I think it may give me the chance I've been looking for."

"How's that?"

"Look, I wouldn't have wished him to go to prison or to get hurt, but if that's the way it's going to be, then I can make the best of it. I have family in Brooklyn and I think I'm going to head down there."

"And do what?"

"My Aunt Lena teaches at a business school," she said. "You know, where you can learn to be a paralegal or something. She's wanted me to go down there for a while, and she said I could stay with her."

"That sounds like a decent plan," I said.

"Duffy, can I ask you something?" She looked at me and smirked.

"Sure."

"Maybe not, forget it."

"You sure?" I said.

"Did I tell you that my cousin Rafael is a barback at Cinderella's?" she said.

"No."

"He used to be an amateur fighter." She sat back in the chair and smiled. "He said he saw you there last night. Doesn't seem to be your kind of hangout."

It wasn't really a question so I let it hang.

"Look, if it's okay with you, I'm not going to waste any time moving to Brooklyn," she leaned forward in her chair. "I guess that means I won't be on your caseload."

"No, we'll transfer your case to the appropriate place in Brooklyn. I'll take care of that."

I hesitated to ask her something because it had nothing to do with her case or her treatment, but I had to know.

"Sherrie, let me ask you something. You don't have to answer if you don't want," I said.

"Go ahead," she said.

"When you were in jail, did you hear anything about what happened to Walanda?"

"I can't say for sure, but I don't trust those three from Forrest Point. I heard them laughing about her being dead. Sick shit like about her brains spilling out and stuff...it was awful," she said. "That's all you know?"

"Yeah, sorry."

"That's okay," I said. "Walanda was on my caseload for a long time and I feel bad."

"Sorry, Duff."

"Hey—that day in the group I noticed something. You don't know what those three had tattooed on their hands, do you?"

"It was a spider's web, a little tiny spider's web."

I felt a chill.

"Duff, you all right?" she asked. "You look like you saw a ghost." "Nah, just got me thinking, that's all."

"Hey, I'm going to run," she stood up. "Can I get a hug? I appreciate everything you've done for me."

"We only had two sessions, Sherrie." She hugged me and held on for a moment more than the customary clinical hug.

"Uh-huh, sure," she said. "Just the same, you were a big help." "Well, thanks and good luck."

"You too, and Duff?"

"Yeah?"

"You might want to ice that hand," she said.

She winked, smiled, and headed out the door to Brooklyn and what I hoped was a new life.

12

I had some amends to make, and despite the fact that I wasn't looking forward to dealing with Kelley's anger, I wanted to face him. I owed him an apology, so I headed to AJ's right after work so I could be there when he arrived.

I also had an ulterior motive. Sherrie said that the tattoos the three from Forrest Point had were spiderwebs. That's a pretty common jail-house tattoo, though it's one usually sported by bikers around their elbows. With that group, it signifies the fact that they had the distinction of having committed a murder, kind of like how Cub Scouts get merit badges. I was dying to know if Kelley knew anything about spiderweb tattoos and if they had any relation to Walanda's "Webster." Still, I was a bit nervous asking Kelley for any information tonight. When it came to favors, my account was in the credit column.

I was distracted from my anxiety by the Fearsome Foursome who were already in mid-evening form, even though it was barely six thirty. TC and Rocco were in a heated debate centered on wedding rice and birds.

"You can't throw rice at weddings anymore because the ASPCA outlawed it," said Rocco. "The rice gets eaten up by the birds and it expands when it warms up in their stomachs and they blow up." "That's bullshit," said TC. "You're thinking about seagulls and Alka-Seltzer. If you give seagulls Alka-Seltzer, they explode in midair because of the fizziazation."

"If you use Minute Rice at a wedding, do the birds blow up faster?" Jerry Number Two said, pausing to sip his Cosmo.

"God, Jerry, you did way too many drugs," said Jerry Number One.

"You're right, there," Jerry Number Two said. "One time I was tripping and somebody gave me a bunch of those Pop Rocks and a Dr Pepper. I was in the emergency room for eight hours. I felt like a seagull at a wedding."

I was three-quarters of the way through my first Schlitz when Kelley came in. Trying not to be obvious, I studied his face for how he felt. As usual, Kelley's facial expression didn't give anything away. He took his usual spot.

I motioned to AJ to set Kelley up with a beer. AJ is often a pain in the ass but he knew his trade. He sensed there was a tension between Kelley and me and he stayed out of it. Almost imperceptibly, he opened Kelley's beer and slid it in front of him.

"Thanks, Duff," he said.

"Kel, I owe you an apology. I'm sorry if—" Kelley interrupted and I didn't get to finish.

"Oh, your little 'Duffy for Hire' deal?"

"Uh, well yeah."

"Well, I know you private eyes kind of live on the edge a bit," he said. "Shoot from the hip, live for the moment. I know, I've read the books," he said.

I deserved Kelley's sarcasm and I wasn't going to argue with him. He wasn't looking at me and he was trying to be nonchalant, but I could tell he wasn't happy with me.

"Look, you were way out of line, and it could have cost me my job," he spun around on his stool and looked me right in the eye. "If you want to get killed living out some vigilante fantasy, that's your business. Next time leave me out of it."

"I'm sorry, Kel," I said.

"It's fine. The guy's going away for a long time so the end result is that another piece of scum is off the street. Besides, I got a special commendation from the chief for my actions...geez."

"I'm glad you didn't get into trouble over it."

I was tempted to make a joke about the heroics but decided against it. Kelley was a man of principles and what mattered to him was that my irresponsible actions could've screwed him. The fact that the results were positive was incidental.

AJ set us up again, again on my tab. Kelley didn't protest. I decided to chance asking Kelley about the tattoos.

"Kel, what do you know about jailhouse tattoos?" I asked.

"Oh, now we're just making conversation?" he said.

"I did a group in the jail and these three tough-looking women from Forrest Point all had small spiderwebs tattooed between their thumb and forefinger."

"Look, 'Duffy for Hire,' didn't we just have a little talk about you retiring from the gumshoe life?"

"C'mon, Kel," I said. "I'm just curious."

"I've never heard anything about it. Bikers have 'em on their elbows sometimes, but that's something different."

"Yeah, I know. Do you think it has anything to do with the 'Webster' stuff Walanda was talking about?"

"Duff, you watch way too much TV."

With that, he half turned to direct his focus on the TV. The Yankees were off, so the TV was on ESPN Classic. They were showing a 1984 USFL game between the New Jersey Generals and the Arizona Wranglers. Kelley acted like it was some storied rivalry akin to Notre Dame and USC, and fixed his attention on the screen. I decided to let it go.

The Foursome, like a dog with a bone, was still chewing on the seagull/rice/Alka-Seltzer dilemma.

"TC, it's a known fact," Rocco said, raising his voice. "Accept when you're wrong."

"How come you don't see dead birds all in front of churches if it's true?" TC said.

"How come you're just an asshole?" Rocco said.

"I heard about a lady," Jerry Number Two said. "She tried to dry off a guinea pig in a microwave and the poor thing blew up." "The guinea pig or the lady?" asked Jerry Number One.

"I don't remember," said Jerry Number Two.

"That happened to me once," TC said. "I put a chicken liver in the microwave for the cat," said TC.

"What the hell kind of voodoo were you practicing?" said Rocco. I couldn't take it anymore. I stood up and was counting out money for my bill and AJ's tip when Kel spoke without looking away from the Wranglers' classic touchdown drive.

"How many times did you hit him?"

"I hit him with a one-two and then a body shot. Then I slammed his head into the bumper twice," I said.

"The one-two landed on the nose? The head slam was on the side of his head?"

"Yeah."

"The scumbag's nose was halfway over to his ear," Kelley stayed focused on the television. "It separated right off his face, you know."

"Yeah," I said. I turned for the door.

"Duff," I turned back around. Kelley was still watching the game. "Nice combination," he said.

I headed past the Foursome and went home. I was halfway home when it dawned on me that my mysterious Crown Vic friend wasn't tailing me. I smiled to myself, thinking about how my imagination can run wild, but I didn't get to smile for long. Just as I was pulling into my driveway, a silver Crown Vic passed the Moody Blue heading the other way.

13

"Hey Duff." I hated it when Sam greeted me first thing in the morning. Actually, as I thought about it, I hated when Sam greeted me regardless of his timing.

"Yes, Sam?"

"How can you tell when a Polack chick has been using a vibrator?" Sam smiled.

"Gee, Sam, I don't know. How can you tell when a Polish-American woman has been using a vibrator?" I said.

"Her front teeth are chipped." Sam really got a kick out of that one, and before I could say anything, he disappeared and went back to the business office.

It was a lovely start to another shit sandwich of a day. It was time for the second Quality Assurance Committee meeting. As I made my way into the boardroom, I saw Sheila talking to Gabbibb, and I think I heard her mention something about Botox. Gabbibb was wearing an authentic Derek Jeter Yankees jersey with dress slacks and polished Bostonian shoes. He was heading to the Stadium after the meeting to catch his beloved Bronx Bombers.

Bowerman led off the meeting with an announcement.

"Before we get started, I wanted to let you all know something. As you all know, we're very excited about our new halfway house and though it's far from being refurbished, we would like to invite everyone out to see the new facility."

Bowerman had her hands folded neatly in front of her. She was doing her best to be ultraprofessional. "We'd also like to present an overview of the type of program we'd like to run, once we get approval from the state and all the construction is done," she said.

There was an effort to unite the various Jewish agencies to coordinate services. For people like Claudia and Bowerman, this was threatening because it meant the possibility that their little empires might be compromised. It was Hymie's idea, and on paper it was a good one. Unfortunately, the inane power struggles that dominate the lives of people who rise to the positions of leadership in these organizations would find a way to sabotage whatever good could come of a partnership.

Besides this committee and a couple of others, the big joint project was the halfway house that Espidera was funding. Anyone in social services will tell you that there's an absolute dearth of residential facilities for women with children. It is probably the biggest single obstacle for women to get help for addiction, prostitution, and physically abusive relationships. There were halfway houses and safe houses, but none where you could bring your kids for longer than a few weeks. It was going to be a great thing, despite the fact that Espidera made it possible so he could get a tax break. I guess sometimes the ends do justify the means.

"I'm just so excited," Espidera said, beaming at the attention he was getting. "The possibilities this new program will offer the women and children of this area are tremendous."

Bowerman and Claudia figured a date for all of us to take a ride out to Kingsville to see the new facility and to discuss some program planning. It wasn't hard enough that I had to get caught up with all this paperwork, I also had to somehow get it done on days when we weren't even in the office. These little field trips to pat board members on the back and stroke the egos of people like Bowerman made me crazy.

I had just gotten back to the cubicle when Trina stopped by.

I liked Trina and, even though she was the Michelin Woman's secretary, she seemed to be on my side. I also liked her because she was twenty-four years old, with shoulder-length brown hair and legs that reached all the way to the ground. Being twenty-four, she gravitated to the hip-per fashions, which was fine by me. Having her pass by the cubicle in some of her tight-fitting pants or significantly above-the-knee skirts had a way of breaking up the day.

Trina was my women's focus group of one. I ran relationship issues past her, got date ideas, and dissected rejections with her. She was eager to help me navigate the minefield that was the fairer sex, and I could tell she genuinely liked me. She smelled nice and was a pleasure to be near. She also had been seeing a guy named Lou for two years and I could sense she wasn't always pleased with him.

"Hey Duff," Trina almost whispered.

"What's up?"

"I'm not supposed to tell you this, but she's going to audit ten of your charts in the morning."

"Shit. Do you know which ones?"

"She usually has me, you know, randomly select them."

"Ugh."

"Duff, suppose you, like, happened to let me know which ten of your files are in the best shape. Maybe I could, like, randomly select them for you."

"Trina, you don't have to do that."

"Let me know by the end of the day," she looked over her shoulder to see if anyone was watching. "It's, like, so not a big deal."

She smiled at me and let her eyes linger on mine a little after we stopped talking. It made me wonder. I didn't feel comfortable having her stick her neck out for me, but I am also not a fool.

The problem was I didn't have ten good files. I could give Trina a list and try to get ten files into some sort of shape. It would mean close to an all-nighter, but it would buy me some time. I came up with ten and discreetly slipped the list onto Trina's desk on my way to get some coffee. She smiled at me and tucked the list away.

Before I started on the files I wanted to see how Mikey and Eli were doing. I got Rudy on the first ring.

"Rudy," he said.

"Geez, you ever think of doing any of those Dale Carnegie courses?" I said.

"Fuck you."

"I'll take that as a 'no,'" I said. "Hey, how are the guys doing?" "Actually, real well. They're in some pain, but they're healing, and best of all, neither of them seem to be having bad effects from the radiation," Rudy said.

"That's good, right?"

"Yeah, as long as the stuff gets after the cancer. If it leaves the rest of the body alone—that's the best," Rudy took a bite out of something and chewed into the mouthpiece. "The cops doing anything?" "Kelley told me in subtle terms that they're doing about the minimum. Eli and Mikey were hit randomly, so it's a very hard investigation to nail down. It also doesn't help that neither one of them are pillars of the community," I said.

"Maybe the community would care if they knew that treating them was going to cost about two hundred large."

"Are you serious?"

"That's conservative, Duff." Rudy took another bite of whatever he was inhaling. "They'll be in here for a month, they'll wind up with several surgeries each, and then there's Gabbibb's bill." "The oncology costs a ton, I bet."

"It's not just that. He gets a cut on all of it because his practice has orthopedic guys, trauma guys—you name it. Ol' 'DAT, DAT' will make a killing," he said.

"Shitty choice of words, Rude," I said. "Hey, what happened to making these guys get out of the hospital in a hurry?"

"Turns out their Medicaid was the right kind, especially with the cancer. They can be here forever."

I signed off with Rudy and went to the file cabinet to get my charts. It was going to be a long night.

14

D: Patient reports eating twenty-two Krispy Kreme donuts and then having sex with the cashier at the donut shop.

A: Patient appears to struggle with self-control and moderation.

P: Patient to make a list of positive and negative consequences of her impulsive episode.

It was heading toward midnight and I was trying to get the ten charts I identified up to snuff. I was putting the finishing touches on Martha Stewart's.

Martha goes nuts over Krispy Kremes. She spent an entire session talking about how good they are. I still remember it clearly.

"They come down that big conveyer belt from the oven and they're still so warm," her eyes were as glazed over as a glazed cruller. "They're awesome and they feel so good going down."

"Martha, it's probably not a good idea to obsess like th—"

"And they have this coating. It's white and it's both crispy and sweet. It's like, uh…like…"

"Liquefied sugar?"

"Yeah, I guess so."

Martha made six trips to the donut shop that day, eating a few warm ones from each batch. She was so overcome with warmth from the deep-fried carbo that she hung around after closing to have a go with Vassily, the Ukrainian guy who works the counter. Martha explained that she became uncontrollably attracted to Vassily and just had to have him. I think my correspondence course in Intro to Psych said that was projection. No, maybe it was displacement. Anyway, I was moving on to the Jewish couple when I heard someone coming up the stairs. I stepped out of the cubicle to see what was going on. It was Trina.

"Hey," I said. "What are you doing here?"

"I saw your car outside and thought you might be here," she said.

"It's almost midnight, isn't it?"

"Well," Trina sounded like she had had a few—not drunk, but glowing. "I think it's past midnight, Duff."

Aside from the glow, she was looking good—faded Guess jeans, black leather boots with a three-inch heel, tight black turtleneck, and a leather jacket.

"Duffy, I worry about you." She took a step toward me.

"You worry about me?" I said.

"I'm afraid you're going to get hurt, or get fired, or maybe catch pneumonia in that can you live in."

"Not to mention get eaten alive by that wild animal I live with." "That too." Trina paused. "It's not my place to say, but I'm going to say something anyway."

She was barely a foot away from me, and I got the feeling up my spine that was part nervousness and part excitement. I guess tonight you could also add part confusion.

"You could do a lot better than Lisa." She moved even closer to me.

"Ah, Trina…where's Lou?"

She stopped moving forward. You could see that whatever state of mind she was in was suddenly changed. She looked away and awkwardly put her hands in her pockets. Her eyes welled up.

"Lou…was out with someone else tonight. He told me…" her voice trailed away as she stifled tears.

"I'm sorry, Trina. I didn't mean to—"

"Don't worry, Duff, he was a jerk. I just have to get over the shock of—"

"Being alone and scared?"

"Yeah."

"I know a little about that too," I exhaled. "Lisa called us off."

I hugged her and she held on to me tightly. She quietly cried into my shoulder and neither of us said anything. She held me even tighter and the pressure of her body went right through me. It was part physical and part something else. Something I couldn't find a label for.

"Trina, is there anything I can do to help?"

She pulled back from me, her eyes wet with tears, bit her lower lip, and smiled. The smile was a genuine one, and it made for a weird combination with the tears.

"Yeah, Duff, there is."

Trina stepped back, tilted her head, and smirked at me. She shrugged out of her leather coat and gently untucked the turtleneck from the top of her jeans.

"Duffy, did I ever tell you how much I love your blue eyes?"

"No, I would've remembered that," I said.

"Or your really strong jaw line?" She ran her finger the length of my really strong-looking jaw line.

"Er, uh, no." That was the best I could come up with.

"Tonight I would love to feel like a very hot, desirable woman." With that she turned on her heel and slowly started to walk through the office. I stood transfixed, wondering exactly what Monopoly square I landed on today. A few steps later, Trina's turtle-neck fell to the carpet and her hands reached up to undo the clasp of her bra. Without breaking stride, a step and a half later, the bra went the way of the sweater.

Though I am quite capable of cerebral pondering, this clearly wasn't the time. I followed Trina's strip march through the agency. I found her in Claudia's office. She was shimmying out of her Guesses in that way that makes men stand back and feel grateful. She slid her thumbs into the thin piece of material that made up the strap of her thong, and in one motion whisked it off and threw it in my direction.

She used both hands to hike herself up on Claudia's desk. Her naked body stood out in stark contrast to all the trappings of an office, especially this office.

"Duff, haven't you always wanted to sit in the boss's chair?"

"Actually, not until this very moment."

I sat in Claudia's chair facing Trina. This was getting very weird.

"Isn't this the position your corner man is in between rounds of a fight?"

I guess so.

"Let's go a few rounds."

With that, there was the tussle of getting out of my clothes, the hurried groping and touching that comes before two people find a rhythm. We did it with an intensity that brought the two of us together and, at least for then, chased away any feelings of aloneness. I felt both in and out of my body as Trina surged through me.

Breathing hard, glistening with sweat, we both got where we were going, seemingly all at once. It was intense and it was passionate. We finished up on top of Claudia's desk, our naked bodies spread over the top of it with all her pens and pencils and knickknacks knocked to the floor. When my consciousness returned and I looked around at where we were, I couldn't help but start laughing. Trina joined me, and we slid off the top of the Michelin Woman's desk onto the carpet, both rolling around with laughter.

"We just screwed on top of the boss's desk, you know," Trina said when she could breathe again.

"Yeah," I thought for a second. "I can't even begin to think of the amount of time in psychotherapy I'm going to need to process that."

"Thank you, Duff. It was what I needed tonight."

"I'm glad I could do you the favor."

Trina punched me in the side then nuzzled her head into the crook of my neck. We laid back on Claudia's carpet amongst the debris from the top of the desk. Trina rolled over on top of me, straddling me with her legs.

"You feel like doing me another favor?"

"If I must," I said. Trina was insistent on another favor, and I did my best to comply. When it was over, we did our best to straighten up the Michelin Woman's desk.

It was the most fun I ever had in this office.

15

"Hey Duff, didya hear about the Polish water polo tragedy?" Sam asked on his way to the coffee machine.

"Mornin', Sam," I said.

"It was so sad," Sam said. "The horses all drowned."

Monique was furiously writing in her charts getting ready for the day. She was so disciplined it fascinated me. I envied her self control. I had tried to emulate her work habits and I just couldn't. Fifteen minutes of dedication was always too much and I'd find something else to do.

"Morning, 'Nique."

"Hey Duff," she didn't look up from her writing. "Didya hear?"

"About what?"

"Three more guys got beat in Franklin Park last night. Two of the guys are on my caseload," she said.

"Aw, shit. Who?"

"Sandy K., and Abdul A.," she said. Monique almost never used a client's last name.

"Any word on them?"

"They're conscious but both will need surgery. They have no suspects, of course."

"Have you heard from Gabbibb?"

"I refuse to talk to him," she said. "He believes I'm less than him because I'm a woman, I'm black, and I'm lesbian."

"He's a fuckin' asshole," I said.

'Nique got back to work, and I sat there and thought. Five guys all severely beaten and no suspects. It appeared to be a simple hate crime. Simple, yeah—real simple.

I called Rudy to see what I could find out. He was at his desk and speaking to me through his jelly donut, which was about as disgusting as anything you could imagine.

"Duff, I'm not sure what to tell you," he paused to swallow. I hated listening to Rudy chew because it was just gross. "Gabbibb is the treating doctor and he barely speaks to me. I know there's multiple fractures and cerebral bleeding in at least two of them. All three will require extensive surgery."

I thanked Rudy and signed off before he could start his second donut. I had some information and I wasn't sure what to do with it. Actually, I wasn't sure if there was anything I could do with it.

With a little breathing room from last night's all-night record keeping, I had a chance to do some goofing off. I had ten charts ready for the Michelin Woman's audit. Of course, that meant I had sixty-five charts woefully behind, but I'd get to them someday. Out of the corner of my eye, I caught Trina walking past my cubicle.

"Morning, Duff," she said, like she did every morning.

"Morning," I said.

She winked at me and went right back to her desk. I got the sense that though Trina was young and hurtin' over Lou, our late-night rendezvous wasn't going to be a Fatal Attraction deal. It was something she needed—hell, who am I kidding—it was something I needed. Neither of us regretted it, but we probably wouldn't make a habit of it. That was okay with me, very okay.

I decided to play around on the computer. I'm no geek, but I know my way around a little bit. I decided to do some searches on the key words I'd gotten from Walanda and the jail. I went to Google and typed in "Webster." It yielded 3,803,000 hits. Even I didn't have that much time to goof off at work. Next I entered "Web." That got me 1,803,000 hits—significantly less but way too much.

I tried "spider"—1,706,000 hits.

This wasn't going to work. I was going to need some help. I knew where to go, but it was going to have to wait until after work.

It dawned on me that through all of this I knew very little about Shondeneisha, Walanda's kidnapped, or at least allegedly kidnapped, stepdaughter. I got out Walanda's file and looked for next of kin information and anything else that might tip me off. It was one of the few times I ever wished I had taken copious notes.

The face sheet on Walanda's file listed six relatives. Four were men and were added as she went from relationship to relationship. There was also a half sister that came in for a couple of sessions early in Walanda's treatment but ultimately gave up on her. She got into Al-Anon, which told people to "detach with love." It made sense for the relatives of addicts to detach, otherwise they'd wind up going down with the addict. What the therapy books don't tell you is that in real life an overinvolved relative who never gives up is often exactly what an addict needs.

The self-help groups call that "enabling" and insist "tough love" is the way to go. Maybe, but I've seen my share of lives that were saved by what they call an enmeshed family member who just couldn't let their addicted loved one go. They followed them around, bailed them out of jail, and even threatened dealers—whatever it took. Often it failed, sometimes it didn't, but telling someone to "detach with love" always felt a little too simple for me.

Jacquie Turner, Walanda's half sister, lived across town from the ghetto Walanda lived in. She was an office manager at an accounting firm and took classes at the local business college. From what I remember, she had managed to create a life for herself that Walanda couldn't. It wasn't clear whether she received the same abuse as a kid, but it was possible. Sometimes abusers focus on only one child, sometimes they don't. Just the same, Jacquie had a career, lived in a nice apartment, paid her bills on time, and seemed to be what us social workers called "functional."

I tried her at the accounting office.

"Good morning, Noonan, Malinowski, and Platt Accounting Offices, Jacquie speaking. How may I direct your call?" She had that professionally efficient tone to her voice. Not quite cheerful but certainly pleasant.

"Jacquie, this is Duffy Dombrowski at Jewish Unified Services. Do you have a minute?"

"Good morning, Mr. Dombrowski," she hesitated. "I'm the receptionist, so I can't really talk for long. How can I help you?" "First of all, I'm very sorry about Walanda," I said.

"I am too, but Walanda made her choices," she said.

"Before she died, she spoke to me about a stepchild named Shondeneisha. Can you tell me anything about her?"

"Only that she's the daughter of a man named Bertrand, another addict she lived with. They had the son together that got murdered." "Do you know where Bertrand is now?"

"I have no idea. He was also an addict. The last I knew, he was drifting from city to city looking for welfare benefits."

"Walanda thought Shondeneisha had been kidnapped by someone named 'Webster.' Do you have any idea what she was talking about?"

"No, I don't. Look, Mr. Dombrowski," Jacquie's tone changed almost imperceptibly. "I loved my sister, but years ago I had to detach from her. I tried and tried and she kept going back. I really didn't know much about her life for the last three years. I don't mean to be difficult, but I really should go."

"I understand, Jacquie," I said. "Thanks for speaking with me."

Jacquie was no help. In some ways I don't blame her for distancing herself from the cesspool of a life that Walanda lived.

She was doing something positive, and maybe her way of changing things meant being the best she could be. Honorable, even if your sister winds up dead, I suppose.

After work I got Al, and we took a trip over to Walanda's old house. I hoisted Al onto his side of the Eldorado and we headed out. I threw in some Elvis from '56. It was the original rockabilly sound that changed the face of music forever. To me, listening to Scotty Moore play the guitar riff to "When My Blue Moon Turns to Gold Again" was just about as good as music got—simple, with feeling.

I was singing along, curling my lip in the exact right spots and adding the bass to my voice when it was needed, when Al started to mess up my rhythm by playing with the power windows. He would plop a fat paw on the switches and then marvel at the hum of the descending window. He did it over and over again, paying absolutely no attention to my interpretation of the King's music. Eventually, Al allowed the window to go all the way down and he stuck his head out the window. The wind blew his ears back as he surveyed the passing landscape with a watchful eye.

I parked in front of Walanda's old place, hooked Al up to the leash, and took a walk. Al's tail started wagging, and he started barking when he realized where we were. I hadn't thought about Al returning to his old home, and it was kind of sad.

It was the kind of neighborhood where people interacted from stoop to stoop, porch to porch, or up and down the sidewalk. Back in the late sixties, urban planners started building high-rise projects in this neighborhood in an attempt to homogenize the poor. That way they could be kept out of sight and up in the air, and they wouldn't be on the street being offensive to the eyes of the suburbanites. The projects removed the way people from the inner city interact, and that's why they were destined to be a failure from the start. Sure, high-rises were a tad more antiseptic, but they took away the humanity of everyday life and attempted to compartmentalize lives. If you don't believe me, go to the projects in your town and see how they're doing. Most are abandoned or turned into something else.

Walanda's neighborhood was always full of activity. It wasn't all positive activity, but the idea that everything going on in the streets of urban areas is drug traffic, crime, or drug use is ridiculous. The street can be a wonderland of personal interactions, both positive and negative.

Kids create playgrounds in their imaginations, using what the city has to offer for their amusement, and it seldom has to do with slides and swing sets. Mothers catch up on hairstyles, recipes, and childcare. Adolescents play hide-and-seek with their hormones as packs of girls and boys spy each other up and down the streets in coming-of-age rituals. Old folks go to church or go through their daily routines in the neighborhoods they've spent their whole lives in.

A group of women were gathered three houses up from Walanda's old place, chatting in a circle. Usually, when a white guy approaches a group of black people in an almost all-black neighborhood, there's a guarded resistance and for good reason. White people usually mean police or some sort of other authority who seldom venture into these neighborhoods to pass out sweet potato pie. I had some slack because I was known as a decent guy who did social work and as a fighter. Most of the local boxers were brothers and I had some respect there as well.

One of the three ladies was a recovering crack addict named Laila. I hadn't been her caseworker, but I had run a few groups she was in and she liked me.

"Hey Duffy," Laila said. "What you doin' out here in the hood?" "I wanted to see what I could find out about Walanda," I said. Al jumped up her leg, getting about as far as her knee. Laila returned the affection. Clearly they were old friends.

"That girl was a shame," the woman to Laila's right said. She was very dark skinned and had tight little braids in her hair. "Started to have it together and then lost it even worse. For real, she shoulda stayed in the Nation."

"You guys ever see her with somebody she shouldn't have been with?" I asked.

"That child never stopped bein' with people she shouldn't been with, Duff," Laila said.

"I guess that was a stupid question. Ever hear her talk about 'Webster' or 'The Webster'?"

"She went on and on about some 'Webster' taking her stepdaughter Shony for hoin'," the third woman said. She was lighter skinned and freckled with a short and very wide nose. "I don't know what that girl was talkin' 'bout."

"Did you know what she was talking about?" I asked the darker woman.

"Nah, that girl crazy from the crack."

"Anybody ever hear about 'Webster' or anybody like that pimping?"

"All her men were pimps and she went on the street when she need to get high. Everybody know that," said Laila.

"Anything having to do with 'Webster'?"

"No," the light-skinned woman said. "But there was one ugly white dude used to come 'round givin' her crack. Big ugly-ass biker dude. They'd go for a ride or something. I don't know if he was pimping her or what."

"I never heard no 'Webster' stuff," the dark woman said.

"Tell you what, though, that Shony a pretty girl," said Laila. "Like a young Whitney Houston. She wasn't Walanda's, but Walanda loved her."

"Shony's a good girl too. Sings in church, volunteers with the old folks, and gets good grades," said the light-skinned woman.

"That's right. My gramma is in the county home, and Shony and the other church girls come sing for her every Sunday afternoon," said the darker woman.

"Duff, that girl was Walanda's hope," Laila said. "It was like Walanda was goin' put every ounce of whatever positive she had left inside her for that child to make up for all of the years she's done wrong."

"I think she was also givin' Shony all the love that she lost when Benjamin was killed in that home," the light-skinned woman shook her head. "That was a damn shame, him gettin' murdered. Walanda ain't never been right after that."

"Anyone know where Shony's father is?" I asked.

"Her natural father was that crackhead Bertrand. He ain't around no more. Walanda was livin' with Tyrone for a while with Shony," Laila said.

"Tyrone? That man is a stone-cold pervert," said the dark-skinned woman.

"Crackhead sell his mother for a rock. I heard he moved to the country or somethin'. That boy need to be locked up," said the lightskinned woman.

"He's that bad?" I said.

"Walanda was always afraid he'd turn Shony out," the dark woman said. "He might too, if it meant getting' his ragged ass some crack."

"Know if he did?"

"Don't think so. You know that Walanda was crazy like a fox sometime. She took a bread knife to him once. Cut up his ass good too," said the dark woman.

"And no one knows about 'Webster' except her going on about it?"

The three of them shook their heads. I thanked them and headed back to the Eldorado. When we passed Walanda's house, Al started for the porch and I had to tug him to come with me. He let out a couple of high-pitched whines and he reluctantly came along.

That night I headed over to AJ's. It was late and I guess I missed Kelley, but the Foursome were there.

"I'm tellin' ya," Rocco said. "They had to wrap Dorothy's tits in a big Ace bandage so her nipples wouldn't show through in that scene with the Munchkins."

"The Munchkins were deathly afraid of nipples for some reason?" TC said.

"You know, if you look close in that scene when the good witch is flying away and they're all waving," said Jerry Number Two, "they're actually all giving her the finger."

"That's because the good witch wouldn't show her nipples," said Jerry Number One.

It was a shame to cut into such an intellectual debate, but I grabbed my Schlitz and went to talk to Jerry Number Two.

"Hey, Jer."

"What's up, Duff?"

"You spend a fair amount of time on your computer, don't you?" "I try to limit it to eight hours a day. That's why I come here at night. I don't want to burn myself out."

"What kind of stuff do you do all day?"

"Depends on the day," he sipped his Cosmopolitan. "Depends on what I'm working on."

Considering Jerry Number Two didn't actually work, I found this statement a bit curious. Just the same, I had to respect the man's sense of balance in his life.

"I spend a lot of time chatting with other Trekkies and finding out where and when the conventions are. I play some online Dungeons & Dragons. A lot of time I spend looking up the family genealogy."

"Are you pretty good at finding things out using the computer?"

"Depends what it is."

"I'm trying to find out something and I was wondering if you would help."

"Sure, Duff, I kind of like hunting for stuff. What are you looking for?"

"That client of mine that got murdered, she said that the 'Webster' took her daughter. I also saw some women in the jail with spiderweb tattoos. I don't know what it all means and it goes beyond my surfing abilities."

"Duff, that's a pretty broad search. You have an idea what you think you're going to find?"

"I'm guessing something perverted. Prostitution, porn, something."

"I'll give it a go. How will I know when I've found something?"

"Just let me know if you find anything interesting."

"Porn and prostitution usually are interesting," Jerry finished the Cosmo and called to AJ for another.

"Hey, Jer, knock yourself out," I said.

I asked AJ to back all the boys up, and I headed to the Moody Blue. It was late, I was tired, and the Schlitzes had worn me down a bit. I wanted to get in bed. When I got to the Blue and pulled into my gravel driveway, I saw Lisa's car. She was standing up, leaning against the driver's door.

"Duff, can we talk?" She had been crying.

"I don't know, Lis, it's been a long day," I said.

"I think you owe me that," she said with a touch of righteous indignation.

I resisted addressing what I "owed" this woman who dumped me by leaving a message on my machine. Instead there was something else I wanted to know about.

"What did you do to your hair?" She had a man's crew cut. Her shoulder-length hair was gone.

"I'm recreating myself," she said without the confidence that she should have had.

"What did you want to talk to me about?" Even as I asked it I regretted it.

"Us," Lisa looked down at her work boots, which I figured were another part of her ongoing re-creation. "I'm not sure I'm ready to let us go."

"Uh-huh…" I had no idea how to address that.

"It's just that, uh, I—"

"I think it's just that you ditched me and were real quick to point out my intimacy shortcomings."

"Duffy, I just don't know what I need right now," she had that fabricated look of urgency I've seen in women before. It comes after they break up with you and realize that being single isn't all they dreamed of. The panic and the pleading come as a reaction to their loneliness. The problem is, it's all about them. Once you go back with them, they return to where they were and soon you're back to being the piece of shit you were before. I've seen it a lot.

I didn't say anything, I let the silence hang. I started to think about Trina the other night in the office. Now that was fun and in a sense more real than this bullshit. It was sex between two people who like each other a lot. No Hallmark bullshit, but no lying about "intimacy" and closeness. It was a hell of a good time.

"Uh, Lisa," I said. "I think you're panicking because you're lonely. I don't want to play the 'go away, come closer' game. Not now, anyway. I think you should go with your first instincts."

I could have said it a lot harsher or a lot meaner, but I didn't want to do that.

"You're an asshole," she said. "You know that—you don't know how good you had it with me." There were no tears this time. This was the ranting of a little girl who didn't get her way. I'd seen it before and sadly, I'd probably see it again. I've learned over the years that it's best not to engage in it.

"Good night, Lisa," I said and headed toward the Blue.

"Fuck you!" she screamed at me. It was getting ugly and honestly, a little hurtful. There wasn't anything left to say.

I heard her car accelerate on the gravel of my makeshift driveway. It had been a long day and I sat with Al on what was left of the couch watching the E! True Hollywood Story about how a bunch of childhood movie stars were now tortured by drug addiction. I had a Schlitz and thought about Lisa and a bit about Trina.

Something told me that life wasn't supposed to be about a bunch of shit that you couldn't figure out. That maybe life was simpler than we made it and maybe that was the best way to live it.

That's as complicated as my thinking got. Next thing I knew, it was morning, Al was barking, and the TV had something on that was guaranteeing to rid your body of unwanted hair forever.

16

It was time to go back to high school, literally. I knew very little about Shony, and even though I suspected that her kidnapping had very little to do with anything she had done, I felt that it would make some sense to get to know what the kid was about. Shony went to McDonough High School, Crawford's public school, which was located four blocks east of the county jail. That put it six or so blocks from The Hill, which meant it was pretty much a ghetto high school.

I had gone to McDonough as did most kids who grew up within city limits back then. Today, the school was predominantly black and Latino, with various other minorities and the white kids making up the balance. Just about anyone with kids who could afford to headed for the "burbs" a long time ago. Most of the white kids with money either went to Central Catholic or to Crawford Academy, which built a new school just a hair within the city lines eight years ago.

My high school years were marked by intense bouts of both anxiety and acne, though the two are probably not mutually exclusive. It was in high school that I found my way first to the karate academy and then to the boxing gym. I think I signed up for karate the day after the sixtieth time I got my ass kicked in a fight after somebody called me "pizza face" or said that it looked like I had an acid fire on my face and my mom put it out with my dad's golf shoe. Today, I still carry a few acne scars on

132

my cheeks that people just assume came from the ring, and if someone comments on them I don't bother to correct them. Funny thing was that by the time I could kick somebody's ass, I learned it wasn't necessary to. That was the kind of effect Smitty had had on me.

With twelve hundred students, McDonough was almost a city unto itself. Its gray bricks looked tired and dirty and the place always seemed to have a cloud over it. It was three floors and the classrooms had those tall windows divided by many panes. Graffiti was left to fade on the sides and back of the building because the city only really put an effort into cleaning off the front unless the writing was particularly vulgar. The first floor on top of the main staircase had the large suite of administrative offices where you were supposed to go and sign in and get some sort of badge before you visited. I didn't feel like doing that so I hung out on the side of the building and waited for some truant to slip out around lunchtime so I could go in and trespass around school by myself.

A friend of mine from the gym, Jamal, worked as a hall monitor and I thought he would be my first stop. Jamal was also a former member of the Nation of Islam, even serving in their elite Fruit of Islam paramilitary outfit. The FOI was sort of a force within the Nation and they provided security and bodyguards and stuff like that. Jamal left the Nation after a few years and though we never talked about it, I got the sense that he got to the point where he didn't buy everything they were selling.

I had to walk up to the third floor and go down the corridor a bit until I ran him down. He was in the process of throwing some sophomores out of the boy's room for smoking.

"Duffy." Jamal smiled when he saw me. "What brings you here to my prestigious domain?"

"I wanted to see the football coach. I still have four years of eligibility," I said.

"Shit, Duff, you know the Wind needs some speed on the

gridiron. How you going to help with that?"

"There you go with your racial profiling."

"No kidding, man, what'ya doin' here?"

"You know a girl named Shony?" I said. "Probably a freshman or sophomore. Her stepmom, Walanda, was one of my clients." "Walanda Frazier, the woman who just got murdered in lockup?" "Yeah."

"She was a Muslim sister for a short period. I think her mental issues kept her from fully embracing Allah," Jamal said.

"That and the crack."

"Yeah, there was that," Jamal said.

"I got her dog now, Allah-King."

"Ol' AK, huh." Jamal smiled. "Dog as crazy as she was. You know he flunked out of the bomb-sniffing program?"

"What?"

"Oh yeah, for a while the Nation was training canines to sniff out explosives."

"How'd Al do?"

"Not bad sniffing explosives." Jamal paused and rubbed his chin. "Al's problem was pissin' and shittin' on everything."

"Still is," I said. "What about Walanda? Did you know about her relationship with Shony?"

"Another Crawford tragedy. Shondeneisha Wright lived with her on and off. She's a freshman, but she hasn't been around in a while." "What kind of kid is she?"

"She's one of the good ones, Duff," Jamal said. "Respectful, don't curse, don't wear foolish-lookin' belly shirts and having all her business fallin' out of her blouse. That girl is proper, like a throwback." "Any idea what she was into?"

"She's quiet. I think she was church-goin'. She liked to sing, and I think she was even in one of the civic groups. Not sure how she got that way—that Walanda was a trip."

"Tell me about it. How'd you know about her mom?"

"A couple times she came down here all raggedy-assed, cracked-up, making a scene. The kid was mortified. She was ashamed that she lived with her and made a big deal about saying she'd never be like that. It was the only time I heard the kid make a lot of noise." "You know where I could find a teacher who really new her?" "Miss Hippenbecker was her homeroom teacher. She's free this period. She's in 206."

I thanked Jamal and headed to 206. I knocked lightly on the door's opaque glass and let myself in. Behind an old wooden desk sat a fifty-something, rather fat woman in half glasses, reading an Oprah magazine and eating a Snickers bar.

"Miss Hippenbecker?"

"You're supposed to have your guest badge. Have you stopped at administration?"

"I don't have time right now to go over any student report cards." She laid the Oprah magazine down and continued to speak while she waved the half-eaten Snickers in her hand. "You really should make an appointment for a parent-teacher conference." "I'm not a parent. My name is Duffy Dombrowski. I'm a counselor at Jewish Unified Services. Was Shondeneisha Wright in this homeroom?"

"I'm not supposed to release that information."

"Yeah, but it has to do with her stepmother's murder."

"Yeah, I heard about that." She took a bite out of her Snickers. "Frankly, the kid's better off. Her stepmom was worthless."

"Has Shony been in class?"

"I'm not supposed to say, but no she hasn't." She picked up her magazine. "You know how they are. They have no sense of responsibility. I've been here for twenty-seven years and I see it all the time." "They?"

"Oh please. Look, I don't know who you are and I'm sure you want to believe all these wonderful things about these people but face it, there's no mistake why they wind up like this."

"Aren't you supposed to alert someone when a kid's absent?"

"I sent the letters." She exhaled impatiently. "They just ignore them anyway."

"Who did you send them to?"

"I don't know. Whoever is the legal guardian."

"That's her father and he's an addict who changes addresses weekly."

"Not my problem. I have thirty of these animals to look after. The letter definitely went out."

She chewed her Snickers, leaned back in her desk chair, and picked up her magazine. Without a word she went back to reading, ignoring me like the chalkboard erasers behind her.

"Uh…Miss Hippofucker?" I said.

"What did you say?" She looked down her nose at me and put her magazine down.

"Have a nice day." There was something about being back in high school that made me do it.

Next, I headed down to the school psychologist's office on the chance that the shrink might have had a relationship with Shony. The office was on the first floor but at the opposite end far away from the administrative offices. The placard on the office door read, *Dr. Nancy Madison-Riverchild, School Psychologist.* The name scared me.

I knocked on the door lightly and waited. I tried again and waited some more. I thought she might be in session, but there was no evidence of a sign to not disturb, so I checked the knob and let myself in. Dr. Madison-Riverchild was sitting cross-legged on a tattered Persian rug starring at a candle. The room reeked of patchouli and though her eyes were open, she made no motion to acknowledge my presence.

She looked about fifty, she had wavy gray hair down to her ass, and she wore a hemp peasant top and baggy pants that gathered around her ankles like a TV gypsy would wear. She was painfully pale, had crooked teeth, and was very thin. She wasn't wearing a bra and her tits hung down around her belt line. It was one of those moments that you know is real but there's part of your mind that wants it to be a dream. I was deciding whether I should split when Dr. Riverchild spoke.

"One moment, please," she said without changing her position or diverting her attention.

I folded my hands in the same sort of way that I do when I'm in line at a wake. I was trying to be reverent and I wasn't sure what to do with my hands.

The doctor stood up and walked over to me.

"I'm Dr. Madison-Riverchild," she said. She had amazingly good posture and the absolute worst halitosis I've ever experienced. "I'm sorry to have made you wait, I was getting centered. How may I help you?"

"Hi, I'm Duffy Dombrowski." For the first time in my life, I felt like I needed a hyphened name in my title to be on equal footing with someone. "I'm a counselor at Jewish Unified Services and I was hoping to discuss Shony Wright."

"Shony is a terribly troubled child." She didn't ask for a release or if I had any permission to speak to her. Apparently, if you're centered enough, regulations are trivial. "She has been parentified from a very early age, and it has forced her into an untenable heroic identity."

"Uh…I'm not sure I understand."

"She comes from a most dysfunctional environment." The breath was worse than anything that ever came out of Al's ass. "She parented her parents more than they parented her."

"I had heard she was a pretty solid kid."

"Mr. Duffy," she gave me an incredibly patronizing smile, which was fine with me as long as she didn't breathe in my direction. "That's what you see on the outside. Inside you have an inner child struggling against that external self-induced parent. She is the best example of a most dysfunctional teenager."

"Her grades were great, she sang in the choir, volunteered, and seemed to be pretty popular?" I asked.

"Exactly," Doctor Riverbreath said with a sigh that nearly made me lose my own center.

"Well, Doctor, you have been a great help."

"You're welcome, Mr. Duffy," she said. "Mr. Duffy, may I

ask you a personal question?"

"Sure."

"Are you in therapy yourself? You seem to have your own internal conflicts."

"I think I'm going to need some real soon," I said.

"My private practice has openings," she smiled. "We take most insurances."

"Good to know," I said, and I was never happier to leave a room.

I was heading out of the school when I heard the bells ring for lunch. Kids rushed out from behind doors at a crazy pace. After the last two hours that I had experienced in their school, I couldn't say I blamed them. I fell in the throng of kids rushing to the doors and not a single one paid any attention to me. There's something about being a teenager that gives you the uncanny ability to focus on the right-now and how it happens to pertain to yourself at that particular moment. A strange adult, out of place in their usual environment, meant nothing to them.

On my way to the car, I stopped to talk to four young black girls. They were all talking at once, snapping gum, and shouting over each other's voices. It took awhile for them to notice me.

"Excuse me, girls?"

They didn't say anything, they just stopped talking and looked me up and down.

"You guys know Shony Wright?"

"Why you asking?" the girl in the middle asked.

"I'm a counselor and I'm looking for her."

"She in trouble?" the girl closest to me asked.

"Nah, I'm trying to find her. Anyone know where she went?" "She stopped coming to school last week but sometime she do that when she go with her father," the middle girl said. She was clearly the leader and I only expected her and the one closest to me to say anything.

"Was she doing okay? Was Shony a happy kid?"

"She's okay. Her family is wack and her mother a crackhead." "That embarrass Shony?"

"What you think, mister?" She scowled at me. "Shony has it goin' on, though. She smart, she pretty, and that girl can sing."

The other three girls gave a series of "uh-huhs" and "Word!" at the notion that Shony could sing.

"She seem happy to you guys?"

"Mister, who you know who happy all the time?" Again with the scowl. "She happy as anybody else around here."

I thanked the kids and they went right back to talking and yelling and snapping their gum. It was the most intelligent conversation I had all morning.

17

The news about the beatings in the park started to get some attention in the local media. The Crawford Union Star carried a story on the front page of its local section about the assaults and suggested that the beatings were hate crimes because several of the victims were gay. Channel 13 ran it as its second lead story on the six o'clock news and MetroCrawford, the local alternative newspaper, ran it as a cover story.

The attention would bring more of a police involvement at least at first, which was a good thing. I found it a little disturbing that before the victims were identified as gay no one was really up in arms about the situation. Eli wasn't gay, but he was beaten just as badly as if he were, and it didn't seem right that when it was alcoholic street bums getting beaten there wasn't a single reporter interested. Then again, there wasn't a united front of street alcoholics in Crawford like there was a united organized front of gays and lesbians.

The Crawford Gay and Lesbian Community Center was a political force to be reckoned with in Crawford. I knew a little bit about the center from Monique, but she wasn't a big fan of the place. She respected some of the efforts the center made but found the people there cliquish and self-serving. Monique was a proud lesbian woman and secure enough that she didn't feel the need to shout it angrily at everyone within earshot.

With the beatings making it to the newspaper and the TV,

the center decided to have a candle-lit march through the park to make a show of solidarity from Crawford's gay and lesbian community. It was a nice idea, but I must admit I found it a tad hypocritical. Guys like Mikey and Froggy weren't really accepted at the center because of their lifestyle. Their flamboyance and their promiscuous park activity were seen as hurtful to the overall gay and lesbian cause in Crawford. Mikey and Froggy fit too many old stereotypes that shamed the yuppified nouveau gays and lesbians, and my guess is that if they ever showed up at the center, they would not be welcomed with open arms. Sure, they would get a free AIDS test, but then they would politely be shown the door or at least made to feel that going out the door would be a good move.

Just the same, the beatings gave the center a visible opportunity to demonstrate to Crawford the power of numbers and the strength of the gay community. Monique was going to go because, as she explained, for all her differences with the center, the cause was a good one and a chance to let people know that what was going on was not acceptable in a civilized culture.

I went too, partly because I felt like doing something to honor Mikey and partly to see if there was anything for me to learn. The march began just after sunset and it went around the whole perimeter of the lake within the park, finishing at the bridge where there were to be some speeches and a prayer or two.

I fell in with my candle in one of the back rows, and I'd like to say I was perfectly comfortable and that being one of the very few heterosexuals in a group of gay people didn't make me feel funny. But it did, in the same way that I feel a little strange when I'm the only white person in a room. I think most people who are honest with themselves will admit feelings like this, although many holier-than-thou super-liberals will say otherwise. It made me start to think about what it might be like to be in the minority and how that could shape your entire view of the world. Putting yourself in a position as a minority is probably a good thing to do once in a while to give you some idea of how a fair portion of the world feels.

The march moved slowly, and I recognized a few faces but not enough to really bond with anyone. I let my eyes wander through the crowd and I saw all types of people. There were men who looked effeminate and men who looked rough and lots in between. There were a lot of women with no makeup, sensible shoes, and short hair. There were some women with exaggeratedly tough veneers with just a little too much leather, denim, and piercings. It seemed like some were trying incredibly hard to make an impression with their appearance, and there were others who seemed to make their statements by not trying too hard to state anything.

As I marched on, I noticed a familiar pair of jeans a couple of rows up ahead of me. I let my eyes travel up the legs to the back and head and realized it was a very familiar pair of jeans. It was Lisa and she was walking hand in hand with a short, squat woman in a leather biker jacket and so many piercings in her face that it looked like she fell down a flight of stairs while carrying a tackle box. I found myself staring even when I didn't want to.

While the march slowed, the squatty tackle box woman ran her fingers through Lisa's hair. Lisa looked her in the eye and then the two of them kissed. At first it was just a quick lover's-type peck, but in short order they were doing the whole tonsil-hockey thing. It was like a bad car wreck—I couldn't not watch, but it gave me kind of a surreal feeling, like it was happening but it wasn't. I've seen old girlfriends kiss somebody new, but it was always another guy. When that sort of thing happened in front of me I usually went off by myself and listened to Elvis sing something like "Are You Lonesome Tonight?" or "That's When Your Heartache Begins." Elvis didn't have a song for this. The closest I could come was "A Fool Such as I," but I wasn't sure that would've worked.

You know, I'll admit that on occasion I've accidentally

looked in porno mags, you know, if there was an interesting article or something. They almost always have some sort of lesbian pictorial. I don't ever recall one of the models being five foot one with a Dick Butkus hairdo and a face that would overwork a scrapyard magnet. Geez, to think all these years the dirty magazine business has been misleading me.

Eventually, Butkus got her tongue out of my ex-girlfriend's esophagus and when their lips parted, a gobber of spit got hung up on the Butkus's second lip piercing from the left. This car wreck was getting worse, and apparently so was my staring because Butkus turned around and saw me.

"Hey, take a picture next time—it lasts longer," she said in her Ernest Borgnine voice.

It didn't register with me because I was in a lesbo-induced trance.

"You, buddy, you got a problem?"

I came out of my hypnotic state and realized I was being confronted by an angry, semi-dwarfed, metalicized Dick Butkus. My mouth opened but nothing came out. In my head, Elvis was singing the first verse of "A Fool Such as I," and I couldn't imagine anybody ever feeling so foolish.

"Uh me?" was all I could get out.

"Never mind," Butkus said. "Asshole."

Next to her, Lisa waved and seemed as awkward as any person who ever lived. I waved back, ignoring Butkus. The two of them turned around, and I could tell that Lisa had to explain a few things. As they walked away, Butkus put her hand on Lisa's ass.

I still hadn't moved when a voice distracted me.

"Mr. Duffy, whatever are you doing here?" It was Froggy. He was standing, thrusting his one hip out and looking at me with his big brown eyes.

"Hey Froggy," I said. "Here to show my respect for Mikey and the others."

"You go, boy. Something gots to stop these rednecks. It's

beginning to cramp my dating life," he said.

"I know."

"Cops won't do anything as long as it's us fags being beat. After this publicity stunt stops, it will be business as usual."

"I'm going to do something, Froggy."

"What are you, the Lone Straight Ranger?"

"Maybe."

"You're not kidding." Froggy had a rare serious moment. "There ain't many like you, Mr. Duffy Dombrowski."

"I get that a lot."

"You all right with me. If I can ever do anything for you— you say so. And I don't mean anything in the bushes, either."

"I'll keep that in mind, Froggy," I said.

After my conversation with Froggy, I decided to leave the park and skip the speeches. The night had gotten weird enough and I just wanted to go home and get some sleep. I was going to have to go through my record collection to find a song too.

18

Today was the day slated for all of us to head out to the new halfway house for a tour of the facility while it was under construction, followed by an all-day retreat with the staffs and boards of both agencies. Retreats are the goofiest waste of time ever imagined, and the only redeeming thing about them is that they afford me time to think. Usually, that meant thinking absolutely nothing about the topic at hand.

The Michelin Woman didn't say a word about my records, which meant she looked at them and they were acceptable. She kind of operated in an evil "no news is good news" mode, except it ought to be more like "no bad news sucks." Trina saved a large piece of my ass with the tip and the fact that she stuck her neck out for me meant a lot. I still had ten good charts and about sixty-five shitty charts, so I was far, far away from being out of the woods.

Hymie asked if he could ride out with me today. Even if he had to bring up the record-keeping business, I still looked forward to sharing the forty-five minute ride out to Kingsville with him. The plan was to meet at Simon's Deli, where Hymie and a handful of businessmen of his vintage held court every workday morning. Simon's was west of Crawford's industrial section, and it was almost exactly the same as it was when it opened in the 1930s. Old man Simon came up from Brooklyn after working in his grandfather's deli, and he pretty much duplicated the business. Crawford had a good-size Jewish population made up of the men and women who migrated from the city, and they made Simon's a little haven of their old home. Sid Simon, the grandson of the original owner, still wrote the daily specials on his grandfather's old chalkboard, still wore the old-fashioned white apron, and still wiped down the wrought-iron ice-cream-store-style chairs and tables after each party left. As America continues to go through its drive-through-ization on its way to the kids' soccer games, Simon's was a throwback and a welcome alternative.

Even though Hymie and his friends were mostly retired and had turned their businesses over to their sons, they kept the ritual that they had started forty or fifty years ago. It's what the opportunistic yuppies of today call networking, except these old businessmen got together because they not only wanted to succeed business-wise, they also cared about each other's camaraderie. Today's yuppie sees every relationship as an opportunity to advance something or to get leverage on something else.

I walked through Simon's front door at exactly seven thirty, and there was Hymie at the corner table with his posse of Bernie, Duke, George, and Henry. I knew each of the guys from these occasional breakfast meetings that Hymie invited me to.

"Abi gezunt, gentlemen," I said, taking the seat next to Duke and across from Hymie.

"This goy protege of yours...Hymie," Duke said. "Did you get him to convert yet? I got a rabbi who will do the circumcision." "You hear that, son?" George said, making a scissoring motion with his fingers. "Do you know what that means to your schmeckel?" "Meshugeh, son, pay no attention to these old men," Henry said. "Get some of Simon's lox. They're very good this morning, though the bagels are too chewy."

I took Henry's advice and got the lox on a sesame bagel with cream cheese. He was right on both counts, the lox were very good and the sesame bagel was a tad chewy. Nonetheless, it was a nice way to start the day.

Hymie finished up and we bid our farewells to the crew with Hymie taking care of everyone's check. The men took turns each morning picking up the tab, and they all accused Duke of ordering more extravagantly when someone else was paying. We climbed into Hymie's 2006 Cadillac DTS, the model that used to be called the DeVille. I guess technically it still was, though GM had gone to great lengths to try to distance the current Cadillacs from the cars of their heritage. It was a silly strategy, in my opinion. I highly doubted that the Generation Xers and the rappers and whatever demographic represents today's youth would be interested in DeVilles, regardless of what they did to them. That's precisely why I liked them.

Now, they're advertised in goofy magazines like Maxim or Stuff and are all muscled up to look "extreme"—whatever the hell that is. The result is you get old guys with osteoporosis and three hairs left on their heads putting on their cardigans and getting into some vehicle that looks like a car that could win at Daytona. The paradox of the situation is that guys like Hymie have been trading in one DeVille for the other every two years and wouldn't entertain a single thought of doing anything else. So you get cars that can go one hundred sixty miles per hour in second gear and they're driven by eighty-year-olds who go forty in the right-hand lane of the highway with their left turn signal on in perpetuity.

"You got any fights on the horizon, Duff?" Hymie asked, puffing on his Garcia Vega.

"There won't be any fights for a little while," I said.

"Why?" Hymie said.

"There was a bit of an incident in Kentucky."

"What kind of incident?"

"The guy said some awful things about Smitty. Then he said some bad stuff about my mom and dad and being Irish and Polish. With all the stuff I've been dealing with, I lost it."

"What happened?" There was concern in Hymie's voice.

"I knocked him out," I said.

"And for that you get suspended?"

"I did it with a thumb and elbow. I broke the guy's jaw."

"You are a crazy Irishman." He looked at me and laughed, playfully slapping me in the face.

"Son, tell me about this paperwork problem you got." He changed the subject, but kept his eyes on the road and didn't change his expression.

"Ah, Hymie, it's my own damn fault. Most of the paperwork is bullshit. I'd rather spend the time with the people than writing about it."

"This Claudia, she's none too happy. It could cost you your job, you know."

"I know that, Hymie, and I make no excuses. I should do it."

"Son, the place needs you. You're the soul of the place. I've never been a big one on regulations, but you can't ignore them."

"You're absolutely right."

"You know I try not to interfere with how the place is run. If she wants you to go for legitimate reasons, I won't intervene."

"I understand that and wouldn't expect you to."

We were quiet for a while after that. He was direct and honorable in how he handled things with people. Good news or bad news, he delivered it directly and without manipulation. Hunched over, short, bald, about one hundred forty pounds, with thick glasses, he was a man's man.

We went out Route 27, which had beautiful trees and an occasional deer and not much of anything else. It's basically two lanes that take you to some of the most forgotten places in the state. About every ten miles there's a gas station with a convenience store, or when you hit the really big metropolises, you'll get an Agway. It's the kind of highway where running into deer and falling asleep due to the boredom run neck and neck for the lead in causing fatalities. Along the way, we passed the sign for Forrest Point and I got to thinking of that trio of women in the jail group. They were clearly linked together. It was obvious not only from the tattoos but also from the way they related to each other. It was more than just a friendship; it was almost some sort of sycophantic bonding. Like they were all united toward something. Whatever it was, it seemed evil to me.

Hymie threw in his Louie Prima CD. He was a huge Prima fan, which certainly didn't fit with being Jewish. Prima's music recently caught fire again when the Gap ran a commercial with Brian Setzer's version of "Jump, Jive an' Wail." Prima was the real deal and was more rock and roll than anything else. Hymie had the CD queued up to "Buona Sera" and he was starting to groove. First his brake foot started to tap, then, as sax man Sam Butera lit into his solo, Hymie replaced the tapping with all-out stomping. By the time Prima joined in on the trumpet, Hymie was slapping his gnarled-up, arthritic hand to his thigh and improvising his own scat. New Orleans jumpin' jazz with a Brooklyn Jew accent is really something you've got to hear. Then he'd throw his head back and shimmy so much that the four or five hairs that went across the top of his head would get messed up.

We pulled into the parking lot of the soon-to-be halfway house with Hymie and Louie dueting on the "The Sheik of Arabie." The building was being renovated so there were several pickup trucks and a handful of contractors mulling around. There were half a dozen cars in the parking lot to the left of the building, and I recognized Monique's older Volvo and Claudia's Camry.

The building wasn't quite in the middle of nowhere, but nowhere wasn't far away. Therapeutically, that had its advantages and disadvantages. On the plus side, it meant very few distractions for the clients, giving them the opportunity to focus exclusively on their treatment.

On the negative side, it meant there were very few distractions, giving the clients the continual nightmare of focusing only on their treatment. Although a lot of human service professionals will have you believe that a person can spend all day doing nothing but focusing on themselves, talking about themselves, and examining themselves, I don't think it's a very practical idea. Short periods away from bad situations help, but after even a short amount of time, people start getting buggy. Spending all day talking about yourself makes you completely self-absorbed, which I never found to be therapeutic for anything. Unless you're a social worker, and then talking about yourself all day is a fun and necessary professional activity. It beats working anyway.

The waiting area/lobby of the building was half done and there were the requisite coffee and goodies set up on a long folding table. The table was filled with simple carbohydrated deep-fried goodies along with fat, tasteless bagels and opened tubs of various cream cheeses. There was one of those fifty-cup percolators going, making what I knew would be horrible human-services coffee.

There were stickies at the sign-in desk for us to write our names and titles on and stick to our shirts. Espidera was there and tried his "shalom" routine with Hymie and gave me one of those fist handshakes that are now in vogue with athletes and celebrities. I saw Monique talking to a woman with shoulder-length brown straight hair and wearing those very thin, nerdy black glasses, the kind that Ashleigh Banfield and that woman who did the news on Saturday Night Live wore. There was something particularly sexy about those glasses. I think it gave the woman that kind of smoldering librarian look, the kind that made you think the woman was just dying to free herself from all the inhibitions and restrictions that the professional world forced on her. That, or she was nearsighted.

I went over to Monique with my cup of coffee. Monique was wearing baggy high-waisted men's pants, a white turtleneck, and a blue blazer, which against her dark skin made her look strikingly handsome.

"Good morning," I said.

"Hey Duff, good morning," Monique said. "Duff, this is Katy. She works at the Eagle Heights clinic."

I extended my hand. Katy briefly smiled but had a look to

her that stated, or at least tried real hard to state, that she was all business and not a flighty girl right out of college. Young women entering the social-work field often work very hard at the feminist thing, and they put a lot of effort into the look of being all business.

"Hi Katy," I said. "How long have you been at the clinic?"

"Four months," Katy said. "But I did my externship here for the previous year."

I never understood the difference between an internship and an externship. For Katy, making the point that she had done her externship here was a way of pointing out that she had far more experience than four months. Being new and young in this business is tough. A lot of counseling skills come from what you've experienced in life, and if you haven't had a chance to experience a lot in life, then your skills will be limited. Counselors like Katy tried to compensate for that by looking serious and immediately adopting as much psychobabble into their vocabulary as possible. It was a futile attempt to cover up the fact that the bulk of their life's experience has been obtained in dorm rooms and on the campus quads. When college kids like this got clients like, say, Walanda on their caseloads, the clients had a great time taking them for a ride.

Bowerman called for everyone's attention and took the time to introduce the board members present and then asked Espidera to say a few words.

"Good morning, everyone," Espidera was doing his best sincerity act. "I just feel so blessed to be able to bring to this area such a needed resource."

"Especially if you need the deduction," I whispered to Monique, who smirked inconspicuously.

"The real credit goes to all of you," Espidera continued turning toward Claudia and Bowerman. "Especially to Claudia and Rhonda for the leadership and direction you've both shown to this organization."

It was nauseating but, thankfully, it didn't last long. From there we were walked through the building where we got to see the suites the patients would live in. They were suites because each bedroom had a small alcove off of it for any children. There was a group dining room that wasn't finished, but I could already tell that it was going to be furnished in that faux-homey way that somehow screamed institutional while trying to accomplish the opposite. There was a lot of that in these types of places.

We got to see the multipurpose room, a room where lectures, multi-family counseling, and probably any type of exercise class would be held. There were two separate rooms for group therapy, one with a two-way mirror for observation. There were three small offices for the staff to do their individual sessions and a large office for Bowerman. There was also an unfinished area that Bowerman told us was going to be another multipurpose area that wasn't complete yet and so we didn't get to see it.

All this excitement was getting to be too much for me to handle, and it was about to get worse. We had another break, and then it was time for the retreat and team-building segment of the day. We all shuffled into the multipurpose area and got ready for a series of goofy lectures and group exercises. The best part of these days was that the lecturers were never well prepared and it usually meant that the day, which was supposed to go to five, would actually wind up by about three thirty in the afternoon.

We were right on schedule to end at three thirty when the Michelin Woman got up and rambled on for an extra fifteen minutes about the importance of a new regulation affecting exactly when treatment plan updates needed to be reviewed by physicians and the importance it was going to have in regard to patient care. She loved the order of regulations, and it kept her from ever having to focus on actually helping a living, breathing person. Talking to the people who came to the clinic was tedious and it was hard to measure if anything we ever did reached them. It was much safer to obsess yourself with regulations.

By the time she finished, I was so bored I felt hypnotized. I couldn't wait to get out of there and get home. I felt like I needed some mental floss.

19

I got back to the Moody Blue just after five, got my rousing greeting at the door from Al, checked my mail, and hit the play button on my answering machine.

"Duff, it's Jerry, c'mon by AJ's tonight. I got some stuff. None of it earth shaking, but I think you'll be interested."

That was interesting, and I was glad to hear Jerry actually got to the project. I was afraid he'd get lost in Star Trek stuff and get abducted by some Klingons. It was too early to head to the bar and there wasn't enough time to head to the gym, so I opened a Schlitz and sat on the good side of my couch. The remote wasn't on the coffee table and it wasn't between the cushions or on the end table. Having to actually get off the couch to change stations seemed like the equivalent of rubbing two sticks together to get dinner going. It was unacceptable.

I got off the couch to search for the remote. Generally speaking, it had to be in the general area of the TV because there was no reason to bring it away from the television. It wasn't underneath the living room furniture or behind anything. On my third search through the sofa cushions, as I tried to heft Al from his side of the couch, it dawned on me.

"You better not have," I said to my new housemate.

Al's eyebrows went up, his eyes got a little shifty, and he let out a high-pitched sigh. I wasn't about to accept that as an explanation. I went to the kitchen and lo and behold, there,

154

next to his food dish, on his special mat with the paw prints were Al's two newest chew toys. Not the rawhide bones I bought so he'd stop eating the couch, not the fuzzy carrot with the squeaky thing in the middle—those objects remained in the spot I left them with absolutely no evidence of slobber. Instead, there sat my multifunction, all-in-one remote covered in slobber with teeth marks up and down its length and missing the six, seven, and nine buttons. I guess this was Al's version of parental controls. Next to the remote was what was left of my cordless phone. There was no antenna, there were chew marks all over the back of it, and there was slobber on all the keys.

I took the remote and stood over him as he slept on the couch.

"Bad!" I yelled with the remote in my hand. That was what the Dogs for Dummies book I bought at PetSmart said to do. I was vigorously showing my displeasure with Al's behavior and associating it with the object.

Al opened his eyes, which from his recumbent posture deeply furrowed his brow, and then he closed his eyes and let out a sigh. He was either overcome with guilt and couldn't look me in the eye or he was practicing some sort of deep breathing transcendental basset meditation.

I pointed the remote at the cable box and no matter what button I hit, it returned me to the Lifetime Channel. Talk about cruel irony. I was either going to have to get up every time I wanted to change a channel, get a new remote, or spend my life watching cable programming for angry women. The thought of watching endless movies about evil men repeatedly wronging victimized women made me shiver. Going to AJ's a bit early was a much better idea.

Apparently, there's no such thing as early for the Fearsome Foursome. It was some sort of existential quirk that no matter what time I got there, they were always present. I guess they merely exist independent of the natural laws of time. They were the only ones in and it was too early for Kelley.

"You have to watch it real close," Rocco said. "But it's

obvious." "Why the hell would the Disney Company have a minister in The Little Mermaid get a boner?" TC said.

"Ministers get boners," Jerry Number One said.

"That's not all," Jerry Number Two said. "In Finland they don't allow Donald Duck movies."

"What the hell are you talkin' about?" Rocco said.

"They got really angry at the fact that he doesn't wear pants," Jerry Number Two said.

"Thank God it's the minister getting the boners!" TC said.

It was a shame to intrude when so much was getting done, but I noticed Jerry Number Two had a very fat binder in front of him. I walked around the group with my Schlitz and sat next to him. I was hoping that sitting exactly opposite my usual position would not result in complete entropy for the universe.

"Hey Jer, what ya got for me?"

"Check this out," Jerry slid the binder in front of me.

The binder was about an inch and a half thick. I opened it up and saw that the first page was a title page, neatly typed like some sort of FBI report.

Report on Internet Sites Related to Webster,
Web, Spiders, and Related Search Words
Prepared by Gerald M. Freeman

After the first page was a detailed table of contents listing websites and separated into categories. The categories included Webster, Web, Spider, and Miscellaneous Related Words, and were further divided into the subcategories Free Access, Pay Access, Member Only by Invitation, and Non-Pornographic.

"Holy shit, Gerald, this is unbelievable!"

"It's the best I could do quickly. With more time, I could have got you more detail."

"More detail? Are you kidding? Where'd you learn to do this kind of work?"

"My old gig."

"I didn't realize you used to work. I mean I knew you must've…" I began to realize how insulting that must have sounded. Jerry didn't seem to care.

"I used to be big into computers. I was really into it."

"Where did you work?"

"In the early eighties I spent some time with the Quantum Computer Services corporation doing Internet stuff," Jerry took a hit off his Cosmo.

"In the early eighties?"

"Yeah."

"I didn't realize there even was the Internet back then."

"Well, there wasn't really, at least not like today. We were working on it."

"What happened?"

"The company changed hands a few times, got bought and sold, and got really commercial. I wasn't thrilled with the commercialization, so I quit."

"What ever happened to Quantum?"

"It became AOL."

"Are you kidding me?"

"No," Jerry downed the rest of the Cosmo and slid it to the edge of the bar. "I took the stock options they paid me and got out in '94. Cashed in the stock in '98."

"You mean you got stock when it wasn't worth much and sold it when it was worth a ton?" I tried to keep my jaw from hitting the floor.

"Pretty much."

"I don't want to pry…"

"Oh yeah, I got a ton of money," Jerry interrupted. "I developed the protocol that eventually was used to create chatrooms and instant messaging."

"I thought you were disabled?"

"Well, I had a few bad trips and spent a little time on a funny farm, but that's not why I don't work."

I bought Jerry another Cosmopolitan and sat thumbing

through the report in front of me. It was overwhelming, and it was going to take a lot of time to go through it. I was about to start going through the report when Rudy came in. As usual, he had deep pit stains under his arms, he had his hands in his pockets, and he shuffled to a barstool with the energy of the participants of the Bataan Death March. He looked like a wrung-out, very fat dishrag.

I bought him his first drink and sat next to him.

"You don't exactly look like the poster child for stress management."

"There's some fuckin' insight," Rudy said.

"How are the guys doing?" I asked.

"You know, remarkably well, thank God." Rudy drank half of the Hennessy in the rocks glass. "Both of them look almost unfazed by the radiation—that's wonderful."

"How about the other stuff?"

"That's time—and a little luck. I'm still worried about Mikey because he's not as stable. They're both in some pain but getting all sorts of good pain medication."

"That'll certainly keep both of them happy," I said.

After that, the conversation wound down. I got the sense that Rudy didn't need the company, that he was there to drink and let the Hennessy do its job. I finished my Schlitz and watched the TV in silence until I figured it was time to go.

I bid my farewells and headed out with my head down and twirling my keys around my fingers, thinking, when a voice jilted me.

"Duff?" It was Lisa. It was late and Lisa was way too much work this time of night.

"Hi." It was all I could think of.

"I miss you," Lisa said. She looked down at her new Doc Martens. "I don't know what else to say."

"I don't either, Lis. It looked to me from the other night that you found somebody new."

"You hate me because I'm interested in a woman."

"Nah, I don't think it's that." I tried to choose my words carefully. "It just seems to me that you found someone new and I ought to move on."

"Do you have to be so closed minded?"

"I don't have a lot of experience with this type of thing, Lis." I never wanted to be in a conversation less. "Look, I got to go, take care of yourself."

I didn't wait for her to say anything else, which seemed a little cheap, but sometimes there's nothing left to say. The situation had gotten to maximum weirdness, and I think I had some hurt around losing a girlfriend. That was then multiplied by the fact that it looked like I lost her to another woman. That wasn't revolting, but it didn't fit neatly into any particular category on the hard drive of my mind.

I was turning left on Main heading toward 9R when the headlights in the rearview took me away from Lisa. My buddy in the Crown Vic was back. He stayed with me, didn't accelerate or slow down until I pulled into the Blue, and then he kept right on going up Route 9R.

20

Not having a home computer meant using my work computer. Considering the vast majority of these websites were pornographic, that meant that I would have to wait until everyone had gone home for the night. No one would suspect anything about me staying late because I was so far behind on my work. Of course, burning the midnight oil looking at porn sites with a spider theme wasn't going to help me get my records up to snuff, but that was beside the point.

At five thirty, the only people left in the clinic were Monique, Trina, and myself. Monique had a women's group to run and Trina was covering the front desk. That meant I was pretty much alone to surf the net.

I had no idea where to begin, so I just started.

Spiderweb.com wasn't pornographic; it was a seldom-used search engine and it didn't look any more exciting then a poorly constructed search engine would be.

Webster.com had something to do with dictionaries.

Web.com had to do with an Internet access company.

Spider.com was a motorcycle parts business.

Webbies.com was a site for computer geeks.

Daddylonglegs.com was the first porno site. It was dedicated to the men who love long-legged women, preferably in fancy hosiery. The woman on the front page was naked except for very sheer stockings and a garter. The stockings had the seam running up the back and she was wearing impossibly spiked heels as she bent over to touch the floor. I'm guessing she dropped a contact lens or something.

The left side of the page featured links to live webcams, white hosiery, black hosiery, fishnet city, body stockings, and message boards. I took a surf through and saw some interesting-looking women with interesting-looking outfits, but nothing that looked like it could possibly have anything to do with Shony. The message boards were filled with messages to the models from lonely men with far too much time on their hands, who somewhere along the way got way too wired on what women wear on their legs.

Daddyslonglegs.com was a very similar site, as was Dadslonglegs.com and Daddylongleggs.com. Who were these people? I mean, a good-looking woman in stockings is nice to look at, but don't these people ever leave the house?

Next came a long series of sites that combined the word "sex" with spiders, webs, and websters. Some were pay porno sites, some were sites featuring amateur models, and some were sites for clubs. There's a funny thing about pornography. I think most men enjoy it; some will admit to it and some won't. I've always thought it was like Mexican food—I really liked it in small amounts. If I eat Mexican food a couple times in a week, it starts to taste crummy. With porn, looking at it once in a while was okay, but too much or too often and it loses its flavor.

Apparently, not everyone thought so. I've had clients who lost jobs, relationships, and went bankrupt because of it. Probably like people who get hooked on crack, porn addicts remember how turned on they got the first time and they keep chasing that feeling.

I was forty-five minutes into looking at women and couples in every position I ever dreamed of and some I hadn't. It wasn't the least bit exciting, in fact it was kind of a drag. I had worked my web through about forty percent of Jerry's report when I came across a site called www.Xcracksterweb.com.

The page opened with a slowly spreading black spider's web. There were no graphics or photos, just a spider's web that continued to grow. When I looked closer, I saw that the web was coming from a tiny spider that spread its web until it covered the entire screen. After a minute or once the web covered the screen, red lettering that said, "If you're over twenty-one and not offended by depictions of sex, enter here."

I clicked on the enter link and the screen went bright white. A large red-and-gold banner began to fill up the top of my screen. It said "Crack Hos for U." Then a series of photos appeared of women, most naked and most engaged in a variety of sexual positions with different men. There were extremely graphic shots of oral sex, anal sex, sexual intercourse—you name it, it was there. In every shot, either the woman or her partner had a crack pipe in their hands.

The photos were not just graphic, they were degrading in the sense that the woman depicted were engaged in sexual activity with crack being held up to them as a reward for what they were doing. The men in the shots were mocking the women while having sex with them.

Crack addiction and prostitution are strongly linked. Selling your body is an almost instant way to get money and why women addicts often turn to prostitution. Men usually turn to crime, not because they object to selling their bodies, but because the market for male hookers is small and made up almost exclusively of gay men. The prostitution we're talking about here isn't the Julia Roberts Pretty Woman kind. We're talking repeated episodes of oral sex in a crack house with the payment being a single rock of crack. That high wears off in about ten minutes and then it's back to more oral sex. A woman in a group session once tearfully told me that she had done over two hundred acts in a single twenty-four-hour crack binge.

Along with child abuse, it was the most disturbing thing to hear about on my job. I hated both of them for the lifetime of damage they inflicted upon people. The fact that there were actually people who wanted photos of this shit was more than disturbing. I understand pornography's attraction and I understand fetishes, but the evil that had to be in someone's heart to find this stuff arousing was despicable.

The background of the website was covered in a spider's web motif. The top of the page had a smaller version of the same "Crack Ho" banner with a little spider sitting on top of the "o" in "Ho." On the bottom of the page, there was a menu of links to other pages on the site. The pages included girl-girl action, group scenes, all oral, all anal, streaming video.

Looking at this shit made me feel like I needed to wash, but I felt like I was on to something, so I kept on. The all-anal page was the toughest, but it also proved to be the most interesting. On the third page, I recognized Melissa, the youngest of the three women from the jail group. I clicked on the photo to enlarge, and there was no doubt it was her. I looked closely and sure enough, she had the small web tattoo. I went back and studied all the photos, and all the women had the tattoo.

Knowing crack addiction as I did, it was obvious what was going on. Whoever set this operation up knew they could get crack addicted women to do just about anything if they got crack for doing it. It sickened me.

After I had worked my way through the rest of the site, I clicked on the "streaming video" link. I came to a page that informed me that this part of the site required payment or a password. I didn't want to put any money into the pockets of whatever scum profited from this, and I figured I had learned enough for tonight. I'd visit Jerry and see what he could tell me about the site and how to get into the other section without a password.

I closed out the Internet from my computer and headed to AJ's. As much as I ever did, I needed a drink.

21

"It's the yellow dye number five that does it," TC explained the science behind the product's testicle shrinking properties. "It isn't anything special about Mountain Dew."

"That was DiMaggio's number," Rocco said.

"Ah, yes," said Jerry Number One. "The Ol' Splendid Splinter." "That was Ted Williams, you ass," Rocco said.

"Not if he was drinking Mountain Dew," Jerry Number Two said.

I took my new favorite seat next to Jerry Number Two, or as I now like to think of him, Gerald Freeman, consultant, formerly of Quantum Computer Services.

"Jer—I found something. I was hoping you could dive a little deeper for me on one of these sites."

"Which one?"

"Xcracksterweb."

"I thought that had some possibility," he said. "What's up?"

"One of the suspicious women showed up. There's also a page that requires a credit card and a password. Can you get me in without that?"

"Yeah, it'll take about two minutes."

"Really?"

"So much for Internet insecurity."

"Jer?"

"Yeah?"

"This page had every kind of porn you could imagine. The part where you needed a password had a silly title too that hinted at kids. I'm suspecting you might find stuff with minors."

"I'm guessing you're not referring to the guys who go underground with flashlights on their heads."

"No. I just don't want to get you in any trouble."

"Thanks, Duff. I'll be careful."

Kelley was in his usual spot. I slapped Jerry on the back and went to my stool.

"What's up, Kel?"

"Hey Duff."

Kel was watching a Classic Sports rerun of a Bruins-Canadiens game from the late seventies.

"This is the one where Bobby Schmautz scores the winning goal in overtime, isn't it?" I asked. When I cared about hockey, Schmautz was my favorite hockey player.

"You know, Duff, I didn't follow the career of Bobby Schwanz all that closely."

"It's Schmautz," I said, defending a hero.

"Schwanz, Schmautz," Kelley said.

"Hey, Kel, what happens if someone comes across child pornography on the Internet?"

"Duff—I think it's time you went to a psychiatrist yourself."

"I'm serious. Who would you report to?"

"Why don't you join Dick Tracy's crime stoppers or something?" "C'mon, really."

"You could call the local police, you could call the FBI. It will wind up in the hands of the FBI and they'll get a task force on it. It takes a long time because they tend to want to round up as many of the pervs as they can."

"Gotcha."

"I don't want to know, right?" he said.

"Probably not," I said.

AJ opened another long-necked Schlitz and I asked him to give me a bourbon, neat, with it.

"A sidecar tonight for the social worker?" AJ said. "Looks like he may need a detox."

I nodded and decided against a comeback. The night had been an ugly one. The photos bothered me but not nearly as much as the concept that there was an element of people that would find them arousing and amusing. The bourbon was an attempt to disinfect my mind a bit. It went down warm and I saved a sip of Schlitz at the end to chase it. The Foursome had moved on from Mountain Dew but had kept somewhat close to the theme. As I walked past them and waved good night to everyone, TC was pontificating something about a gerbil, a toilet paper tube, and Richard Gere.

I didn't stick around to see how it came out. Instead, I left AJ's and took a walk around the block. For four or five square blocks, there were warehouses and factories and one or two houses. Except for the baked-goods factory, nothing was open after six and the whole area was lit with those amber streetlights that are now popular in urban areas. The amber hue gave the place an eerie feel. I looked in and out of parking lots and in the few residential driveways that there were. I did three laps around and got the same results. A silver Crown Victoria was nowhere to be found.

Three times was enough, and I decided to head home. In the Eldorado, I slipped in the eight-track From Elvis in Memphis, Elvis's double album from '69 that represented his return to serious music. A lot of it was dark and thoughtful music, and I particularly tuned in to "Long Black Limousine," a song that told the story of a tragic death and a funeral.

Just before the Route 9R turn, the Crown Vic showed up. It lay back about two city blocks but made the turn onto 9R with me. Whoever it was was too far back to recognize and whenever I slowed down, the Crown Vic slowed down with me. It was making me crazy, but I did my best to ignore it.

At the Moody Blue, Al greeted me with enthusiasm at the door, jumped on me and then off, and then spun around in a complete circle while letting out a high-pitched cry. I had no idea what he was talking about. After taking a second circle, he sprinted to the bathroom and got himself a drink. I sat on the good side of the couch and flipped on the TV, forgetting that it would go to its now-default station, Lifetime. Robert Stack was talking about two sisters who had never met getting together for the first time. I wondered why everyone on this show always seemed to have a Southern accent.

My Unsolved Mysteries reverie was shattered when Al jumped on the couch and came over to give me a big toilet-water-laced slurp on my ear. His nose, face, and long ears were sauteed in el agua del bano. It was cold and a bit shocking and a fitting ending for what had been overall a pretty disgusting day.

22

"Hey Duff," Sam said. "Did you hear why the new Polish navy got a glass-bottom boat?"

"Again with the nautical theme, Sam?"

He didn't even pause.

"So they can see the old Polish navy."

"Good one, asshole," I muttered. I was a bit hungover, which surprised me because I hadn't drank all that much. It might have been the mixing of bourbon and Schlitz, though that didn't seem to bother me much in the past.

I was dredging through the paperwork and trying to get done with the tortuous Aberman file. In a session a couple of months ago Mrs. Aberman was complaining that Mr. Aberman seldom did anything romantic. Best I could remember it went something like this: "He never gets romantic," Michelle Aberman said. "Ever."

"I rub your bunions," Morris Aberman said.

"That's not romantic. It's nice, but it's not romantic."

"What would you consider romantic?" I asked therapeutically.

"Roses, champagne, you know, sweet talk, fancy dinners…"

It went on like that for over an hour. I was looking at Michelle and trying to figure out what she would have to do for me to get me to even consider rubbing her bunions. Just the thought of her bunions was disturbing enough that I had to force myself to sing "Don't Be Cruel" for the rest of that day to not think about her bunions.

Writing about it was bringing about a similar revulsion, and I was to the part where the Jordanaires do the "ooooooos" right before Elvis growls when Trina's voice, thankfully, took me away from it all.

"Meet me in the parking lot in five minutes," she said. "Don't say anything to anyone."

"Wha—"

"Don't say anything!" Trina said.

At first, I thought Trina might be inviting me to something kinky in the early morning of a workday, but her urgency made me dismiss that quickly.

I nonchalantly made my way to the parking lot, not sure what I was about to get into. Trina was standing next to her Honda, nervously smoking a cigarette.

"What the hell's going on?" I asked.

"Were you looking at porn in the office last night?"

"Are you with the bishop's office or something?"

«T> * »

"I'm serious."

"Well—"

She didn't let me finish.

"Claudia knows. She checks that shit every morning with some program. She's going to fire you. She's already called Hymie and Espidera to meet with her. It's in the policy manual."

"I was looking at it because of Walanda."

"It doesn't matter. She thinks she's got you now. She's checking the browser history and she has the board guys coming in around four this afternoon to review it with them."

"Shit."

"Look, I gotta get back inside before she figures out I'm gone."

I didn't think a small office like ours checked computer activity, but it was just like the Michelin Woman to be hung up on something like that. Looking at porn at work is almost indefensible and I couldn't let on that I was trying to solve a murder. I was screwed.

I had a couple of hours to come up with something, and I quickly figured out that it was time to call Rudy. He wasn't in, but I left a message for him on his service and told them where I wanted him to meet me. Rudy would do anything for me and often did.

I met Rudy for an early lunch at AJ's and ordered two double orders of AJ's hot chicken wings. Rudy loved them and attacked them more than he ate them. Whenever we had wings, he wound up with orange stains all over the front of his shirt and covering the lower half of his face. He looked like some sort of Stanley Kubrick circus clown when he ate wings.

"What's goin' on, Duff?" Rudy asked. "What kind of trouble you in now?"

"C'mon, Rudy, what makes you think I'm in some sort of trouble?"

Rudy just looked at me.

"All right—I need a favor."

AJ slid the two orders of wings in front of us. Rudy asked for extra bleu cheese, like he always did.

"You know, kid, I got my own troubles. What kind of favor are you looking for?"

"I need to get time off from work."

"C'mon, kid," Rudy rubbed his forehead. "That shit hasn't died down from last time."

"I'm not taking a fight, it's something else."

"What is it then?"

"It's not important, it's work bullshit. I think they're going to fire me today."

Rudy was cleaning the wings right down to the bone like a kind of sabertooth, prehistoric, short fat guy. There were already speckles of wing juice dotting his shirt. The scary clown face was starting to form.

The wings were good. AJ changed the oil in his Frialator

about every solstice, which, as disgusting as it sounds, added to the taste.

"All right, but I can only give you a temporary thing. You're not going to be able to go out on a full disability. This will give you about a week."

"I'll take it."

"All right, let's see...depression, nah too easy to question...fibromyalgia flare up...nah...better not...I got it."

He started to scribble on one of his prescription pads. He wrote as illegibly as any doctor and when he handed the note to me I had no idea what it said.

"What is this?"

"Irritable bowel syndrome—stomach cramps, the shits— often brought on by nervousness. You can't go into work because of the cramps and the shits and, of course, the stress in your life."

Rudy was stripping the last evidence of DNA from the saucy drummette he held between his fat thumb and forefinger.

"Will it work?"

"Of course it will work. IBS is very hot these days." "Rudy, you're the best."

I finished up lunch and headed to Kinkos. I didn't want to chance showing up and giving the Michelin Woman her chance to can me, so I decided to fax the note in. I hated the idea of Hymie thinking I was some sort of perv, but I could straighten that out later. They can't fire you when you're on disability, so I was in the clear—for a week or so.

23

Back at the Moody Blue, I was having problems settling down. There were just too many things happening at once. I was going to get fired from my job for any one of a number of reasons, people were going to think I was some sort of smarmy pervert who spends hours looking at porn sites, Mikey and Eli were still recovering, Shony was still gone, and Walanda's murderers may or may not have something to do with one of those porn websites.

Coincidence is a funny thing. The fact that Melissa from the jail was on a porn site and in jail with Walanda at the same time didn't mean her and her friends had anything to do with killing her. At the same time, it was hard not to jump all over the conclusion that they did.

I was pacing back and forth inside the Blue, which wasn't exactly a mansion so I had to turn around quite a bit. I'd walk the length of the trailer, starting in the yellow formica world of the kitchen/ dining area, past the built-in sofa and TV, through the narrow hallway by the bathroom, take a right into the living room, through the bedroom door, and finally turn around at the foot of my bed and start over. Al was asleep in the bedroom away from my pacing, which was just fine with me because he would probably find it objectionable and let me know it. I was working myself into a lather when there came a knock on my door.

I opened the door cautiously. I didn't feel like taking any chances. "Hey Duff." It was Trina and she looked uncomfortable. "What's up, what brings you out here?" I said. "C'mon in. The place is a mess."

"Look, after work, I was thinking." She sat on the couch and ran a hand through her hair. She had on a pair of faded jeans and black shiny boots with a significant heel.

"Do you want me to warn you of stuff like today? I mean, I don't want to be the one who brings you bad news and I don't want to feel like I'm, I don't know…" she said.

"No, I appreciate it. You probably saved me, at least for a little while." Trina's foot tapped nervously. "How'd my doctor's note go over?" I said.

"Claudia was pissed, but said something about that it wouldn't be enough to save you this time."

"Figures. Did she tell Hymie?"

"She called him—so I think so. She also had an emergency meeting of the Quality Assurance Committee."

"How does my looking at Internet porn become a quality assurance issue?"

"She said it put the agency at risk for public relations."

"Geez, talk about bullshit."

"They met and she had me print out the history on your computer to show the committee."

"Great."

"Duff?"

"Yeah?"

"Why were you looking at porn for four straight hours in the office?"

"It had to do with Walanda and who killed her—but don't tell anyone that. I don't want them to know," I said.

"You'd rather have them think you're an Internet pervert?"

"For now, yeah."

"Duff, you're not a pervert, are you?"

"No, I'm not, Trina."

"Good." She sighed.

"Is that what brought you out here? You were worried that I was some sort of wack-job pervert?"

Trina's chin started to tremble and a single tear ran down her face. She didn't make a sound.

"That stuff was awful. Why would anyone like that?" It wasn't a question for me, it was just a question she couldn't answer.

Trina put her face in her hands and started to sob. I moved to the couch and sat next to her and held her. It was a bit awkward because I had the side with no cushion. She buried her face in my chest and let go. I let her cry.

It took awhile, but it subsided. She pulled back from me and kissed me on the cheek. I kissed her back lightly on the lips and when I did her lips parted ever so slightly. I felt her hand on my back as she pressed herself into me like she wanted to go through me. I held her head in my hands and kissed her hard.

Trina held on to me with one hand while she untucked her shirt with the other. She was in a hurry and there wasn't much grace to the movement. She moved my hands under her shirt, first to her waist. Her skin was warm and smooth and she was lean with a hint of muscle like a woman should be.

Trina pawed at my shirt from the back to try to pull it off my head, and when it got tangled around my head we slid off the couch and down to the floor. She pulled off her shirt and undid her bra with an economy of motion. She rolled over so that she was on top of me and we were both naked from the waist up. This time there wasn't the playfulness there was in the office, this time it was intense.

Trina ground into me as she sat up on me, and she seemed to be almost in another world. She was with me, very much with me, but at the same time she was focused on herself. She slid off me and undid my jeans and pulled them and my underwear off with a strong tug. Trina stood and reached to pull the zipper down on each of her boots before she kicked them off. There was no strip play to this, this was a woman with purpose. She undid the snap on her faded jeans and did that same little wiggle to get out of her slightly too-tight pants that she did that night in the office. Trina climbed on top of me and let out a half sigh, half whimper. She pulled her hair back with both hands and tilted her head to one side as her face contorted with intensity. She had found her rhythm and was riding it.

Trina's pace picked up along with her breathing, which became shorter and more labored. I had entered my own world of intensity and was completely in the moment when Trina screamed.

"Ahhhhh! What the hell is that?" Trina screamed while abruptly bucking off me in a way that bent and twisted me and turned pleasure into pain in a hurry.

Shocked out of my blissful carnal state, I sat up quickly to see Al lapping away at the soft white skin of Trina's ass.

"Stop that, stop it, I said." Trina pushed Al's nose away from her butt and Al looked at me with an expression of confusion.

"C'mon, Al, geez," I said.

"Make him go away," Trina said. In a matter of seconds we had passed through a world of intense bliss into a world of unending awkwardness.

"Al, go—C'mon, Al, go." Al looked at me, then looked at Trina, and then back at me like he didn't get why he wasn't invited. "Sorry, Trina—it's not that easy," I said.

I got up and walked Al to the bedroom while Trina sat with her arms around her knees covering up. Once I got back to the living room Trina looked up at me from the floor.

"I'm sorry," I said. It was all I could think of.

"I can honestly say that that has never happened to me before."

"You should be flattered. Clearly, Al likes you."

Trina went to punch me and when she did I grabbed her and pulled her on top of me as she giggled and play-acted resistance.

"Now, where were we before the dog licked you on the ass?"

Trina and I got dressed and I walked her to her car. It was that awkward moment after, and we found ourselves making small talk. I kissed her goodbye and she smiled at me. When she started up her car, I felt her eyes on me as she pulled out of the driveway. She smiled and reluctantly broke off the contact almost nervously and headed out Route 9R.

As far as getting my mind off things, it worked, but only for a little while. Pretty soon I was back to pacing and thinking of everything. From what Trina said, it sounded like Claudia was circling her troops to get me in a pretty tight corner. The only way out now was to somehow find out about this Webster bullshit. The phone rang again and it was Jerry Number Two.

"Duff, I got something you should see," he said.

"What is it?" I said.

"I think we better do this in person."

"Jer, you're scaring me."

"Maybe we should be scared."

"I'll be right over," I said.

I got directions to Jerry's place and headed over. My mind was racing and I was trying to slow my thoughts and, I guess, my fears down a bit. Elvis was doing "It Hurts Me," the one from the Comeback Special, not the studio one. It was the type of song that calmed me down and helped me focus.

Jerry lived in a basement apartment in the college ghetto part of town, which was kind of puzzling considering what he told me about his wealth. The neighborhood was filled with two-family homes that were rented to college kids who promptly littered their front lawns with beer cans, pizza boxes, and empty Doritos bags. Many of the houses were once the old homes of Crawford's working class who took great pride in their appearance. Now, these homes were either bought up by real estate investors or handed down to sons and daughters whose only goals were to make money. You can charge each kid seven hundred dollars a month, put five of them in each apartment, and they never bother you about fixing anything as long as they can have their weekly keggers. Once nice neighborhoods become ugly, any property owner who does care about their house finds the fastest way possible to move to the suburbs. Of course, there were the college ghetto perks too. Down the corner from Jerry's place there were two ultra-cool coffee shops, a place to get a tan and your nails done, and three places to buy used CDs.

There was one door to his place and it was at the end of a five-step cement stairwell. The building was a hundred-year-old five-story apartment building with about ten apartments. Jerry hollered for me to come in, and I did.

His living room consisted of a futon couch, a futon chair, and one of those big circular rattan chairs with the pillow in the center. The place was filled with big plants, hanging in front of the basement windows and standing on either side of every piece of furniture. As I looked around, it dawned on me that I was standing in the middle of a bumper crop of marijuana. Jerry called to me from another room and I followed the sound of his voice.

Jerry's office looked like something you'd see in the Batcave. There were four computer monitors going, there was a stack of black metallic boxes with lots of wires and blinking lights, and the room hummed from the sound of all the fans within the computer machinery. I had no idea what all the stuff was, but I knew it wasn't cheap and it wasn't simple.

"Hey Duff" It was weird seeing Jerry without a Cosmo in front of him. "Thanks for coming over," he said.

"Sure, Jer. What have you found?" I said.

"Pull up a seat. This will take some explaining."

I wheeled over one of Jerry's four office chairs. Jerry called up www.Xcracksterweb.com on his computer and pivoted the twenty-inch monitor so we could both see.

"Okay, try to follow me, Duff. When you look at this webpage you see the usual stuff, in this case, porn. The menu on the bottom brings you to other pages, like the page that asks you for a password and user name."

"I gotcha so far."

"I got into the pay site with some hacking software."

"How'd you do that?"

"Basically, I have software that throws the dictionary, the alphabet, and numbers zero through nine at the user name box. When the software finds a user name it starts the same process with the password."

"Does that always work?"

"It does because most people are very lazy when it comes to password security. They use birthdays and initials and common names. This site required at least an eight-character password, which is very unusual. It means they were really concerned with getting caught."

"Go on."

"So anyway, I got in and this is what was there."

Jerry went to the pay page and I braced myself to see something really disturbing. When the page appeared, I let out my breath and became confused. It was the web pattern again being spun by a spider.

"What's this? Why would anyone pay for this?" I said.

"That's what the Webmaster wants you to think. There's something else to it," Jerry said.

"What?"

"All right, this is where it gets a little complicated. Looking at this, all you see is the little spider spinning an endless web, right?" "Yeah."

"If you go to the menu on the top of the browser and click on 'view' and then click on 'source' this is what you get."

Jerry pulled down the menu and it revealed line after line of that cryptic computer language, some in different colors. Some of the words said things like "table," "head," "width," and "style." "Jerry—now you're getting weird on me. I have no idea what this shit is."

"All it is, is the code for techs to understand how the page was constructed. It's sort of like a blueprint to understand its construction."

"So?"

"If you scroll all the way down, you see this called 'area shape poly'?"

"Yeah."

"That means there's a hidden link in the page."

"What do you mean hidden?"

"You know when you're on a webpage and there's a menu and you can just click on it and it brings you to another page?"

"Sure."

"Well this is a link that's not labeled."

"So—where is it?"

"It's the little spider. If you click on the spider it takes you there." Jerry clicked on the spider. At this point the suspense had me on edge and I wanted Jerry to just get to the point, but I realized knowing the hows and whys had some value.

The hidden link was a plain white page with the following web address:

briefcase.yahoo.com

Under the address there was a simple line of directions that said:

Username: Webster Password: 4#crackgirls

Jerry went to the briefcase webpage and put in the instructed username and password. It immediately went to a page with a series of folders marked simply with dates.

"This is where it gets bad." Jerry's voice got low.

"Open it up, Jer."

Jerry clicked on the folder and it opened to a series of photos. They were young girls, in various forms of undress. Many had tears coming down their face. In each of the photos was a black guy I guessed was Tyrone, Walanda's ex, the pimp. He was smiling and had his arm around the girls in some pictures. In others, he had their shirts lifted up, and in others he had skirts and pants pulled down.

Jerry took me through a bunch of the folders showing what women and girls were available. On the "Newcomers Page" there was a photo of a pretty young black girl and under it was the name Shony. Tyrone the pimp was next to her. Shony was crying.

I almost got sick. Jerry was silent and a hush fell over the office.

Jerry clicked out of the folder and went to the folder labeled "instructions."

He clicked on it and a white page with simple lettering appeared. In part in read:

Young daughters of crack hos available for your pleasure. Do the mother and daughter at the same time, if that's what you're into. E-mail us, we'll send you the details: Webmaster@xcracksterweb.com.

Don't miss our upcoming video feed.

"Jerry, close it out."

Jerry closed out of the site and went to his desktop. Neither of us spoke or moved for what seemed like a long time.

"All right, Jer, tell me: once one of these assholes gets the passwords, what keeps him from telling all his asshole friends so everyone could get in free?" I asked.

"The webmaster has it set up on a randomizer so that the password changes probably every couple of minutes or seconds. You would have to go through this process every time you wanted access," he said.

"Why did they bother with the briefcase piece?"

"A briefcase is sort of like an extension of e-mail. It won't be picked up by search engines. That way, if the FBI or whoever is scanning the Internet for child porn, it won't be recognized."

"Someone who knows this stuff went to some trouble to do this, didn't they?"

"Yeah. I think the pervs who get nailed are the idiotic ones who put their stuff out there in the open. Either that or they're so brazen they don't care."

"Do these guys make serious money doing this?"

"Are you kidding, Duff? You're the addiction expert. Porn might as well be crack, and when it comes to something forbidden like children, I'm betting these guys just can't stop," he said.

"That and they have all the women hooked on crack so they can't do anything. What they're doing to those kids is the devil's work," I said.

I thanked Jerry and headed home. Jerry had suggested that when I had time that I should go through some of the links listed on the page because they might give me some more information. I really couldn't stomach any more at that point, so I left that project for another day. I had a sick feeling in my gut, and I wasn't sure what to do about it. According to Kelley, I could call the FBI or the local authorities and they'd do an investigation, but that would take a lot of time. In the meantime, Shony was about to be turned into something that could ruin her for life. I didn't like the sound of this upcoming "video feed" thing, either.

I was going to do something, I just didn't know what.

24

Al greeted me with his usual flair at the Moody Blue. He brought me the chewed-up remote and I couldn't tell if he did that to flaunt how he wounded it, to present me with a gift, or just as some sort of pacifier he employed to calm himself when he felt overcome with joy at the sight of me.

Smitty was on the machine, wondering where I was. He had some sparring for me with some young heavyweight and it sounded like there might be some money in it. Monique called from the office, checking on me, and someone else called wanting to sell me some aluminum siding, which was interesting considering I lived in an all-metal Airstream.

I wanted to give Hymie a call, but realized, when I gave it some thought, that my story might not be believable. In a few days, things might sort themselves out and a call wouldn't be necessary. I had no idea how that actually could happen, but I decided that's what I wanted to believe.

Lifetime was showing a movie about a pair of pathological twins who seduced women and stole their money. Meredith Baxter Birney was resolving to not let them get away with it when I left the couch to change the station. ESPN Classic was showing Ray Robinson and Jake LaMotta and even though I'd seen it a hundred times, it was the best thing on and I didn't feel like getting up to change the channel anymore. Tomorrow, I'd get a new remote.

It was after ten and between the day I'd had and the fact that the TV didn't hold my interests, I faded off on the couch. Some nights I stayed on the couch, never making it to bed, which I usually regretted the next day when my back was all twisted into knots. Tonight, I didn't care about what the morning was going to bring; I was content letting the day end quietly on the couch.

I was jarred out of sleep by a series of loud bangs followed by the sound of my side door flying open and banging against the wall. Next, I heard Al barking and growling like I've never heard him before. I was trying to get my bearings, still bleary-eyed from sleep, when I saw this huge form in front of me swing something. The form, which developed into man, was standing over Al and whacking him with something short and black.

I leaped off the couch and right into the swinging arm of whatever or whoever had invaded my home. In one motion, he whacked Al with the object and backhanded me right on the left temple. I saw a flash of white and a fiery pain went all through my head. I was on my knees. I could hear a half howl, half cry coming from Al when I felt a kick in the ribs. The guy was wearing steel-toed boots, and he kicked me hard three or four times in the floating ribs and a couple of times in the gut.

I rolled over on my back, struggling to breathe and not being able to, with a searing pain in my head, when whoever my visitor was knelt on my chest. The knee sent a convulsive flinch through my body. He was wearing a leather vest, old jeans, and big motorcycle boots, and he also wore a stocking mask over his bald head. I noticed tattoos on his arm. Everything was coming in and out of focus.

"Stay off the fucking Internet. You hear me?" He adjusted his stance and kicked me one more time for good measure. "Stay off the fucking Internet or the next time you'll get more than a beating," he said.

The beating stopped and he went out the door. I heard a car start up and I got up in time to see a white pickup truck pulling out of my front yard. Parked on the other side of Route 9R was the Crown Vic, and when the pickup pulled out, the Crown Vic fell in behind it. That was all I saw. I leaned into the wall, coming to the realization that it hurt to breathe. My mouth was full of blood and I was bleeding from the head. My concentration was rattled by the sound coming from the back of the Blue.

I found Al in the bedroom. He was shaking, convulsing really. He had blood coming out of his mouth and when he saw me, he let out a moan like I've never heard an animal make. He was in trouble and in a lot of pain.

I scooped him into my arms, which sent an excruciating pain into my ribs and a rush to my head that made me stagger. He cried harder from the pain of being lifted. I struggled to the car and laid Al down on the front seat. The moving around made his pain worse and he let out another one of those sick, pained howls.

I started the car and I had to drive hunched over because I couldn't sit up right. There was an emergency vet clinic near the Y that was open twenty-four hours. I ran every light and made it there in just about ten minutes. I lifted Al out of the front seat and noticed his nose was covered in blood and a puddle of his blood had formed on the front seat. He yelped again as I got him in.

I handed him to an assistant and they rushed him somewhere to the back of the building. I was breathing fast but with very shallow breaths and I felt the dried blood crusting to the side of my face. I heard another assistant say:

"Sir, why don't you sit down?"

"Will he be okay?" I heard myself say. Things were getting fuzzy. "The doctor is checking on him. Sir, you're bleeding."

"Make sure my dog's okay. Make sure he's in no pain." I felt nauseous and dizzy.

That's all I remember.

I came to in a hospital bed with Rudy standing over me. Rudy was checking on some of his patients and had seen my name on the admissions list.

"What the hell's going on?" I said.

"Don't sit up," Rudy said.

I ignored him, sat up, and puked all down the front of me. "Where's my dog?"

"What are you talking about?" Rudy said.

"Al, my dog, where the hell is he?"

"Duffy, you don't even have a dog."

"Yes I do. He was Walanda's. He's at that emergency vet."

I swung my feet around to get off the bed and threw up again, this time on the floor.

"You're not going anywhere. You've got a concussion and some cracked ribs," Rudy said.

"I got to check on Al," I said.

"No way—no fucking way am I discharging you."

"Look, Rudy, I'm leaving. I appreciate you being here, but I gotta go. Hand me my pants."

"No, you ain't getting your pants. You're not leaving."

"Rudy," I motioned at him with my finger. "Give me my fuckin' pants."

"Nope—you got no business leaving this hospital."

"Fine. You should know me better. You think I need my fuckin' pants to leave? Watch me," I said.

I headed out of my room barefoot with that stupid half-dress thing they give you with no back. The nurses were a bit startled when I blew past them and I was all the way to the elevator when Rudy caught up to me with my pants, shirt, and shoes.

"Fuckin' stubborn Mick-Pollack," he said.

"I need a ride to that vet by the gym," I told him.

"Let's go," Rudy said.

I puked in the parking lot just before climbing into Rudy's SUV. I've been concussed before and I knew what to expect. The midmorning traffic was making me crazy. We pulled into the vet's lot twenty minutes later and I bounded in the door and went right to the counter.

"Where's Al? Is he okay?" I said to a vet assistant. I didn't remember her from last night, but considering my state then, that didn't mean much.

"I'll get Dr. Perkins to speak with you," she answered.

I paced the small waiting room, waiting for the vet.

"Mr. Dombrowski?" the vet said.

"Is he all right?" I said.

"He's going to be, but it's going to take a while. He's had some internal bleeding along with the cracked ribs. He also was hit on the head pretty hard. I think he probably has a concussion."

"Can I see him?"

"Sure, he's still groggy from the pain medication. We bandaged him up and he'll be okay, but he's going to be in some pain for a while."

I walked into a small room off the examination room and there was Al in a small cage. His eyes were closed; he had a bandage on his head that was soaked through with blood, and his midsection was all wrapped up in gauze.

I got close to the cage and put my fingers through to pet him. His eyes opened and he saw me. When his eyes could focus, he tried to get up but couldn't. His tail started to wag, but then he started to whimper from the pain.

Seeing that hurt more than anything I'd experienced in the last twenty-four hours. Right there, I decided someone was going to pay dearly for this.

"When can I take him home?" I asked.

"You can take him now if you can keep him quiet, give him his medication, and watch him all day. If you want, I can get him ready."

"Please," I said.

I waited while they changed the dressings on Al and gave me his medications and directions for what I was supposed to do. The assistant up front, a cute blonde woman who couldn't have been twenty-five, asked me if I'd be paying cash, check, or charge.

"I hadn't even thought of that. How much is it?"

She slid the invoice in front of me and started to explain the bill item for item. I didn't hear any of it. I was transfixed by the number on the bottom of the computer printout. It said $3,892.

"Um…what happens if I can't pay this?" I said.

"Then we can't release the animal," she said.

"You keep the dog?"

"Sir, we will hold him until you pay and charge you for boarding."

"Give me a second," I said.

I went out to see Rudy. He was reading The New York Post and sitting behind the wheel.

"Hey Rude, I need a favor," I said.

"What else is new?" he said.

"You got a credit card, don't you?"

"How much is it?"

"Around four thousand dollars."

"Are you out of your mind?"

"I wouldn't ask if I didn't need it."

Rudy walked me into the vet's and handed them his Visa Platinum. They handed me Al in a carrier.

25

I stayed home with Al, spending most of the day in bed with him next to me. I iced the egg on my forehead and my bruised ribs and tried to do the same for Al. He slept most of the day, probably from his medication, and periodically let out whimpers when he breathed heavily. One time when I dozed off and rolled over, I bumped him and he yelped.

I ran the series of events through my mind. This is what I knew: The women on Walanda's block suspected that Tyrone, her ex, the perverted pimp, was up to no good and that he had made overtures toward Shony in the past. I knew that there were three women linked by a tattoo in the jail and that they were all from around Forrest Point. I knew that the same design as that tattoo was featured on a website that also had photos of one of the women from the jail, probably Tyrone, and definitely Shony. I knew that the term "Webster" was used by Walanda and was the user name for the perverted pay site that featured a mother/daughter prostitution ring. I knew that some big bald-headed biker type gave me and Al an awful beating shortly after I put this all together. I also remember Laila, the woman from Walanda's neighborhood, mentioning that Walanda took rides with a big, bald-headed biker guy. Then there was the fact that the guys in the park got beat up by a guy with the same description. Sure, the percentage of guys who commit hate crimes who are shaved-headed biker types might be skewed in such a way as to suggest that there may be more than one of them, but I didn't like coincidences. Then, of course, there was the Crown Vic.

I didn't know where they housed the women in the porn ring or who ran it. I didn't know for sure how they got women to be part of it, but that was probably the easiest thing to figure out. People who get addicted to crack will do just about anything to keep using the shit. If it's made available to them, they will keep doing whatever it is that makes it available to them. Most crack addicts don't even try to stop until the supply runs out. If whoever was running this operation could keep the women who were tricking for them supplied, then they could keep the operation going endlessly. Add in the usual pimp mind games and abuse, and you got yourself a very captive audience.

I called Jerry to make sure he was okay. He told me that he had not been visited by the biker guy and assured me that he hadn't mentioned anything to anyone about my Internet explorations. He also gave me an impromptu tutorial on Internet security or, better put, insecurity. Though it wasn't easy, someone who cared enough could track who was visiting their sites and from what server. It meant being pretty vigilant, but if you're running a kiddie porn site and facing years in prison with people who take a dim view on the mistreatment of children, you might go the extra mile with security measures.

So maybe they tracked my computer and sent the bald bastard to give me a calling card. That told me a little about how, but it didn't address who or why. The women from jail were from Forrest Point, so I guess I could drive around Forrest Point looking for a child pornography/crack ring. There probably wasn't a sign over wherever they were doing business that said "Child Porn 'R' Us," and Forrest Point was mostly rural, so I could drive past a lot of forest and farmland and not see anything. I guess I could start knocking on farmhouse doors and if I turned anything up, it would put a particularly perverted spin on the old "farmer's daughter" jokes.

I could look for Tyrone. Perverted pimps usually weren't masters of disguise. There probably weren't a ton of black people in Forrest Point, and I think he might have a tendency to stand out. I could also drive around looking for a bald biker-type guy driving a white pickup truck. That guy might stand out, but there were more than a few white pickup trucks in Crawford and even more out in the country.

I could also try to talk to the people at the Eagle Heights Jewish Unified Services. There was a high probability that someone involved in this horror show was mandated into treatment at some point for addiction, child abuse, neglect, or some other less-than-socially-redeeming lifestyle characteristic. Of course, I was on a five-day disability pass, so showing up at our sister clinic wouldn't be cool. I thought about my irritable bowel syndrome diagnosis, and thought that maybe if I went there and shit my pants in the waiting room I could get away with it. I decided against that.

I needed a computer to use and my office was out. I figured if I checked out some of what Jerry had to say, it might jog my mind into doing something. Jerry had said that the password for the webcast site changed frequently, but I had to be sure. I couldn't deal with one of those college "cyber cafes," so I headed to Crawford Medical Center. They had a medical library on the third floor, and I had gotten a little friendly with the librarian there from my visits with Rudy.

Deborah Speakwell was a little bit of a strange bird. Don't get me wrong—she was helpful in that librarian way. I always felt like librarians acted like all the books belonged to them and they were constantly wary about your intentions. Debbie had this weird compulsive disorder that had her perpetually grooming herself. She was either behind one of the shelves brushing her thick red hair or she was forever applying moisturizer to her hands from this gigantic container. She must have gotten the moisturizer at some sort of warehouse club because the thing was like an industrial drum. Whenever you entered the library, you'd hear these fart noises coming from behind the shelves. I found it disturbing until I realized it was Speakwell depressing the moisturizing container top.

I said hello to Debbie, who was behind the shelves making fart noises, and asked her if I could use the computer. She yelled "okay" from behind the shelves just like a woman who was in the shower would. It was a bit risky checking out porn sites in the hospital library, but I figured I couldn't get fired from a place where I wasn't employed. Speakwell would be moisturizing and brushing the whole time so she wouldn't be on my back.

I went to Yahoo! Briefcase and tried the password Jerry had given me. Unfortunately, Jerry was right about their security measures and the password had expired. I surfed around a bit, went to www.Xcracksterweb.com, didn't see anything new, checked my e-mail and Fightnews.com, and signed off. I thanked Debbie and

started to head out when something dawned on me. I wanted to check out the links Jerry mentioned that were on the site to see if they might tell me something.

I signed back on and headed to the browser window to click on the Xcracksterweb address instead of typing it all in again. The window displayed the history of where the most recent surfers had been. The first four or five addresses were the ones I just looked up. Right underneath those were some strange websites.

There were:

www.inthefeetofthenight.com
www.toesrus.com
www.stinkyfeet.com,
www.Xcracksterweb.com
www.boobworld.com
www.alfinuu.org and
www.bankofcanary.com.

The position of www.Xcracksterweb.com was such that it looked like someone else had been there before me. Mine was up just below my e-mail site and above Fightnews.com. Unless the computer did something out of order, that had to mean that someone in the library was on www.Xcracksterweb.com in addition to what looked like a bunch of foot-fetish sites.

"Deb, can I ask a question?" I asked while she hit the top of the moisturizer.

"Sure, Duff—that's why I'm here," she said.

"The history displayed on the Internet browser goes in chronological order, doesn't it?"

"It should go according to the order in which sites were downloaded, though sometimes it doesn't record every site," she said.

"But it wouldn't skip out of order, would it?"

"It shouldn't."

"Who was on this computer just before me?" I asked.

"You're the first one to use it today," she said, brushing her hair.

"Who would have used it last night?"

"There's only one doctor who generally comes in after hours." "Who might that be?" I asked.

"Dr. Gabbibb."

26

My head was spinning. I kept trying to tell myself that the fact that Gabbibb was on the computer looking at www.Xcracksterweb.com was a coincidence. All it proved, along with his penchant for sexy feet, was that Gabbibb was an even creepier wack-job than I originally guessed. Just because the guy's idea of a turn-on involved toe punk, it didn't mean he was a kidnapping rapist. Not necessarily anyway.

A call to my increasingly busy information technologist furnished me with more background. Jerry researched the Alfinuu site and determined it was some sort of radical, anti-American deal based in Pakistan. The Bank of Canary was an offshore bank that Jerry explained would be a good place to launder money or to avoid taxes on money earned illegally.

I thanked Jerry for his help. I had some information that felt like something, but I didn't know what it was or what to do with it. I also had to find Shony and I didn't have enough information to know where to start. I wanted to find out as much as I could about this India-Pakistan thing, and I wanted to find out from someone who lived it, not just read about it. I couldn't very well ask Gabbibb, and though there were a few other Indian doctors and students at Crawford Medical Center, not only did I not know them, I didn't exactly get a great vibe from them, either.

Every now and then when I didn't know what to do, I'd give

Smitty a call. If he didn't know the answer to something, he often knew how to find the answer. I called him late at night when I knew he'd be up and I got his usual cheerful greeting.

"Yeah?" he said.

"Man, I can see why you never made a fortune in the telemarketing business," I said.

"You know, just because your sorry ass got suspended doesn't mean you can't workout," Smitty said.

"Ahh geez, don't you ever let up?"

"No."

"Maybe if I didn't throw a hook like a bitch."

"Yeah, that's part of it," Smitty said. "Look, what are you calling me for?"

"This is goin' to sound a little weird, Smitty."

"Comin' from you—I doubt it."

"You know anyone from India?"

"You're getting weird on me, son."

"I told you—do you?"

"What are you, with the census bureau all of sudden?"

"Nah, I want to find out something about India and Pakistan and all that terrorism shit," I said.

Smitty was quiet for a moment.

"You free Tuesday morning?"

"Yeah."

"Meet me at the Y at seven."

"For what?"

"Be there at seven." Smitty hung up. I knew better than to ask a lot of questions. With Smitty it was simple—I'd see him Tuesday morning at the gym, about five minutes to seven.

That Tuesday morning I met Smitty in front of the Y at five minutes to seven and got into his Ninety-Eight. Smitty always drove and it wasn't something you asked about. I had my coffee and I got in his car and, like always, the two of us didn't exchange "good mornings" or make a lot of small talk. I didn't ask him where we were going or who we were going to speak to. We knew each other on a different level, and I knew that soon enough my questions would be answered.

We drove for about half an hour, without talking and without the radio. Smitty was the only guy I ever felt comfortable being with for periods of time without speaking. Out past Schorie County and almost to Mariaville, Smitty turned down a dirt road and slowed the car until he pulled into a gravel parking lot in front of a prefab steel building. On the lawn in front of the building was a sign that said "Hatha Yoga."

With anyone else, this would've been ample fodder for a couple hours of ball busting. I knew better.

"Before you go inside, take your shoes off," Smitty said.

I nodded.

We went through the front door, and sitting on a plain carpet in a twenty-by-twenty room in front of us was a very dark and shinyskinned man who looked like Gandhi, or at least like the guy who played Gandhi in the movie. Smitty stood with his hands folded and his head down until the man greeted him.

"Horace, it is good to see you," the Gandhi-guy said. For twenty years I knew the man only as "Smitty," and now I think I knew why.

"Good morning, Yogi," Smitty said quietly. "This is the man we spoke of. This is Duffy."

For some reason I felt like genuflecting or curtsying but I didn't do either.

"Please sit," the man said.

Smitty and I sat cross-legged on the carpet with my new friend, Yogi.

"How can I help you?"

"I want to know about India and Pakistan."

"Mr. Duffy," the Yogi remained amazingly still and expressionless. "India and Pakistan are vast lands. Could you be more specific?"

"Do you know anything about a Pakistani organization called Alfinuu?"

Yogi looked down and studied his hands. His expression did not change.

"Alfinuu is a fundamentalist Islamic organization that has caused much unhappiness in both Pakistan and India. It is made up of rigid people who feel that those not like them do not deserve to live. They believe they are superior and need to dominate those who do not follow their beliefs."

"Are they a large organization?" I asked.

"It is difficult to tell; they are not open in their dealings."

"What do they do?"

"They take the Koran, which I respect as a holy book, and they use scripture to do unholy things. In parts of Pakistan, women are jailed for what is perceived as adultery, though adultery can be seen as any type of expression. If a woman is raped against her will, she is seen as an adulteress."

I noticed the Yogi hardly ever blinked and I had to look real carefully to see if he was breathing. Smitty had his eyes closed and was breathing very slowly as well.

"How does Alfinuu support their efforts financially?" I asked.

"Several ways. They take the women who they have labeled as adulteresses and, because the women are seen as unforgivable, they often force them into prostitution. They also take the children of these women and either sell them as prostitutes or slaves where they are abused or forced into pornography."

This was beginning to sound familiar.

"Mr. Duffy, the Alfinuu is not India or Pakistan any more than the Ku Klux Klan is America. They are poisonous venom within Pakistan," Yogi said.

"I understand," I said.

"From culture to culture, people devalue others as a perverted way to overvalue themselves. It is the disease of the world."

"I agree, Yogi."

"Mr. Duffy, do you realize the way women are treated by

the Alfinuu? If a man believes his spouse has been unresponsive to his needs, it is now commonplace for the man to douse the woman with acid so it disfigures the woman's face. It is horrible."

"What is being done about it in Pakistan?"

"The Alfinuu work underground and they have spread enough fear to intimidate."

"What's their ultimate goal?"

"To rule the world and have everyone think like them," the Yogi wiped his hand across his forehead. "Mr. Duffy, I have people coming in that I must prepare for."

"Just one more question, please. Do you know the Indian doctor Gabbibb from the Crawford Medical Center?"

"I know of him. He does not associate with others from India. He avoids anything involving the Indian culture. None of my associates know much about his life in India." Yogi paused and scratched his ear. "There was an incident several years ago."

"An incident?"

"An Indian woman approached him at his office to invite him to an Indian social event. He spat on the woman and physically pushed her through the door."

"Did anyone know why?"

"He yelled that she was an unclean whore for wearing Western makeup and lipstick."

I thanked the Yogi and Smitty motioned to the door quietly. We left without saying a word as the Yogi closed his eyes and folded his hands again. Smitty and I drove to Crawford in silence. As we pulled in front of the gym, he spoke.

"You find out what you wanted?" Smitty asked.

"I'm not sure," I said.

Smitty was about to pull away and I couldn't resist.

"Horace?"

Smitty gave me his coldest, meanest stare and drove away.

I needed to weasel some information out of some social workers, and you would think that would be tough because of the stringent regulations on confidentiality. Well, sometimes it was and sometimes it wasn't. If you had a good friend in the field, you could kind of speak off the record or in code and get whatever info you wanted.

For instance, I wanted to find out what happened to those three skanks that were in Walanda's jail therapy group. I called Jane and she pretended to give me a hard time about it, but then I got her to give in. I gave her the ol' "...suppose, hypothetically, of course, that there were three skanky women in your jail group. Suppose their names were Melissa, Stephanie, and Lori..."

In just a few minutes, I knew Melissa got released a week ago, Stephanie would get out tomorrow, and Lori would get discharged in three days. All three were sent to the Eagle Heights clinic.

Jane was all right.

Now I had to find out if that new counselor with glasses, Katy, was. I wanted to pump her to see what she could tell me about the trio, but I was afraid that because she was new to the field and didn't know me, she might be tight with the information.

Young social workers like Katy overcompensated for their lack of experience by developing their vocabulary and playing the part. I'm guessing she went home crying once or twice a week feeling overwhelmed and incompetent. She probably grew up in a nice suburb and always wanted to help people, she just didn't picture it would be these kind of people. The Katy's of the profession usually last about a year or so before they find themselves a doctor or lawyer to marry. Then they're pregnant and they just don't have the time to work anymore despite how much they're going to miss it.

I didn't want to risk not getting the info I wanted from Katy, so I didn't bother playing on a friendship we didn't have. Instead I called and spoke in a very official and bored tone and told her I was following up on some cases. I pretended to be filling out a post-aftercare continuing follow-up form and asked her a bunch of methodical questions.

It worked.

I found out Melissa started in treatment earlier in the week, that she was driven by her significant other, a large man with a shaved head who didn't leave the car, and that she was placed on Bower-man's case load. Apparently, according to Katy, Bowerman fancies herself an expert in women's issues.

I took my chances and asked if she had any contact with a client named Tyrone whose last name I just couldn't remember but who Michelin wanted me to find out about. I explained that the file was way over in the chart room and I didn't feel like getting it.

She bought all of it and gave me the entire deal on Tyrone. I guess my man Tyrone had been thrown out of treatment a long time ago for inappropriate sexual advances on the female clients.

Imagine that.

27

I took some time to process what I had just learned and started strategizing what to do about it. As I had guessed, my bald biker friend had something to do with the evil babes from jail, probably was the same guy who used to pick up Walanda, and almost assuredly was the guy that paid me and Al a visit at the Moody Blue. I wasn't sure what I had, but I had a piece of thread to start pulling at. If Stephanie was due out tomorrow and headed for the Eagle Heights clinic, then I had a pretty good guess who might be taking her. I was guessing that if I hung out around the clinic long enough, I'd see a white pickup truck with a bald bastard behind the wheel who had something coming to him. As this ran through my mind, I glanced down at Al. He was uncomfortable and continued to struggle with his breathing.

The county jail discharged prisoners at 12:01 a.m., which was one of the classic strokes of incredible bureaucratic idiocy. A very high percentage of the people who wound up in county jail got there because of drugs, drinking, or other nocturnal happenings.

The jail was located at the bottom of South Hill in Crawford's worst ghetto. The inmates only had to walk out the door and head a block up the hill to get their first hit of crack or heroin. There was even a scum subset of dealers who waited on that block at 12:02 every night. Some women would leave the county lockup and wait for the first john to cruise by. There would be a ten or fifteen dollar transaction and then the usual sexual procedure. That payment got them a couple of bumpies, as they were sometimes called, and a briefly interrupted crack addiction was reignited.

I had a couple of hours to kill before midnight and I was starving, so I headed over to AJ's. Al was going to have to come in with me and AJ was probably going to give me shit for it, but I didn't care. I parked right out in front, lifted Al off his seat, and carried him in the front door.

"Hey," TC said. "Meat deliveries in the back."

"Duffy—get the hell out of here with him. It's against health laws," AJ said.

"He's a seeing-eye dog," I said.

"For who?" Rocco said. "Midgets?"

"Look, AJ, he's hurtin' and I can't leave him alone. Give me a break this time, will ya?"

AJ shook his head and muttered something and walked to the other end of the bar. He acted disgusted, but that was predictable and he didn't put us out.

"Hey Duff, he's one of those basket hounds, isn't he?" Jerry Number One asked.

"That's bassoon hound, jerkoff," said Rocco. "They were originally bred to accompany the soldiers in the French and Indian War. The bassoonist called the men to battle."

"I think it's bastard hound, because they drool so much," TC said.

"What the hell would drooling have to do with bastards?" Rocco said.

"It pisses everyone off and so that's what they called them," TC said. "God damn bastard hounds."

"Fellas, he's a basset hound," I said. "They're originally from France, and they're bred to trail small game for hunting." My Dogs For Dummies reading was paying off.

"That too," Rocco grumbled.

Eventually they got around to asking me about the bumps and bruises Al and I had. I mentioned something about a fender bender and a bad day at the gym. That was enough for the Foursome because they were already on to their next discussion/argument—something about a choking dog spitting up a burglar's fingers.

I decided to talk with Kelley.

"Hey—Kel."

"What's going on, Duff. Tough sparring session?"

"I guess you could say that."

"That's not from the ring." Kelley didn't ask—he was making a statement.

"Well…"

"I don't want to know, do I?"

Before I could answer, Rocco interrupted us.

"God damn bastard hound!"

I spun around on my stool to see Al chomping through Rocco's cheeseburger. He had ketchup on his nose.

"Shoo, shoo!" Rocco yelled.

"Rocco—he's not a pigeon," TC said. "What the hell are you telling him to shoo for?"

Al finished the cheeseburger and was sampling Rocco's fries.

"Shoo, you bastard!" Rocco said.

I grabbed Al and gingerly carried him away from the bar and to one of the tables. Everyone thought it was hysterical, that is, everyone but Rocco.

"Sorry, Rock," I said. "AJ—can you make Rocco another burger and get him a beer on me?"

"Bastard hound," Rocco muttered.

"Certainly seems more fitting than bassoon hound now, doesn't it, Rock?" Jerry Number Two said.

Rudy came in sweating up a storm, sat on the other side of the Foursome, and ordered a Foster's and a sidecar of Hennessy. Poor Rudy looked like he was getting fatter as he sat there. The back of his neck looked like a pack of hotdogs and the fabric on his clothes looked as stressed as he did.

"Hey, Rude. What's happening?" I asked.

"Bullshit, Duff. Nothin' but bullshit," he said, taking a pull off the Hennessy and leaving just about a sip left in his rocks glass.

"Gabbibb found cancer in two more of the park-beating victims." He wiped sweat from his forehead. "Something weird is happening and I don't know what. Either these guys are all eating something bad or the park is radioactive or something," he said.

"How could all of these guys have such bad luck?" I asked.

"Well, it's possible, just not very likely."

"Hey Rude—why would Gabbibb have money in an offshore account?" I said.

"What are you talking about?"

"He was on the computer before me and I saw that he was on the Bank of Canary website."

"That doesn't necessarily mean anything, Duff." He swallowed the rest of the Hennessy. "He might be doing something shady with that electronic business he does with his cousin."

"He was also on some Pakistani extremist site."

"Duffy, what the fuck are you doing?" He wiped sweat from his brow. "You think he's some sort of money-laundering political extremist trying to take over Crawford, New York?"

"I think he's a shady asshole," I said.

"I think there's a lot of shady assholes around, but that doesn't mean they're all doing it on a giant scale."

"Hey, how's that shit going at work?"

"They've called a meeting with the hospital board of directors to decide whether they rescind my privileges."

"I'm sorry, Rudy," I said.

"Yeah, me too, Duff," he said.

I finished off my third Schlitz and realized I'd better head out if I wanted to catch the 12:01 jail releases. I bid my farewells to the boys, scooped up Al, who winced a bit when I put pressure on his ribs, and walked to the Eldorado.

I slid in a compilation eight-track I made years ago of some of Elvis's stuff. Colonel Parker, Elvis's manager and guru, was one of the stupidest music people ever. He had a tendency of burying some of Elvis's greatest songs on albums that really sucked. "Burning Love," for instance, was on an album with movie hits. I decided I would create my own compilations of my favorites and tell the Colonel to stick his marketing plan.

As Elvis went through his paces on "In the Ghetto," I cruised into Crawford. I went right past Walanda's house, which still had a washer on the little five-by-five front lawn, and the porch door was still banging off the wall in the wind. The rest of the neighborhood looked like it needed a shower and a good night's sleep. This part of town was where my Polish grandparents lived, and in their day it was a poor but proud neighborhood. Folks from my generation who wouldn't think of walking a block through one of these neighborhoods now like to point out that their ancestors had little money but kept the neighborhood looking beautiful.

That sort of mentality had elements of truth to it, but it also seemed oversimplified to me. Growing up black and poor was a whole lot different than growing up Polish or Irish or Italian and poor. I'm not exactly sure why, but I believe it has something to do with one's ancestors being sold as property for centuries. I know that doesn't happen now, but I think the residual effects on our culture linger. I'm sure people a whole lot smarter than me could explain it better.

I parked my car near the top of the hill three blocks from the jail. My '76 burnt orange Eldorado was a lot of things, but inconspicuous wasn't one of them. Al and I walked down the street to get a look at the front doors of the county jail. The two-block walk took us past three guys selling crack and two women who offered to gratify a very specific desire of mine for ten dollars. Interestingly enough, the crack dealers were selling two rocks of crack for the same price.

The second woman dropped her price down to five dollars, and when I looked closer at her I realized she was a former client of mine whose case I recently closed.

"Teresa?" I asked.

"Yeah? Oh, Duff, it's you…er…this isn't what it looks like, man…I…uh," she stopped in mid-sentence. Though her mind was fixated on nothing but crack, she still realized the absurdity of denying what she was doing, especially after just offering to perform an unmentionable act on me for five dollars.

"Teresa, be careful, please. Come in to the clinic tomorrow. Promise me."

She started to cry and turned and walked up the street. I couldn't think of anything sadder. By the time she reached the corner, she was already offering herself to the crackheads and johns walking by.

I would've pursued her, but I wanted to be in position by midnight and we had just five minutes. Al stood in the darkness next to a tree one block from the jail. I would've turned up my collar and smoked a cigarette like any self-respecting private eye, but I had on a hooded sweatshirt and I don't smoke.

A Lexus SUV pulled up in the "No Parking" area in front of the jail at 11:58. The Lexus SUV was the pimpmobile of our times, replacing the Cadillac and Lincoln. I suppose today's pimps did a lot of camping.

A black guy wearing a bright blue, baggy FUBU warm-up got out of the Lexus, lit a cigarette, and leaned against the front fender. He was a ways away but he looked like he could've been the guy from the website with Shony. The Lexus had gold trim all over it, and someone had taken great pains to wax the thing.

At 12:01, half a dozen people walked out of the front door. There were five men and one woman. Two of the men hooted and hollered when they walked out and gave each other high-fives. The other two men went in opposite directions, both lighting up cigarettes as if choreographed.

The woman was Stephanie, and she walked toward the Lexus. The black guy put out his cigarette and, without any acknowledgement toward Stephanie, got in the Lexus and started it up. Stephanie got into the passenger seat and the Lexus drove away.

I looked down to my private-eye partner, Al, and said, "I think we just met Tyrone."

I didn't have a whole lot of time to bask in the pride of my tremendous detective work. Before Al and I could step off the curb in the direction of the Eldorado, there was a screeching of tires and the slamming of doors, followed by a bunch of yelling.

"Hands up, hands in the air!" the guy jumping out of the silver Crown Victoria said. He was wearing a blue blazer with gray pants, though I didn't get the color of his tie because I was busy looking at the gun pointed at my chest. He had a partner who had circled around the car and he, too, had his gun drawn.

I tried to put my hands in the air, but that pulled Al's leash, which caused him to yelp and then bark. Both suits focused their guns on Al momentarily, then back at me. I could tell they couldn't make up their minds which of us was more dangerous.

"Sorry—what do you want me to do?" I said.

"Make the dog shut up," came from blue blazer who seemed to be in charge of talking. He had a Middle Eastern complexion with slicked-back, very dark hair and very bushy eyebrows.

"I don't know how to do that," I said.

The other guy who looked about twenty-five was about five foot eleven, one hundred eighty-five pounds. He had blond hair and it looked like he didn't shave yet.

Al just kept barking and the two guys looked bewildered. I probably would have been much more frightened if Al wasn't making such a racket. Too much was happening too fast.

"Tie the dog to the streetlight and get in the car," Blue Blazer said.

"He's not going to like that."

"You think we're playing games here!" He waved the gun

toward the pole.

I tied Al to the pole, which thoroughly pissed him off. Then I got into the back seat with the two guns pointed at my face. The Middle Eastern guy had a pockmarked face and perfect white teeth, which made for a strange combination. Blondie had a slightly turned-up nose, which made him look even more juvenile than he already did.

Al wouldn't shut up and the noise was deafening, even with the windows up.

"What do you know about Alfinuu?" Pockmark said.

"Not much, just—"

"Stop fucking around, sticking your head where it doesn't belong." He didn't wait for an answer. "Leave things alone."

"What are you talking about?" This was getting weird.

"Alfinuu is nothing to mess with. Stay away—it's a matter of national security."

"Don't you guys have to tell me who you are?"

"Duffy, you watch too many movies," Pock said, which caused his pubescent partner to snicker. "Never mind about the girl too."

"The girl?"

"Don't fuck around with us. Do what you're told. Go to the gym, go do some counseling, I don't care, but stop looking into things that ain't your business." He paused for emphasis. "You hear me? Leave it alone—all of it."

The car got quiet, which all of a sudden made me realize Al wasn't barking. I looked at the streetlamp and Al's collar and leash were there and he was gone.

"Al!" I yelled and went to bolt out the door but they were locked. "He's gone—let me out."

Pockmark laughed at me. "Word to the wise, Duff—do what you're told and leave things alone. Now, get out of here and go find your fuckin' dog."

I heard the electric locks disengage and I ran out the car and into the street screaming for Al. I had no idea how to find a runaway dog, and in my panic I wasn't being terribly strategic. I sprinted up one street and down the other, getting funny looks from the street whores and low-level crack dealers.

"Allah-King, Allah-King!" I screamed until I was hoarse. I was looking down driveways, in alleys, and behind abandoned buildings. Between the running and my anxiety I could feel myself running out of gas.

In the distance, a couple of blocks over, I thought I heard something. I didn't waste time running around the block—I ran right through four backyards, jumping fences, and two streets over, I saw him and it dawned on me. This was where I should have started the search.

Al was on Walanda's porch scratching at the front door, whimpering and then barking out of frustration.

"C'mere boy, it's all right, it's all right," I said. It took him a little while to come to me, and when he did, he looked up and whimpered.

"It's okay, buddy. Let's go home," I said.

We started to walk and he stopped and looked back at the house a couple of times.

I thought about the jail, I thought about Tyrone, and I thought about my visit from the men in the Crown Vic. I thought about Walanda and I thought about Shony. I thought about Al.

And I thought I'd be damned if I was going to leave anything alone.

28

It was Wednesday and I had until Monday to nurse my irritable bowel syndrome, which didn't give me a whole lot of time. I had learned that there were some connections, but I still wasn't sure what they connected to. There was definitely some skuzzy business going on involving three scumbag chicks from Forrest Point, there was a bald biker guy who was connected to them who also beat me and Al, and there was Tyrone, a former significant other to Walanda whose highlighted resume sections included pimp and pervert. He was connected at least to Stephanie and Melissa, but maybe most disturbing was that he had voiced a desire to get Shondeneisha into prostitution or something equally as vile. Then there was the Crown Vic.

I needed to find out more about the connections, and I figured my best bet was to hang around the Eagle Heights clinic because eventually Stephanie had to show up there. Usually, post-jail assessments occurred within forty-eight hours of release, and because it was part of probation, the clients usually kept those appointments,

even if they dropped out of treatment shortly after that. Probation officers had a habit of checking on the first-visit attendance but after that losing track of the clients on their caseloads.

If I was going to keep my eye on the Eagle Heights clinic, I had two choices. I could sit outside the clinic for the next forty-eight hours, which was going to be very tedious and there was always the danger of being spotted by Stephanie, Tyrone, and Baldy, or by the clinic staff. If the first group spotted me, that could cause them to be suspicious and might bring on another surprise visit from Baldy. This time it might mean more than a warning.

If the clinic staff spotted me and it got back to Claudia, then that would probably blow my sick-time claim and I'd get fired faster than Claudia could buy a new pair of elastic-waist pants. The best chance I had was to get ahold of Katy and see if she could get me some information and be quiet about it. If it got back to Claudia, I was in trouble, and if it got to Rhonda, I was probably in trouble. The fact of the matter was that I was likely to get in trouble no matter what I did. I guess I was already in my fair share of trouble and was probably going to lose my job for a bunch of reasons, so—what the hell?

I poured myself a cup of coffee and figured I'd call Eagle Heights around 9:20. If I called right at nine, I would look too anxious. There was also a good chance that, Eagle Heights being a not-for-profit, no one would be there until ten after nine. Human service workers usually have so many issues that getting to work on time is almost impossible.

Al's health was showing some improvement. He was walking okay and whimpering less. I still had to lift him on and off the sofa and bed because the few times that he jumped it caused him to make this awful yelping sound. Right now he was lying on the kitchenette floor, sleeping.

Before I could call Katy, my phone rang. It was Jerry Number Two.

"Duff—I think I got something you better see."

"What is it?"

"The website has announced their special monthly event."

"What are you talking about?" I said.

"I went to the members-only pay site—the one with the kids and the sicker shit," Jerry said.

"Yeah?"

"They were promoting their next webcast featuring the newest girls."

"Jesus."

"Yeah, and they're making a big deal about Shondeneisha losing her virginity live with somebody named Tyrone."

I froze. I felt a sickness in my stomach that quickly spread all through me. This was beyond sick and had to be stopped. It didn't matter if I lost my job or got in trouble or took a beating. Concern for that now seemed ridiculous.

"Duff—you there?"

"Yeah, Jer. When is this all going down?"

"It says on the webpage that it's supposed to happen on Saturday, but the time won't be announced until sometime that day. It looks like they take care in not letting out too much information. They're pretty sophisticated in the security measures they take."

"Jerry, can you look into Dr. Gabbibb?" I asked.

"I can find out something on just about anybody," Jerry said. "What kind of stuff are you looking for?"

"I know that he has at least checked out the site. Can you find out about the alfinuu.org site and the offshore banking stuff?" I said.

"I can try, Duff, but without being real sure what I'm looking for, I'm not sure what I'll come up with."

"Whatever you can come up with will be great."

I signed off with Jerry and told him I'd be over to see him after I took care of something else. I called Eagle Heights and asked for Katy.

"Hi Duff, what can I do for you?" she said.

"Hey Katy, how's it going? I was calling to see if Stephanie's eval was scheduled," I said.

"Uh...Duff, aren't you supposed to be out on disability or something?"

Shit. She had found out. I had no idea what this was going to do. I decided to go with it and see where it took me.

"Yeah, I'm just following up with what I can from home."
"Rhonda told us that Claudia called her and they want us to let her know if they hear from you. Duff—I think you're in some trouble."

"Probably."

"I don't know if I feel comfortable talking to you."

"Can you just tell me what time her eval is? I promised Jane at the jail."

"I really shouldn't. You're putting me in an awkward position." "I won't tell anyone I talked to you. Please, it's important to me." "I don't feel right about it…"

"Look, Katy, do you really want to spend your life being afraid of assholes like Claudia and Rhonda? Do you think they care about helping people or do you think they care about protecting their own little pathetic bureaucratic power? Don't become one of them—it means death to your soul."

I lost my cool. My little tirade probably would mean she'd run right to Bowerman. She was young and impressionable and was still scared.

"Hang on," Katy said and I heard the call go on hold.

I didn't have any idea what to expect and I waited for a few minutes that felt like a month.

"She's coming in at eleven today."

Katy hung up before I could thank her. I was impressed. The kid was all right.

I went to Jerry's and we reviewed the site and it was as sick as I imagined. There were images of a very frightened Shony with Tyrone next to her with all sorts of promises of all the things he was going to do to her in the upcoming simulcast. There were images of other young girls—some looked barely ten—who were also to be featured that night. Apparently, the simulcast was the big event for the losers who belonged to this club of scumbags.

I asked Jerry if there was any way of telling where something like this could take place. He said there wasn't, that was what made Internet porn so difficult to track. Nothing pointed to the physical presence of things, and any evidence of whereabouts was limited to servers and domains and that bullshit.

I asked Jerry what he had found out about Gabbibb.

"I didn't come up with a lot, Duff," he said. "He's been a doctor for twenty-seven years, went to medical school in Pakistan, is part owner with his cousin in an electronics store, and he paid cash for his three hundred fifty thousand dollar home."

"Must be nice," I said.

"I found a way to translate alfinuu.org, and it's an extremist site—anti-Jew, anti-American. It's either terrorist or terrorist related."

"Is there any sign that Gabbibb is involved in any way?"

"No, but I would doubt if anyone who was going to get involved in terrorism in this day and age would leave their name and address," Jerry said.

"What's their aim?"

"The usual shit. Death to America, death to the Jews, et cetera, et cetera…"

I thought it over for a minute. There's lots of reasons a guy could go to a site like this. Maybe he read about it in Newsweek, maybe Tom Brokaw was talking about it, or maybe he wants to keep a handle on what his enemies are doing. I didn't want to jump to conclusions.

"What about the Bank of the Canary or whatever it is?" I asked.

"Like I said before, maybe he has money that he doesn't want the government to know about," Jerry said.

"Like if you invested in a very profitable porn site?"

"Yep, that would be a reason," Jerry said.

29

I got done at Jerry's at about five minutes to ten, which gave me just enough time to make the drive to Eagle Heights. I asked Jerry to loan me his video camera and he gladly gave me some space-age thing that fit neatly in one hand. It was ergonomically shaped so that it was easy to carry and maneuver.

In the middle of my ride over to Jerry's, I had a startling moment of sanity. Kelley was right about me sticking my nose into things. I had come a long way, but this whole deal was getting way beyond my scope. I figured if I could catch Stephanie and Tyrone or Baldy or all three of them on tape and show the FBI and the cops the website, it would make arresting them relatively easy. The whole evil thing could be stopped, and they could do it better than a goofy social worker pug who read too many comic books. Maybe my friends in the Crown Vic would be the guys who would ultimately be the saviors in this deal after all, and, though I wasn't following their directions, the ends would justify the means.

Al took the ride with me because I didn't feel it was okay yet to leave him alone. With the forty-five-minute ride, the company wasn't bad as long as he kept the flatulence to a minimum. Al's new habit of playing with the power windows and power locks was getting on my nerves. On long drives, he'd throw a big, fat paw up on the switches and then watch with fascination as the window went down or the locks clicked up and down. He tried sticking his head out the window like he had before, but lately his ears kept slapping him in the face, which would make him howl as if some evil force in the universe was doing it.

I pulled into Eagle Heights at 10:40, giving me plenty of time to watch Stephanie's arrival. The clinic was on Ninth Street, which was a busy street, and I parallel parked a block and a half away. The Eldorado was no doubt conspicuous, but the narrowness of the street made it difficult to spot. I waited for Elvis to finish up the last verses of Dylan's "Don't Think Twice, It's All Right," a song most people would be surprised he did, and I turned off the eight-track.

I distracted Al and got him to turn around and have his head face me so he would stop with the window deal. He settled in, happy to drool on the velour elbow rest. At exactly eleven, the white pickup truck pulled up on ninth from the opposite direction. I fumbled around to adjust my seat to get the video camera in position.

My shuffling around got Al to sit up and look in the direction I was looking. He started to whimper and shift his weight from side to side in what appeared to be some sort of nervous fit. He scratched at the passenger door and tried to get at the window switches. I grabbed his head and tried to calm him down. He had remembered the white pickup.

I got the camera pointed at the truck and, though we were down the street and it was being shot from a distance, it was very clear that Stephanie and Tyrone were getting out of the truck, which was driven by Baldy. Tyrone and Stephanie headed into the clinic and I was relieved when Baldy took the right turn on the side street before passing Al and me.

That was what I needed. I had the connection between Tyrone and Stephanie together with the bald guy. When I turned this over to the authorities it would be a piece of cake for them to wrap this up.

I didn't waste any time getting out of Eagle Heights. I drove about eighty home and stopped just once along the way to let Al do some business and to call Kelley from a pay phone. I got lucky—Kelley was there and available. I set up a meeting over lunch at AJ's.

Al was sleeping so I left him in the car and went in to meet Kelley. Kelley was already there sitting at the bar. He didn't look pleased.

"Look, I only got a half an hour. Why do I have a sneaking suspicion that this is going to involve your new private-eye bullshit?"

"Kel, you're right, but let's put that aside for now, this is too important."

I set down the video camera so we both could view the playback screen. I hit play and watched as it showed the white pickup pulling up in front of the Eagle Heights clinic.

"That bald guy is the asshole who paid Al and me a visit and probably the same guy doing the park beatings. The black guy is Tyrone, an old perverted boyfriend of Walanda who always wanted to get weird with Shondeneisha. The woman is Stephanie and she's one of the women I told you about from the jail."

"Geez...Duff, slow down. What the hell are you talking about?" I pulled out the webpage printouts I had made at Jerry Number Two's.

"Here's the porn webpage they're running with underage kids, and this is what they're planning for this Saturday night."

I explained all the security stuff that I went through with Jerry Number Two. I explained the relationship of the three characters on the video and how they came to go to the Eagle Heights clinic. I knew I was going at a frenetic pace, but I couldn't control myself.

"Whoa. All right, all right. I see what you got. I won't lecture you now about getting in over your head, as you clearly have, I'll save that for later."

"Kel..."

"Don't interrupt, Duff. We have the bald guy on an assault.

We have Stephanie on a porn site, but she's not doing anything illegal. We have what we think is 'Tyrone' going to a clinic and promising to be involved with child porn on the web page."

"Right."

"Where does Tyrone live?"

"I don't know."

"What's the bald guy's name?"

"I don't know."

"Where is this webcast going down?"

"I don't know."

"So what we have connecting this trio is the video tape shot from what looks like a hundred and fifty feet with a guy that could be the guy on the website, a guy who is most probably your assaulter, and a woman who we can definitively say is the woman from jail and the website."

"Yes."

"If we could find the bald guy we could arrest him. Busting Tyrone immediately will be harder because any task force will want to be sure that what they got him on sticks. He hasn't done anything worth arresting him for yet. Stephanie is a creep, but I don't see what we can bust her on now."

"Kelley—C'mon!"

"Duff—I'm telling you how it works. The images on the tape are shot so far away any lawyer will have it thrown out. You can't read the license plate number on the truck and even if we could, it's probably stolen or untraceable in some other way. The child porn stuff is awful, I agree, but those task forces move slower so that collars stick."

"You're telling me nothing can be done?"

"I'm telling you what will happen. I'll bring the information to my supervisors, but they're going to tell me the same shit, only less politely."

"Shit. This sucks."

"Yeah, I know."

"The other thing—and I have even less proof of this one—

but I think Dr. Gabbibb is financing the whole thing."

"Duff, you are out of your league. What the hell am I supposed to do with that kind of information?"

"Kelley—I don't know, but this just can't be allowed to go on." "Look, I'll do what I can, but this isn't how this stuff works, you know," he said.

Kelley left to get back to his job and I sat there for a minute or two thinking. I had no idea what to do, but I was going to do something. I didn't blame Kelley; he was just being real and giving it to me straight. It meant that if this webcast was going to be stopped, I was going to have to do it. I thought for a while about just going to the police and telling them exactly what I had found out and being a good responsible and safe citizen.

I also thought about Walanda. Her whole life was one big shit sandwich and the cruelest and coldest things in this world had eaten her up. She asked—no, pleaded with me—to help her not have that happen to Shony. Shony had already been subjected to the scummiest of the earth and was about to go through a trauma that she would carry with her forever.

Fuck being a responsible citizen.

30

The next morning the lead story on all the news broadcasts was that with the anniversary of 9/11 coming up in the next couple days, the Department of Homeland Security had raised the warning level around the country to orange. They noted that "chatter" had led to "specific and credible" threats and that all Americans should be "cautious." That and, oh yeah, no "need to change your daily plans" but be "vigilant."

Like everyone else, I found that this type of announcement did little except make me feel creepy. Lately, there wasn't much that could make me feel any creepier. I decided I was much better off listening to Elvis and put in Elvis in Concert, a tape of one of his last shows and poured myself a cup of coffee.

Just for the hell of it, I gave Clogger McGraw a call to see what he could tell me about the brothers Gabbibb. He described the electronic store in Staten Island as a dirty storefront with lots of odds and ends, closeouts, and brands he never heard of. When it came to Enad, Clogger was much more demonstrative in his descriptions.

"Dude, the dude's way intense, man," was the way the Clogman put it. Then the Clog went on to describe how patriotic and zealous Enad got when he talked about his home in Pakistan. That struck me as odd.

"You mean India, don't you Clog?" I said.

"No way, dude's way negative on India," Clogger said.

I signed off and wondered what that was all about. It might have been that Clog smoked some inferior weed and got things wrong. Or maybe it meant someone was lying.

I decided to take a trip to the country. East Dunham was about as diametrically opposed to Staten Island as you could imagine. It was a ski resort town in the winter and a small artsy-fartsy community the rest of the year. The East Dunham grocery was also the exact opposite of Enad's electronic store. It looked like it used to be a Trading Port, one of the small neighborhood grocery stores. Trading Ports come from the era before supermarkets had to be the size of 747 airplane hangars. It was neat and clean and cheerful and had everything you needed without the unnecessary bullshit that today's megastores have.

Tunad looked very Americanized with his nametag and shirt and tie as he walked up and down the four aisles asking folks if they needed help. I asked him where the frosted strawberry Pop-Tarts were, and he gladly directed me to aisle two, with barely a trace of accent. I grabbed a box of Pop-Tarts for Al and headed back toward Tunad to see if I could engage him in some conversation.

"Excuse me, sir," I said in my best consumer voice.

"How can I help you?" Tunad asked with a big smile.

"I love your store."

"Thank you very much."

"Did you own a grocery in Pakistan?" I asked. I knew it was forced and awkward, but I didn't know what else to do.

"I'm from New Delhi, India, sir, not Pakistan," Tunad said.

"Oh, I'm sorry. Were you a grocer in India?" I asked.

"I worked in importing, actually...spices," he said.

"Ah...well, I love your store," I said and went and cashed out my Pop-Tarts.

It seemed as though it was important for the brothers Gabbibb to pretend to be Indian. Why, I wasn't sure, but I'd guess there were some complex political reasons. I got Al out of the car, gave him a couple of Pop-Tarts, and we strolled around

East Dunham. Al was recovering nicely and I admired his recuperative powers. He was still sore, but he got around well.

There were coffee shops, New Age bookstores, a hemp store, and an organic butcher shop. It was a neat little place with lots of crunchy people walking around. I always wondered what these people did for a living because no one ever seemed like they were in a hurry to do anything, nor did they seem to ever get intense about anything, except maybe when yoga class was cancelled.

Al was thrilled to be smelling new smells and meeting new people. A fair number of the crunchies smiled at Al and stopped to pet him. A pair of forty-something New Age housewives loved him until he slobbered on their peasant blouses. They acted disgusted and abruptly left in a huff. I guess organics have their time and place.

We were swinging around the back of Tunad's grocery, heading back to the car, when Al stopped short. He lifted his head in the air, looked around, and then put his nose to the pavement and started sniffing the ground as he went. He was on a scent, and I was waiting to come up on a dead raccoon or something.

A man was unloading a van near the double back doors of Tunad's shop. Al was pulling hard on the leash and was getting difficult to control. I held him up and he struggled, not barking but making an intense whining sound. I watched the guy swing four of the boxes into a hand truck and disappear into the back doors. I let Al lead me over to the van.

There were a half-dozen boxes on the ground, and it looked like the driver would be back in a second to get them. Al sniffed all around them, stopped dead, and sat in front of the boxes, staring straight at them. I didn't want to hang around and explain to the van driver what my dog was doing, but I had a good idea.

I pulled on Al to get him going, but before he would come he lifted his leg on the stack of boxes. I pulled him even harder and began running to get away from the back of the grocery and onto the main street again. I had to find a pay phone.

There was a pay phone just outside the hemp store. I dialed as fast as I could.

"This is Jamal."

"What did Allah-King do when he smelled a bomb?" I said.

"Duffy?"

"C'mon man—what did he do?"

"Easy, man, take it easy," Jamal was caught off guard. "Oh yeah, uh...the dogs were trained to sit and stare at whatever had the explosives."

I hung up without saying goodbye.

31

I had to find Kelley. The Gabbibbs were lying about where they were from and one of them had explosives. I'm sure that being from Pakistan wasn't a crime, but I thought the authorities might be interested in today's combination of events.

By the time I got to AJ's it was nine o'clock, the prime Foursome hour, and I was also in luck because Kelley was there. I didn't say hello to anyone, I went right to Kelley.

"Kelley—you gotta hear this," I said.

"What makes me think I'm not going to want to?" Kelley said.

"I found explosives in Gabbibb's cousin's grocery store, and his other cousin, the one who runs the electronics store in Staten Island, admitted that he's not Indian—he's Pakistani."

"What the hell are you talking about?"

"Don't you see? They're covering up being Pakistani, one of them has explosives—they've got to be up to some sort of terrorist thing."

Kelley just stared at me for a second. He didn't blink and his mouth hung open a little bit.

"Let me get this straight. Dr. Gabbibb is masquerading as an Indian because he's really Pakistani. He's financing a porn site, and he's planning a terrorist act with his two cousins, one of whom has explosives in his grocery store?" Kelley said.

"Yes—there's a Pakistani extremist organization known as

Al-finuu. They make their money exploiting women they've deemed as 'unclean' through prostitution and pornography. It looks like he's set up the same operation here and his cousins are in with him. They're financing something big, damn it— something horrible."

"You are out of your league—can you prove any of this?"

"Al sniffed out the explosives in East Dunham."

"Al the cheeseburger-eating hound is doing your intelligence work?"

"I'm serious, Kelley!"

"You're fucking nuts—that's your problem."

"Nuts! I'm not fucking nuts!" I could feel my forehead throb. "A little girl's life is going to be ruined, some scumbags are fucking around with terrorist bullshit, no one can do anything, and I got federal guys threatening me—and I'm fucking nuts?"

"What do you mean you got federal guys threatening you?" Kelley said.

"I've had a Crown Vic following me home for the last two weeks. The other night, two federal types cornered me, jumped out of the car, put a gun to my head, and told me to leave things alone."

"Who were they?"

"I have no idea, they didn't identify themselves."

"They show you ID?" Kelley said.

"They didn't show me shit, they didn't say shit—except to threaten me."

"What did they look like?"

"Blue blazers, gray pants, one guy looked Middle Eastern, the other was young and blond."

"Middle Eastern?"

"Yeah, but no accent."

"Duff, the car, the outfits—they sound like FBI. I'd do what they say."

"Can you find out anything about who they are, Kel?"

"No—the FBI doesn't answer to us."

"Then what the hell do I do? I'm not sitting back while something happens to this kid. And what if these guys are planning something? Then, what do I do?"

"Call the FBI anonymously and tell them about the explosives," Kelley said.

"What will that do?"

"In this day and age, a lot. They will follow up."

That made some sense. I didn't know where the Crown Vic was from or what they were up to. Maybe they were on to the Gabbibbs and I was in the way. If the Crown Vic boys were from the FBI, then the FBI should know what I knew. And if those guys weren't from the FBI, who the hell were they?

I wasn't letting go of going after Shony, though. I wasn't sure what I was going to do next, but I was going to do something. This had gotten way too personal, and it wasn't time for me to let it go—not a chance.

I asked Kelley for the number for the appropriate FBI contact. He fished a small piece of paper out of his wallet and pointed to it. I borrowed Rocco's cell phone and went outside. I called and spoke quickly to some clerical type and then I hung up.

There, I had done something a responsible levelheaded citizen would do.

I came back inside AJ's and got a fresh Schlitz.

"Did you call?" Kelley said.

"Yeah."

"Did you tell them everything?"

"Yeah, then I hung up without giving my name."

"See, being a responsible citizen isn't so hard."

"Shut up and drink." I bought Kelley a round and asked AJ for a sidecar of bourbon. I wanted desperately to chill out before the vein in my temple exploded all over the bar.

With the Yankees game over, it was time for the eleven o'clock news. The bar got quiet as the talking head anchor told us about the nation's alert level going to orange. This was the type of fuel that the Fearsome Foursome thrived on.

"They're goin' to botulize the reservoirs," Rocco said. "Bushel full of bad mushrooms in the water system and we'll be shittin' our pants for months."

"Thanks for the visual," Jerry Number One said.

"I did some bad mushrooms once," Jerry Number Two said. "I didn't shit my pants, but I did hallucinate."

"What did you see?" TC asked.

"Spiro Agnew and Golda Meir having sex," Jerry said.

I ordered another Schlitz and watched the rest of the local news. The Foursome just wouldn't let go.

"They could hit the bridges with explosives," Rocco continued. "I heard something on the news about how they could infect all the hookers with a small ox."

"Geezus, Rocco," TC said. "You got to get the Miracle-Ear serviced. That's small pox, jackass."

"Or they could blow up a dirt bomb in Times Square." Rocco was on a roll. "We might not get hurt, but all that dirt would be a pain in the ass and fuck up the economy."

"Unless you were a dry cleaner," Jerry Number Two said, sipping his Cosmo.

"Actually, that dirty bomb shit is pretty scary," TC said.

"You're right," Jerry Number Two said. "A pretty simple way to cause not only a shitload of damage, but also mass panic."

"With dirt and gravel?" said Rocco.

"No, Rock. A dirty bomb is regular explosives with radioactive material put in it," Jerry said. "When the explosives go 'bang,' the radioactive material gets spread all around."

The conversation suddenly drew my attention.

"Jerry—where do you get radioactive material?" I asked.

"Lots of places. It's in construction materials, some gauges, and in medical stuff."

"What kind of medical stuff?" I asked.

"Again, gauges, measuring material, and the stuff you treat

some cancers with," Jerry said.

I froze. My stomach did a flip and I could feel the hair on my neck stand up.

"Rocco, give me your phone," I said.

"What am I tonight—Rocco Ma Bell?"

"Just give me the fuckin' phone, huh?"

I ripped it out of his hand and called Rudy. It was almost midnight and he'd just done a double shift. It couldn't be helped. "What?" a groggy Rudy answered.

"Meet me at the medical center in ten minutes," I said.

"Fuck you, Duffy," Rudy said. "I just got out of there."

"I don't have time to explain. Be there in ten minutes."

I hung up before he could answer.

32

Rudy kept me waiting and pacing in the emergency waiting room. When he came I pounced on him.

"We've got to go check on Eli and Mikey," I said, grabbing Rudy by the arm and hustling him to the elevator.

"I'm not going anywhere." He stopped dead in his tracks. "You mind telling me what the hell this is all about?" Rudy said.

"You remember telling me how well Eli and Mikey were handling the radioactive treatment?"

"Yeah—Duff, that's good news."

"It's good and bad news. It's good news because they probably don't have cancer in the first place and bad news because they're being used as pawns. I'll bet you anything that they're not getting any of that radioactive stuff at all," I said.

Rudy just stared at me. I woke him up and he was exhausted and he wasn't processing my rapid-fire information yet.

"But Duffy—why?"

"Let's just go check," I said.

We walked out of the sixth-floor elevator and down the hall. Rudy had woken up and had some urgency in his step. We didn't speak all the way down the hall.

"Wait here," Rudy said, heading into Mikey's room. He came out in less than thirty seconds and walked right past me and went into Eli's room. He wasn't there as long.

"All right, Duff you're right." Rudy was all business now. "You mind telling what the fuck is going on?"

"Gabbibb is building a dirty bomb and he's taking the radioactive shit from here."

"What the hell makes you think that?"

"Look, one of his cousins has a store in Staten Island. Clogger delivers stuff there, and he says the Gabbibbs aren't even Indian—they're Pakistani."

"So—"

"Let me finish. The other cousin owns a grocery store in East Dunham. I checked it out and it looked all on the up and up until I saw them loading explosives in the back room."

"You saw that?"

"Well, Al used to be a bomb-sniffing dog and he—"

"You're fucking kidding me—right?"

Rudy rolled his eyes and let out a huge exhalation. He wiped his hand through his sparse hair and spun around, pacing back and forth across the hall.

"Not only that, Rude." Now, I was pleading with him. "The guy who beat Eli and Mikey and the other guys in the park is the guy who beat me and Al up in the Blue. He also is tied up with the women in the porn site," I said.

"You're losing me."

"Remember you told me how much Gabbibb was making from the all the surgeries and cancer treatments?"

"Yeah, so? He's a doctor."

"I bet anything he's behind the beatings. He's paying someone to bring him business, and he knows if he does it to the guys in the park, no one is going to make a lot of noise about it," I said.

"So why a dirty bomb and why such a high-tech scheme for a bullshit little city like Crawford?"

"Rudy, what is Crawford known for? What's our city's trademark?"

Rudy rubbed his chin. "You think because of the wind they

229

chose Crawford to set off a dirty bomb?"

"We're under an hour from the city," I said.

Rudy looked right into my eyes and shook his head.

"You better be right, Duff. This ain't no bullshit irritable bowel syndrome disability diagnosis. If we're wrong, we're dead."

"If we're right, a lot of people are going to be dead."

It was Friday afternoon, which meant I had twenty-four hours, give or take a few hours, to find the location of the webcast. I also had to pray that the FBI or somebody would find Gabbibb even faster. I called Rudy at the hospital. He told me that Gabbibb didn't come in today, that he didn't have any scheduled time off and no one knew where he was. That was scary, but I thought it over and I decided that I had to go after Shony and let the government work on Gabbibb.

I started with dropping the video camera off with Jerry. I asked him to see if he could enlarge or enhance the picture to make the people and the license plate more discernible. Jerry told me that he could enlarge the digital image, but because of some sort of issue with something called "pixels," the resolution would be poor as the images were enlarged. He also said there was a chance he could work around that, but that it would take a little time.

I thanked Jerry and as I was heading out, I asked him if he had a cell phone I could borrow. He went into a closet and came out with a small box that had a half dozen or so.

"Take your pick," Jerry said.

"What are you doing with these?" I asked.

"Somebody I did some work for didn't have any money, so he paid me with these. It was a nice thought, but I don't have much use for them."

"Thanks, Jer, I appreciate it."

Now it was time to get to work.

The one thing I knew was that Stephanie was connected with the Eagle Heights clinic and Tyrone and Baldy chauffeured her there for her first visit. I had nowhere else to start, so I decided to see what more I could find out. I called Katy and I knew there was a good chance I was about to go to the well one too many times, but I didn't have any other wells to pursue. I gave her a call at the clinic.

"Katy speaking."

"Katy, it's Duff."

"Whatever it is, the answer is 'no,'" she said. "I'm hanging up."

"Wait. This is important."

"Important?" she said. "Does it have to do with your Internet porn obsession? Here I was, giving you all sorts of information and God knows what you were doing with it."

"I was looking at porn on the Internet because I think one of my clients was involved in something ugly—that's what I was doing," I said.

"I'm sure. I don't think it's going to matter much. From what I hear, you're getting fired as soon as you get back to work."

"Where did you hear that?"

"Rhonda was on the phone with Claudia. I heard them talking about posting your job within a week."

"Great—it doesn't matter anyway. Look, can you tell me when Stephanie is due back in?"

"Why should I tell you anything? You sound like you got some issues and I don't think I trust you."

"Katy, listen to me. The last time we spoke, you wound up giving me info that you knew was against the rules. You didn't want to, but something inside told you it was more right than wrong. You're a good person, don't become one of these asshole social workers. Your instincts had you go out on limb for me because you believed something about me was right. Listen to your instincts," I said.

The phone went quiet.

"Stephanie is going with a bunch of the women to look at the new halfway house. Rhonda wants her to be part of the first group of eight that gets admitted there. They're leaving in half an hour," Katy said.

She hung up before I could thank her.

I didn't have time to tail them to the halfway house. It would be tough to hang around the halfway house and not be seen, and I just couldn't pull up in front of the place and say hi to everyone there. I put on my sweats, my knit cap, and decided to do some roadwork.

I wasted no time getting there. I parked the Eldorado about a mile and a half away in the parking lot of the only Kingsville grocery store. I told Al I'd be back and I started to run. At about an eight-minute-per-mile pace, I came up on the halfway house in a matter of minutes. Thank God, the van with the clinic lettering was still there.

I put my hooded sweatshirt up and turned up the block before the house. I swung back down the street that led right to the clinic. Rhonda was leading a group of women toward the parking lot back to the van. Stephanie was in the middle of the pack with a group of rough-looking young women, most of whom were dressed in cheap, tight, acid-washed jeans. Most of them had that big eighties hair look that seems to be so popular with uneducated women who spend a lot of time on the street.

I pulled up my run about a half a block away and pretended to stretch as if I were cooling down. I turned my back to the group and bent over to stretch my back before I turned back around. That's when I saw the white pickup truck parked on the other side of the van. When I had come down the street, the angle I was looking from made it impossible to see the truck. Wandering across the street, doing my stretching gave me a different point of view.

Stephanie was talking to Tyrone, who was on the passenger side of the truck, and though I couldn't say for sure, I would bet that Baldy was behind the wheel. The women were getting in the van and Rhonda came over to the pickup truck to get Stephanie, who was lagging behind. It looked like Rhonda said something quick to Tyrone before Stephanie finally got in.

The van took a right out of the parking lot and then the pickup took a left, which surprised me. I decided to run after the pickup as long as I could without being too obvious. They continued down Route 44 and didn't turn for as long as I watched them. That was the opposite direction from the clinic.

I ran back to the grocery store and started the Eldorado. Al was nervously shifting his weight from one foot to another in what appeared to be the basset equivalent of pacing. He was glad to see me and gave me an enthusiastic lick to let me know. I headed to the clinic, which was about a fifteen-minute drive from the halfway house. Even with the head start it wasn't going to be hard to catch up with an Econoline van. I pulled up on Ninth Street and waited for the van to show up. I got there just minutes before they did.

The women slowly got out of the van and headed back into the clinic, presumably to sign out and get their purses. I didn't have anything else to do, so I hung out to watch them all leave. In a matter of minutes, the women were back out the door. Only two had their own cars; the other five walked down to the next block to catch the fifty-five bus. Stephanie hadn't come out.

It seemed unlikely that Tyrone or Baldy would be coming back any time soon because they had left the halfway house heading in the opposite direction. It was heading toward six, so maybe Stephanie and Rhonda had a session, or maybe Stephanie had to go to another group. That seemed like a lot of therapy for one day.

At ten minutes to seven, Stephanie came out of the front door, followed by Rhonda. Rhonda had her keys and was walking toward the small parking lot across the street. Stephanie walked with her. Rhonda hit the automatic locks and the lights and horn briefly went on in her dark blue BMW.

Then Rhonda and Stephanie both got in the car.

33

It wasn't normal procedure to drive a client anywhere. In fact, it was against the rules because it supposedly meant developing inappropriate boundaries. I had driven clients places and even got written up by the Michelin Woman once for doing it. I found it hard to believe that Rhonda was ignoring the rules; she was an administrator and seemed too much like Claudia to be doing something human.

I waited at that corner down the street from Bowerman's town house for an hour. The Yanks were in the middle of a home stand with the Mariners and it was the top of the third and they were already down five to nothing. Announcer Suzyn Waldman was going on about the merits of the aluminum bat used at the collegiate level and somehow that broke into a discussion of steroid use in the major leagues. John Sterling brought up the fact that just because Barry Bonds's head was the size of a sixteen-pound medicine ball, it didn't necessarily mean that he was doing anything unnatural.

Waldman was about to use an eleven-syllable word to keep the conversation going when the national news broke in with a special report.

"We interrupt our regularly scheduled programming for this special report from NBC. We take you now, live to our New York studios and Brian Williams."

Ever since I was a kid, the sound of a special report scared the shit out of me. It wasn't like they ever interrupted things to bring you good news.

"Good evening. In Crawford, New York, a city fifty miles north of New York City, four Pakistani nationals were arrested an hour ago. They had in their possession several hundred pounds of explosives and an undisclosed quantity of cesium 147. Cesium 147 is a radioactive isotope used in the treatment of special types of cancers. If combined with explosives, it can disperse large quantities of radioactive material while also rendering damage from the conventional force of the bomb.

"The four arrested are all employees of the Crawford Medical Center. They are Afu Mohammed, an oncology nurse, Faid Ru Abdul, a nurse's aid, Said Farook, and Nasseem Abdul, both facilities services workers.

"Details are still coming in, but Special Agent Carlisle of the FBI was quoted as saying, 'The suspects are in custody and the radioactive material is accounted for. The situation is under control.'"

The report continued on but it was mostly interviews with the usual experts talking and debating about the seriousness of a "dirty bomb" and the ability of the four to have been able to carry out their plans. They also went to great lengths explaining how the wind currents in Crawford are ideal for the terrorists' plans and that it showed that the terrorists had done their homework.

Nothing was going on outside of Bowerman's house, so I got Rudy on the cell phone.

"Yeah, this is Rudy," he said.

"Did you hear the news?" I said.

"I'm at the hospital now," he said. "Everyone is, there are all sorts of mandatory meetings and debriefings."

"Is Gabbibb there?"

"No, but he phoned in. The FBI is saying it was these four guys and they are directly connected to some sleeper cell of Al-some-thing. It wasn't Al-Qaeda, but it was something like that."

"Does that mean Gabbibb is off the hook?" I said.

"It certainly looks like it, Duff." Rudy exhaled loudly. "Thank God we didn't do anything rash."

"The guy's still a creep," I said.

"Yeah, but that doesn't make him a terrorist. Look, I got to run. Why don't you cool your secret-agent-man hijinks for a while?"

I let Rudy go and breathed a sigh of relief. I wasn't happy that Gabbibb wasn't arrested, but I started to come around to the fact that just because a guy is an all-around douchebag, it doesn't mean he's involved in all things that are evil. Perhaps I had overreacted to what I saw on the hospital computer. Either way, I had to save Shony.

Around ten o'clock, the lights went out inside Bowerman's house and I figured the two of them had turned in for the night. I suppose it could have been nothing more than a little over-involvement on Bowerman's case, but I doubted it. I didn't see the use in hanging around all night, so I headed back to AJ's. I was back there by eleven and I was happy to see that not only was Jerry Number Two and the rest of the Foursome there, but so was Kelley.

"The fact that you could see her bush was what got to DiMaggio," Rocco said.

"I thought it was because JFK was seeing her bush," Jerry Number One said.

"Wasn't Bush the head of the CIA during that period?" TC asked.

"Jackass," Rocco said. "We're talking about Marilyn Monroe in the Seven Year Itch" Rocco said.

"I know, but didn't J. Edgar Hoover eventually buy that dress?" TC said.

"Shut up," Rocco said. "DiMaggio got pissed when that fan blew up Marilyn's dress and because of the bright lights you could see the bush through her panties."

"I never trusted Bush," said Jerry Number Two. "Not any

of 'em."

I sat next to Jerry Number Two. There's no point in waiting for a polite break when the Foursome is at it. So I broke in between Bush segments.

"Jer, did you find anything out about the pickup?"

"Hey Duff. Yeah."

Jerry foraged around in his pockets and got a wrinkled piece of lined paper.

"The pickup license plate is LMQ-56 and it is registered to a Daniel Dunston. Dunston's last address was 3A Rd. #2 in Crocketsville," Jerry read the information from a neatly typed memo. "Some more digging around also brought up that this guy has spent at least three-quarters of his adult life behind bars. Various assaults, drug charges, and a pretty serious manslaughter. He did eight years in Attica for his involvement in the bombing of that federal office building in Manhattan."

"What bombing?"

"It was foiled—it had to do with some extremist group."

"Charming," I said.

"That's not all, Duff. He killed a guy in prison. They ruled it self-defense. The guy's throat was slit from ear to ear."

"Oh good. Anything on the black guy?"

"Duff—all I know is that he's a black guy with the name Tyrone," Jerry sipped his Cosmo. "Most search engines don't turn up a lot of good information with that query," Jerry said.

He was right, of course, but after working with Jerry on computer stuff, I think I kind of believed he could find out anything.

"Jerry, one more thing. Can you find out as much as you can about a Rhonda Bowerman, the director of the Jewish Unified Services in Eagle Heights?" I gave Jerry the address.

"You got a social security number?"

"No."

"All right, but it will take a bit of time."

"As fast as possible, if you could. Anything on exactly when the webcast is going down?"

"No, just the same sick shit advertising."

I thanked Jerry and sat for a moment with my Schlitz. I had to go ask Kelley questions that he wouldn't like, and though I wasn't looking forward to it, I copied the information down Jerry gave me. Kelley was watching ESPN Classic's ABA feature. The Kentucky Colonels were up against the Virginia Squires and even though Ticky Burden had thirty-six points, his Squires were still down by eighteen. I sat next to Kelley, but if he saw me, he didn't acknowledge my presence.

"Kel?"

"Hey Duff."

"Anything about the website and the child porn stuff?"

"The sergeant told me to stop trying to be a hero and just do my job. He said he'd turn it over to the sex crime task force."

"Here's some information Jerry got on the pickup and the bald guy."

"Oh great, now you got Jerry working for you, illegally obtaining information. What's next? You going to have the whole Fearsome Foursome form a SWAT team? They can talk all the villains to death."

I filled Kelley in on everything as fast as I could, just in case, and then I left him alone. I finished off my Schlitz and headed home.

34

The next morning I went to see Rudy and borrowed his new Lincoln Navigator. I wanted Jerry to be able to reach me the very second he found something out about Bowerman and when he figured out when the webcast was going to go down. I thought the best use of my time was to find out for certain if Dunston and Baldy were one in the same and if he lived at the address Jerry gave me.

In New York State, when someone lives on a street that has a road number instead of a name, it's a pretty good bet that they live in a very remote spot. Dunston probably lived off a series of dirt roads in a cabin, a trailer, or some sort of prefab. Pulling down a dirt road in my Eldorado and not being noticed was not going to be easy. I guess if I'm going to pursue the life of a private eye, I'm going to have to consider a new set of wheels. Until I go full time, I am going to have to borrow Rudy's rig.

The foolish SUV weighed about ten tons, and it was hard to get used to being twenty feet in the air, driving. Rudy had power everything, a CD and cassette player, but no eight-track. Through the years, I have made a handful of Elvis cassettes for just such circumstances so I would have something to listen to. Al was happy that there were power windows because it would give him something to do.

I figured I had a couple of choices. I could stake out Bowerman and Stephanie, but there was no guarantee that they would be associated with the webcast. Stephanie had been on the website in porn poses, but there was a chance that she wouldn't have anything to do with this event. There was still a chance that Bowerman had taken her to her house for some quasi-legitimate social work reason. I doubted that, but there was a chance.

My other option was to track down the address that Jerry had got me for Dunston. So far, it seemed to me that he was always on the scene. If there was something that needed security or enforcement, I'm guessing he was their guy. There was a chance that the bald guy wasn't Dunston or that the address was bogus, but I decided checking in on him would be the first thing I would do. If I could determine that he really did live at the address Jerry gave me earlier, then I could decide what to do from there.

The Rd. #2 address was another seven miles east of Eagle Heights. I hoisted Al into his copilot seat, which, with the height of the Navigator, was no easy trick. Al really liked Rudy's SUV. He sat right up and looked out over the dashboard while hitting all the power switches, making the doors lock, the windows go up and down, and the moonroof slide back.

At ten, I made the turn off Route 44 and started to head down the dirt roads. I got to the end of County Road #2 and decided to walk in the rest of the way. The Navigator wasn't as conspicuous as the orange Eldorado, but out in these boonies another breathing human being was noticed.

I left Al in the SUV and headed in. There were worn-looking houses with appliances on the front lawns, old rusted car chassis, and dogs tied on chains. There were houses about every five hundred yards. Most of them looked like two-bedroom deals laid on slabs. At least half of them had a motorcycle or snowmobile or both on the front lawn.

About a mile and a half in, I came upon Dunston's house and sure enough, the white pickup truck was parked outside his dirty white house. He had a homemade carport with three motorcycles in various states of disrepair underneath it. His lawn was overgrown, and there was a rusted refrigerator that the grass had grown around.

I stayed back a couple hundred yards and tried to take in as much as I could. I wasn't exactly sure what to look for, but I felt compelled to study his house, make a clear mental image, and store it in my brain. When I felt I had it, I went back to the Navigator.

Al was sleeping as the soundtrack to Blue Hawaii played on. Over the last three weeks, Al seemed to mellow out when Elvis went into "Can't Help Falling in Love." I wasn't sure what to do next, but I felt like it was time to check in on the Eagle Heights clinic. I figured Bowerman might have taken Stephanie back there. I hit the McDonald's drive-through on the way there, and Al and I split two quarter-pounders with cheese and an order of fries that was big enough to feed a family of six.

I parked a block and a half away from the clinic. My new wheels made hanging out without being noticed easier. Sure enough, Bowerman's blue BMW was parked outside. Staring at the front door of the clinic for the next four hours wasn't easy, and I was going out of my mind with boredom. My lower back was starting to ache and I had to take a leak.

It was almost four o'clock, and just when I thought I couldn't take it anymore, Bowerman left through the front door of the clinic. I watched her head to the parking lot, but instead of getting in the BMW, she went for the clinic van. She was alone.

She took off in the same direction that she did last night when she went home. I followed her from a safe distance and she took the exact same route.

I was a quarter mile behind her when she turned into her development. I didn't follow her, I kept going straight. There was only one way out of the development and there was no point in risking getting spotted. I did a U-turn and parked off the side of the country road, a half-mile down from the entrance to the development.

I waited. I had already spent about eight hours in the car today, most of it doing absolutely nothing. I don't know how guys make a career doing this sort of shit because it was making me crazy.

I killed time devising strategies for beating some of the alltime best fighters. I figured to beat Robinson I would crowd him and make him move to his left. That would make me vulnerable to his hook, but it was worth the chance. Against Joe Louis—easy, I would give him a lot of side-to-side movement. With Ali, I'd be all over him with elbows, forearms, and cuffs. He hated the rough stuff. I was just about to beat Marvelous Marvin Hagler when the phone rang.

"Duff—it's going down tonight, at eight thirty," Jerry said.

"Shit. What else can you tell me?"

"Duff," Jerry was speaking fast. "They're saying all sorts of sick shit about what's going to happen to Shony. She's the feature and there's three other girls about the same age."

"It's a little after four. That gives me four hours."

I hung up and watched Bowerman pull out of her development.

35

Bowerman headed back the same way she came. My mind was racing and my stomach flipped. I had a heart-pounding desire to do something, I just didn't know what.

Bowerman went straight back to the clinic and went inside. She stayed in there for about forty-five minutes while I waited down the block for her. She came out alone, but with several duffel bags and headed back out. Al must've picked up on my nervous energy because he was sitting up, looking over the dashboard, rocking back and forth like he was trying to see what I was getting excited about.

It was now five thirty and Bowerman was headed out on another county route to God knows where. I had a horrible fear that I was following the wrong person and that I wasn't even going to be near a place where I could help Shony. The phone rang again.

"Duff," it was Jerry. "I found some shit out on Bowerman."

"What is it?"

"First of all, Bowerman is her maiden name. Her married name is something else."

"What?"

"Dunston. She's married to the bald guy."

"Holy shit—anything else?'

"I can't find any record of her social worker certification. She's listed as one in several employment references, but when you go to the Department of State website she's not listed. I'm betting a lot of nonprofits never actually check certifications. There are also gaps on jobs and residences."

"Jerry, the second you find anything else, call me."

I couldn't believe what I had just heard.

I followed Bowerman as she headed south for about fifteen minutes. She then turned off the main road on to another series of dirt roads. I laid back and gave her a good mile head start because I didn't want to get caught following her. I made two left-hand turns and wound up at a fork. It was hard to see, but when I pulled up close enough to read the street sign everything started to come together. I was outside County Road #2, exactly where I was this morning. Bowerman had just gone a different way to get here. She had come to meet her husband.

I drove the SUV down the road and parked it on the side in the tall grass. If I was going to go to Dunston's house, I was going to have to do so without being noticed. I was also concerned about being able to maneuver Rudy's car on these narrow dirt roads. If I played it wrong, it wouldn't be hard to be cornered or run off the road.

I went in on foot and I didn't waste any time. I left Al in the SUV, which he wasn't pleased about, but I didn't want anything else to think about.

I ran, trying to make up for the time I lost trailing Bowerman. I got within a hundred yards of Dunston's house in about six or seven minutes. The van was parked behind the white truck and there were lights on in the house. I thought I heard some conversation, and I could see the silhouettes of several heads through the living room shade.

After about five minutes, Bowerman came out the front door with four young girls behind her in single file followed by Dunston and Tyrone. From where I stood, it looked like Shony was last in line, closest to Dunston. They loaded the kids into the van, Tyrone got in the driver's seat and Bowerman rode shotgun. Dunston drove the pickup truck. They pulled out together and headed up the dirt road.

I gave them just a minute to get out of sight and I sprinted up the road behind them. I didn't want to be seen, but I was more afraid of losing them. It was about five o'clock and the webcast was due to start in a matter of hours.

They must have been going pretty fast, despite the dirt roads, because before I knew it, I had no sight of them. I had misjudged how fast they'd be moving, and now I was scared I had blown it.

I sprinted the mile back to the SUV. When I got within a couple hundred feet of the Navigator, I could hear Al and he was going off in a big way. He must have caught sight of Dunston's truck and remembered his visit. When I got closer to the SUV, it obviously was something else.

Parked in front of the Navigator was the silver Crown Vic, and as I got to it my two old friends banged open the doors and headed straight toward me.

"Dombrowski, what did I tell you?" Pockmark said without breaking his angry stride. "I tried to warn you."

That was it.

I had had it with this asshole. It was clear that he thought he was some sort of badass, probably because of his badge, but I've learned that when someone thinks he's a badass, he picks up bad habits. Pockmark stormed at me, all full of piss and vinegar like I was supposed to shit my pants in fear. During his strut he got lazy reaching for his gun.

I rushed him hard and fast and he wasn't ready. His eyes went wide and he went back on his heels, and that was just what I wanted. I faked a right by just cocking my shoulder and drilled him with a straight left. That was all it took and he went down and out.

"Hands in the air!" Blondie yelled. I had forgotten that he was even there. I looked him straight in the eye and he was trembling. Even though he was in a textbook shooter's crouch like you see on TV, something in his body language told me there was no way he could pull the trigger.

There was too much adrenaline in my system to feel fear. Al was barking and I was focused on Shony.

"Hands in the air!" Blondie said with even less conviction.

I ran to the Navigator and took off. In the rearview mirror, Blondie went to check on his partner, and at that moment I'm sure he felt he had made a poor career choice. Lucky for me that I had come across a fresh academy grad with no stomach for the job.

Al was beside himself with a bad case of sensory overload. There was the sight of Dunston, the Crown Vic boys, and me belting Pockmark. That was a lot of stress in his world, but I didn't have time to be real nurturing and I floored the SUV, barely keeping control on the dirt roads.

I came out on Route 44 and took a guess and went left. I had the SUV up to ninety-five, which on a country route is pretty frightening. After a few minutes, I saw some tail lights up ahead and I slowed. I didn't want to kill any innocent bystanders, but also I didn't want Dunston and his gang knowing it was me. I followed the taillights from a quarter-mile distance for another fifteen minutes until they went around a bend very close to the entrance to the town.

I was just a few hundred feet before the stoplight that marked the beginning of Kingsville and there was no one at the light. They were nowhere in sight and a shot of panic raced through me. I went another block through town, trying to keep the vehicle at a speed that would get me somewhere fast but allow me to keep looking for things.

I was coming up on the new halfway house, and what I saw made the little hairs on my neck stand up.

There, in the small halfway house parking lot, was Bowerman's van and Dunston's truck.

36

I parked the Navigator three blocks away from the parking lot and killed the engine. Al recognized the pickup truck and started whining and shifting his weight back and forth again. I called Jerry to see if he had any new information. He said he was still working on it, but I let him know that I was outside the halfway house and I was getting ready to go in.

When I shut off the cell phone, I saw Dunston come out to the van and get the duffel bags that Bowerman had loaded. Then he went to the back of his pickup and got three tripods and a couple of brackets that held lighting. This was it; this was where the webcast was going down.

I sat in the Navigator trying to think things through. Chances were that there was going to be more than just a few people in there. Shit, Dunston was enough to worry about, let alone if he had any friends with him. I had ejected my Elvis tape and had the radio tuned in to the Yankees pre-game show. It was September 11 and the Yankees were playing the Mariners. They were doing a special moment of silence before the game. It was ironic—this was the game Gabbibb had offered me tickets to. Funny what a difference a couple of weeks made. Up until a little while ago, I was convinced the guy was about to set off a dirty bomb and ruin my hometown and maybe a good stretch of New York with it. Then, I thought of Clogger's routine and how much it had changed his life around for him. I don't know if he was the poster child for recovery, but he did seem to be happy with the slight changes he had made in his life. He had his wings back, he got to be involved with the Yankees, and was even making a decent buck flying Gabbibb's electronic shit.

Hold it—

Clogger's been delivering packages of electronic stuff for Gabbibb...He flies over Yankee Stadium, circling in front of sixty-thousand fans, before he delivers the packages to Staten Island...

I called Jerry.

"Yo, Sesame Street, this is Bert."

"Jerry—how do you set off a dirty bomb?"

"You do it like you would a conventional device."

"How?"

"Uh...let's see, a remote device, an electronic transmitter...anything really...the new trend in the Mid-East is cell phones."

"Oh no."

"What's the matter?"

"Clogger is delivering a box for Gabbibb. Gabbibb has given him a cell phone. Gabbibb may be setting off a dirty bomb in Clog's plane with Clog in it over Yankee Stadium."

"Holy shit...That would kill thousands and make the area around the stadium uninhabitable for years. But I thought they got the guys with the explosives and the radioactive shit," Jerry said.

"Gabbibb has all that shit at his disposal through the hospital and the medical college. It's got to be what's happening."

I signed off with Jerry and started to dial the FBI number. I stopped before I finished. If they knew Clogger was carrying a bomb they'd blow him out of the sky. I had to call Clogger.

I got his number and dialed.

"Hello," it was a female voice. Probably his new live-in, Foon.

"This is Duffy from the clinic. Is Clogger in?"

"No, game night, he gone already."

"Isn't it early?"

"Clogger gone…" The language gap wasn't going to make this very easy. I didn't have the time to translate.

"I know, thanks."

I hung up. I didn't dare call Clogger for fear that his cell phone was rigged. What the fuck was I going to do? My mind raced, my body went cold, and I started to sweat.

Holy fuckin' shit.

Holy fuckin' shit.

Holy fuckin' shit.

All right, the only thing left to do was to call the FBI and let them do what they had to do. I couldn't let them blow Clogger out of the sky, but I couldn't let a capacity-filled Yankee Stadium get blown away with some bullshit dirty nuke. I watched my fingers shake as I hit the keys.

9-1-…You're fuckin' kidding me…

The low battery light went on and then the phone went dark.

Holy fuckin' shit.

All this and the Yanks were already down in the top of the first.

With nothing else left to do to help Clogger, I decided to do something about Shony. I gave Al a few strokes and told him to be cool. I left the car turned on so he would be warm and so he could listen to the Blue Hawaii soundtrack. I had no idea what I was about to do. There was no activity going on outside the building for now, so it made it easy to approach. I crossed the street and ran down the right side of the building. The outside of the building was surrounded by heavy brush, and as I shimmied my way along the wall, branches and switches raked across my face. There was no light coming from this side of the building, but by cupping my hands around my eyes I could peer in the windows and make out a bit of the interior. These were windows to the small bedroom suites and each suite had a single bed, a padded wooden chair, a small bathroom, and an adjacent room with a child's bed in it. I peered in each of the windows as I made my way down the length of the building, hoping to find something that would help. All the bedrooms were dark and looked uninhabited until I got to the last window.

Pressing my face to the window, I could see the four girls were all sitting on the bed. Their hands were duct taped behind them, they had tape over their mouths, and they were all blindfolded. They sat side by side on the bed, and I was almost positive that the first one closest to the wall was Shony. The four of them twitched and rocked and, without being able to make a sound, still exuded the terror they were feeling.

I went along the back side of the building, and about halfway down I could see bright lights coming through the windows and I could hear the sound of two or three voices. I approached the corner of the first window carefully and looked in. It was the multipurpose room—the one we weren't allowed to see on our tour. Now I understood why.

They were setting up cameras and lights at different angles and there was a king-size mattress in the center of a stark floor where I presumed the webcast would be staged. I didn't recognize the three guys setting up the cameras and the lights. I looked at my watch and it was seven forty-five.

I went back around the building, passing the bedroom where the girls were kept. I headed out to the front of the building and looked across the sidewalk to the parking lot. I heard a couple of voices, one male and one female, followed by the sound of car doors closing. The car started and I jumped back, pressing my back against the side of the building. I saw the van pull away from the halfway house with Bowerman and Tyrone in it.

I walked around the front of the building back toward the parking lot. I guessed that the equipment was unloaded and there would be no reason for anyone to be coming out to the parking lot, except maybe for a smoke break. I figured they had just started, so it was unlikely they'd be taking a break soon. I tried to picture where the bedroom that the girls were in was in relation to this side of the building. I would have to go through a lobby, a small corridor, a dining room, and then another hallway to get to the bedroom. If they were all busy setting up, there was a chance they wouldn't notice someone coming in. My one shot was to sprint in, get the door open, and rush the kids out. I sure couldn't stand out here all night. Pretty soon there would be more people coming, and it would make any kind of rescue even harder.

I went through the side door quietly with my back sliding against the wall. I got through the lobby, looked around carefully, and headed up the corridor. At the threshold to the dining room, I looked both ways and ran through the dining room to the threshold on the other side. Through that threshold I could see the door that led to the multipurpose room where the webcast was going to take place. To the right was the corridor to the bedrooms.

I checked both ways and ran as fast as I could down the corridor to the last door on the right. I got to it and turned the knob, but it was locked. I slammed my shoulder as hard as I could into the door, but the jamb held. I slammed into it again and a small piece of the jamb broke away. I was all sweat and heartbeat when I threw myself into the door a third time. The jam splintered more, but not enough. I could hear the muffled sound of the girls screaming through their taped mouths when I heard another door close and footsteps up the corridor.

"Fuckin' asshole, you just don't learn, do you?" It was Dunston and he had a bat in his hand.

"You didn't fuckin' listen the last time," he said. "Now you're going to die. I just wish that ugly fuckin' hound was here so I could kill him first in front of you so that was the last thing you ever saw."

Dunston walked down the hallway without rushing, holding the bat in two hands and flexing his arms. My mind raced, and I had no idea how to defend myself. I put my guard up, figuring taking a bat on the arms was better than taking it on the head. Dunston's face contorted as he swung the bat at my head. I turned my body away, lifted my arm and tried to raise my shoulder muscle. The bat landed across all three areas but I still caught fifty percent of it on the left side of my head. A flash of light seared across my eyes and I wobbled into the other side of the wall.

Dunston reared back and sent the bat into the ribs he bruised on his last visit. That made my whole diaphragm feel like it was caving in. I stumbled forward but somehow managed to keep my feet and moved up the corridor.

Dunston kicked me in the ass, moving me up to the end of the corridor to the lobby before the multipurpose room.

"I'm going to make this last," Dunston said. "Why rush all the fun?" He swung the bat into my left thigh. The force moved me into the dining room and dropped me to one knee.

"Not hard to see how you got the boxing record you got, asshole. You don't even fight back." Dunston punctuated it with another kick, this time to the other side of my ribs, pushing me out of the dining room and into the corridor. I could hear the sounds of the street and the occasional sound of a car passing, but it was at such a distance, a yell for help wouldn't have done me any good.

Dunston stepped over me dramatically and leaned on the threshold at the end of the corridor, resting the bat on his shoulder like he was on deck at Yankee Stadium. He had a big grin come to his face as he stood in front of me with his back to the door.

"What the fuck do you care about a bunch of crack whores anyway?" he said, shaking his head. "I had the girls do your friend Walanda inside because she talked too much. Stupid whore blabberin' about the 'Webster.' Didn't even get the name right. Probably had no idea what a webmaster is. Then there's all your park buddies—fags and bums. Duffy, you're a fool," he said.

Dunston paced in front of me with the bat on his shoulder.

"Why'd you want to ruin a good thing? Now you're going to

die, and for what? To save a bunch of crack whores?" Dunston shook his head in mock disbelief and gripped the bat and took a step toward me.

I was trying to think how I could protect my head and stay alive, but I wasn't sure I had the strength. Dunston spit into his hands like a hitter and cocked the bat.

That's when I heard the barking.

Looking up through Dunston's legs I saw the blur of black, brown, and white, and I heard a growl that was not of this earth. It was Al and he was airborne, teeth bared and headed for Dunston.

Before Dunston could react, Al had Dunston's arm between his teeth and was working it like one of my sofa cushions. Dunston dropped the bat and Al scooped it up in his mouth and ran back out the side door. I was on my feet, the life was back in my veins, and the pain was on hold. Dunston stood five feet in front of me, and without a weapon in his hand he looked like an entirely different man.

"Now you're mine, motherfucker," I said.

I stepped toward Dunston and he threw a big right hand. It was probably the type of punch that made him legendary in bar fights or on the tough-guy bike circuit. It was hard and it would hurt, but it was way too wide and way too slow. I stepped in on it and buried a jab right on his nose. I felt it break under my knuckles and I heard Dunston let out a half moan, half whimper.

The jab sent him into the wall where he tried to cover up. I dug a punch to his solar plexus that took the wind right out of him and brought his guard down. I came back up top and drilled a left cross into his already shattered nose. The speed of my punches and the wall behind him kept him up as he tried in vain to protect himself.

I hit him again with the straight left and this time instinctively I added a right hook. With my left hand recoiling back to my chest and my lower body pivoting, I let go of my right hook and for the first time—the very first fuckin' time—I felt the click in my hips that Smitty had been telling me about for fifteen years. It was a wonderful click.

The hook landed just over his ear and it forced Dunston into the space between the wall and the threshold. He was still standing, wedged into the wall and trapped. It wasn't a time for mercy and it wasn't a time for justice, it was a time for something else entirely.

Something inside of me released and I let go with a fury that transcended the physical. This piece of shit in front of me was evil, and I felt everything in me let go. With Walanda's memory, the girls he and Tyrone were about to defile, the guys from the park, and enough of my own personal business all running through me, I beat Dunston with everything I had.

I don't know how many more hooks I threw to Dunston's head. Blood gushed through his mouth and his nose was in three different bloody pieces of tissue across his face. Each shot forced more blood to come out of him like water comes out of a drowning victim. I wound up for one more hook when I heard the blast and a piercing flash of heat in my left shoulder. The force of it spun me off of Dunston and on to the ground.

I had been shot in the shoulder.

I rolled back around and saw Dunston's limp body slide down the wall and a figure step out of the darkness of the dining room. Stepping into the light of the corridor I couldn't believe my eyes.

"Espidera, you asshole," I said.

37

Espidera paced back and forth dramatically, holding the gun like a villain in Miami Vice.

"Duff, I tried to send you a message," he said. "When Bower-man called me in about your porn activity at work, I tried to give you a break. Duffy, don't you know all your activity on the Internet can be traced? You've got to become computer literate, my man." The door to the multipurpose room opened and out stepped Gabbibb. He was wearing his Derek Jeter Yankees jersey and flashing his big toothy smile as he walked over to stand next to Espidera.

"Doofy, du are a stupid man." He paused for a second and looked at Dunston. "Dees people are nothing. Dey are trash you care about." He walked over to Dunston and put his fingers to his neck. He looked back at Espidera and shook his head.

"He's dead, Duff. You killed him. I guess the rap on you not being able to hit is gone," Espidera said. "Too bad for you, though, because now I can kill you and walk."

"How do you figure that?" I said.

"I had to shoot you to keep from killing poor Dunston here." "You're behind this whole thing, you scum. You're the webmaster Walanda talked about. The whole 'spider' bullshit, that's a play on your last name. You narcissistic fuck."

"Very good, Duff. Too bad you're going to take that one to your grave."

"You won't get away with this, you sick bastard."

"Oh, I will. There's nothing that ties this to me. Dunston did the heavy work, Tyrone and the girls took care of Walanda and recruited the kids, and the crew is just hired help. Face it, Duff, I'm a pillar of the community."

"You're a piece of shit."

"Maybe, Duff, but I'm not the loser you are. You lose in the ring, you lose at work, and you're about to lose it all right here."

"Go fuck yourself."

"LT, I got to go for an hour or so," Gabbibb said. "I will be back for day show." He walked past to the door and stopped. "You are a silly person, Doofy, you waste your time with trash."

"Fuck you, asshole," I said.

"DAT, DAT, DAT, DAT, shit…excuse me." His little seizure deal faded as he headed out the door.

I looked at Espidera, and I didn't think he had any idea of what Gabbibb had in mind.

"Espidera, don't you know what he's about to do?" I shouted. "What's that, Duff?" Espidera did his best nonchalant bad guy routine.

"He's about to call Clogger on the cell phone. He's placed a radioactive bomb on his plane and his call is going to set it off just as Clogger does his thing in front of a full Yankee Stadium. He's going to kill thousands and destroy the Bronx for decades," I said.

Espidera laughed. "Duffy, I gotta hand it to you. Under stress you come up with some good ones. Too bad it's going to be the last story you ever tell."

Espidera lit a cigarette, mostly for effect, and steadied his arm. Dying was going to be bad. Dying at Espidera's hands was going to be worse. He was raising the gun to shoulder length with a big happy smile.

And I heard the barking again.

From the side door came Al, growling and barking and

running as hard as he could, straight for Espidera. He went airborne, his trajectory headed for Espidera's crotch, when Espidera fired straight at Al's head. Al landed full force into Espidera's balls but yelped and rolled over from the violent force of the gunshot.

Al's split-second distraction was enough. With just my right arm good, I gave all I had into my newfound hook. Twisting and torquing all the way from my ankles, I let the hook fly just as Espidera was swinging the revolver back around toward me. The gun went off the instant my fist crashed into the point of his chin. Espidera's head whipped around and he went down hard. I've seen that look before, and he was out before he hit the ground. I always figured the asshole couldn't take a punch.

I saw no sight of Al. I feared the worst but I didn't have time to deal with it. I took away Espidera's gun and ran to the back bedroom. By now I had lost enough blood from the gunshot and the beating to feel woozy. It didn't matter right now.

I got to the back bedroom and slammed my body into it. I tried again and each time I hit my body into the door I had to keep myself from throwing up. Finally, the jamb splintered and the door flew open. The four girls had retreated as far as they could on the bed and pressed themselves against the wall. I could hear their muffled screams through the duct tape, and they struggled against the tape to somehow protect themselves. One of the girls stepped off the bed and fell hard to the floor. The other girls heard this and I saw them struggle even harder against the duct tape and heard their muffled screams even clearer.

I went to Shony and undid her blindfold. Her eyes were wide and filled with tears and I could see her jaw muscles flex throughout her whole face as she screamed against the tape. I undid the blindfolds on the other three girls. Two of them cried and screamed and the other fainted.

"Listen to me," I spoke as calmly as I could. "I'm here to take you away from this. You don't have to be afraid of me."

The girls looked confused and only a little less terrified. The fainted girl stirred, opened her eyes, and looked up at me from the floor.

"I'm going to take off the tape now, but it's very important that you stay quiet. Do you understand?"

They all nodded.

I carefully undid the tape and took it off their mouths as gently as I could. The tears ran down their cheeks and they all threw their arms around me at once. It was a reflex more than an emotion. A reflex based on terror.

I held all of them as tight as I could in a way that was as comforting as I knew how. Shony pulled back and looked up at me, confused.

"Who are you?" she said through tears, her voice still trembling.

"Walanda sent me."

"My stepmom? She was killed."

"The last thing she ever said to me was to get you."

"She was a crackhead."

"She was a whole lot more than a crackhead, Shony."

One of the girls interrupted.

"Mister, can we go?"

"You sure can," I said. "Let's get you guys out of here."

For a quick second, they were back to the teenage girls they should have been. A few squeals of joy and a few high-fives, and the four of them started racing to the side door. They ran about fifteen feet ahead of me toward the parking lot.

Through the kids' squeals, I heard some other voices. I tried to call out to the girls and I tried to run to catch up. It was too late; coming through the side door were Tyrone, Bowerman, Stephanie, Melissa, and Lori. Tyrone had grabbed Shony and held a knife to her throat. They let the other three girls run away.

I pulled Espidera's gun out from the back of my pants and pointed it at Tyrone.

"Drop the knife, Tyrone," I said. "Leave the girl alone."

"You ain't seein' things right, my man. You drop the mother-fuckin' gun or I open her neck."

Shony was shaking and tears ran down her face, though no sound came out of her mouth. I held on to the gun.

"I ain't playin' with you. You wanna see her bleed?"

He stuck the tip of the blade into the flesh of Shony's neck. A drop of blood followed by a small trickle flowed around the blade and down the front of her shirt. I slid the gun down and up against the wall.

"You see, you ain't done nothin' here. Ain't nothin' gonna change here, motherfucker. We own these people."

Tyrone ran his tongue down the side of Shony's cheek. She tried to recoil but he held her tighter and put more pressure on her neck.

"I'm even goin' get me some of this tonight, man." Tyrone started to slide his hand down Shony's body as she let out an almost silent cry and the tears ran down her face. He was moving his hand to the snap on Shony's jeans, still holding the knife to her throat, and smiling up at me. He undid the top of Shony's jeans and began to pull down the zipper.

That's when I heard the blast from the doorway.

Half of Tyrone's head blew off and landed somewhere behind me. My ears were ringing and the room was filled with the smell of cordite. A shower of blood sprayed the wall and Tyrone fell face—or at least what was left of his face—first down on the floor. His blood sprayed all over the women next to him.

"Police. Up against the wall, hands in the air. You're all under arrest," yelled Officer Michael Kelley.

Shony ran to me and wrapped herself around me and let the tears come. She buried her face in my chest and sobbed and shook. In a matter of seconds, there were half a dozen police cars and a dozen or more cops at the halfway house. The cops had them all face down and cuffed, and then ushered the group of handcuffed scumbags into a paddy wagon. Blankets were thrown over the bodies of Dunston and Tyrone. Two cops carried a groggy, handcuffed Espidera past me. He was crying like a baby.

Kelley was too busy to talk, but it was great watching him work. When Shony had calmed down a bit, we walked to the parking lot where there seemed to be nothing but sirens and cops and confusion.

It was then that I noticed that only one of the police cars was from the Crawford Police Department and the other five were from Eagle Heights. Kelley was out of his jurisdiction.

I ran out the door to the parking lot just in time to see the Crown Vic pulling up. It was the same two guys from before, but this time they had four more guys with them. When they got out of the car I could see they now all had windbreakers with "FBI" in gigantic letters on the back and "Office of Homeland Security" on the front. Pockmark had a lousy tape job on his face supporting his nose and it was caked with dried blood. He had "Special Agent Singh" embroidered on the front of his jacket. His partner had "Agent Wilkinson" stitched on his. They weren't coming for me this time.

"Dombrowski, where is Gabbibb? We need to find him immediately," Singh shouted at me.

"I don't know. He got away and he has a cell phone on him. He was here about twenty minutes ago."

"He's got to be found. We have new evidence supporting his involvement."

I looked toward Kelley's patrol car and saw four civilians standing on the passenger side. With all the lights I couldn't make out the faces.

"Hey Duff, busy night?"

"Jerry? Holy shit—what are you doing here?" Next to Jerry Number Two were TC, Rocco, and Jerry Number One.

"We took the ride with Kelley." Jerry Number Two smiled. Shony's three girlfriends were in Kelley's squad car with blankets over their shoulders.

"Turn on the fucking Yankees game," I yelled.

"Duff, I'm as big a fan as you, but man, forget about the Yanks for tonight," TC said.

"Not that—it's Clogger. Gabbibb has his plane wired to be blown up with a cell phone call and we can't find the asshole. He's got a dirty bomb ready to blow up Yankee Stadium."

Jerry tuned in the Yankees. It was the bottom of the fifth and there were two outs. Singh and his agents gathered around Kelley's car, listening.

John Sterling had the call.

"Striiiiike three. Giambi goes down looking to end the fifth. No runs, one hit, and one man on—"

"Fucking Giambi, lookin' at a called strike," Rocco said.

"Rocco! Jesus Christ..." I said.

Sterling continued.

"End of five and you know what that means...It's time to flush out the Clogger. Annnnnnd here he comes...taking a wide sweep of the Stadium...the Clogger's in special form tonight...and he heads for the center of the Stadium..."

Sterling did his trademark long pause. It was the longest and most dramatic pause I ever went through.

"Annnnnnnd Clogger cans it!"

And then we waited. The Foursome, Kelley, Singh and his men, the girls, the cops—everyone was silent and holding their breath.

And nothing happened.

Clogger literally flew off to the horizon on his way to Staten Island. A spontaneous cheer rang out in the parking lot. There were high-fives all around. I exhaled as hard as I can ever remember exhaling and slid down the side of Kelley's car. I was exhausted in every way you can be exhausted.

All at once I remembered Al. That dog had saved my life twice tonight and took a bullet in the head for me. I had remembered hearing something about how animals will go off alone when they know they're going to die and my tears just came. That dog had given everything for me. Everything. The whole fucking month seemed to collapse on me right there, especially the loss of Al. I cried so hard it was hard to breathe, and I sat with my head in my hands as the exhaustion hit me.

I was reaching the point of not being able to cry anymore when I heard Jerry Number One say something.

"What the hell is that noise?"

"What noise?" Rocco said.

"Listen." Jerry Number Two hushed everyone.

From deep in the woods beyond the halfway house there was a commotion that was hard to make out. I got up and headed toward the woods. I could barely walk but I headed for the tree line about a quarter-mile away.

Singh and his men were behind me with the Foursome and Kelley. As I got closer, the racket became clearer. I stopped to make it out.

"DAT, WOOOF, DAT, WOOOF, DAT, grrrrr. Shit...excuse me. DAT, AHOOOOO, DAT, SHIT!!!...excuse me DAT, DAT, WOOF, DAT, grrrrrrr, shit...excuse me."

It was.

I sprinted as hard as I could with everyone behind me.

"DAT, WOOF, WOOF, DAT, DAT, grrrrrrrrr...shit, excuse me." It was loud and it was beautiful.

There, about twenty-five feet into the woods, was Gabbibb, pressed against a big oak tree, shaking. His Yankees' jersey was in shreds and underneath was a Red Sox T-shirt that said "The Yankees Suck." Gabbibb was doing his "DAT, DAT, DAT" routine like he had overdosed on Sudafed. In front of him, five feet away was Al, teeth bared. A howling, barking, growling machine.

Between his legs was a slightly chewed cell phone.

Al stopped his noise long enough to see me. His tail went into overdrive and he grabbed the cell phone between his teeth and ran as fast as he could toward me. Gabbibb took off into the woods.

"The dog has got the phone. He could set off an automatic call," Singh yelled and crouched in a shooter's position, aiming at Al.

Rocco was right next to him and as Al sprinted toward me with the cell phone in his mouth, Singh pulled back the hammer. As Singh was aiming, Rocco—crazy-ass bastard-hound-loving old Rocco—delivered the most perfect elbow strike I had ever seen to a man's already broken nose.

I watched from the corner of my eye as Singh's legs went out and he crumpled to the ground, writhing in pain and holding his nose. Al was so happy to see me, he went airborne. Ears flapping, tail wagging, he flew to greet me, crashing as hard into my nuts as he ever had and spitting out the cell phone. It bounced harmlessly to the grass.

Al crushed my nuts and the pain went through my entire nervous system as he walked the length of me to lick my face. It felt wonderful.

"Assalaamu alaikum, my brother," I said to the best friend a man ever had.

Al barked right back at me.

On top of his head was some dried blood from where Espidera's bullet had only grazed him.

38

I got patched up at the hospital; they gave me some blood and took some x-rays. The x-rays came back and it was clear that I had gotten my ass kicked, that some ribs were cracked but nothing was seriously messed up. The gunshot was a flesh wound, and though it stung like a bastard, it wasn't going to cause any permanent problems.

I spent about three hours telling various detectives and FBI agents what had happened. They wrote it all down and each and every one of them told me that I had acted inappropriately and could've been killed. I thanked them for the advice.

Toward the end of their questioning, around three in the morning, Kelley came in with Al. He lifted Al onto the bed and this man's best friend proceeded to lap my face. Kelley had a hint of a smile going.

"Duff, you're fuckin' nuts," Kelley said.

"Tell me something I don't know."

"All right, how's this? The FBI just confiscated a dirty bomb from Clogger's plane. It was large enough to kill thousands and render Yankee Stadium and the surrounding area uninhabitable for decades." "What happened to Gabbibb?" I asked.

"He went with the FBI Homeland Security guys. They're trying to figure if he was with the other hospital employees or if he acted independently. How's this for weird? When they were putting him in the car and taking him away, in between all his

DAT, DAT shit, he was cursing about the Yankees."

"You don't think this was all about destroying the Yankees and the stadium?"

"Hey—you ever been to Fenway? You know what those assholes are like. Anyway, the FBI will look into everything and we may never know."

"Are you going to be in any trouble?" I asked.

"I don't think so. Even cops sometimes realize there are things more important than procedures sometimes. I've got some other good news."

"What's that?" I said.

"The DA says they don't plan to charge you in Dunston's death or me in Tyrone's."

"Holy shit, I forgot about that. What's it say when you forgot that you killed a man?"

"That the piece-of-shit that you killed wasn't worth giving any thought," Kelley said.

I didn't say anything and the room got quiet. Kelley and I were a lot alike and a lot different. I killed a man tonight, and I wasn't convinced that killing a man like Dunston was wrong, but I also wasn't convinced that killing him was my job.

"What was the deal with those Homeland Security guys? Are they regular FBI?" I asked.

"Way I understand it—yes and no. I know they don't have many rules to follow," Kelley said.

"Yeah, that's for sure. I gotta tell you the blond guy froze when I went after Singh. I attacked his partner and he couldn't shoot."

"Says a lot about security, doesn't it?"

The nurse came in and told me that my vitals were good, that they thought I was dehydrated and my blood count or something was approaching normal. They also told Kelley he'd have to leave and that the dog wasn't allowed. The nurse moved on to the next room.

"No dogs? That seals it. I'm out of here. Give me a ride to

AJ's," I said.

"I know better than to say 'no' to you," Kelley said.

The nurses at the desk threw a bit of a fit and they made me sign a bunch of forms, but they knew they couldn't keep me. I was moving a bit slow and so was Al, but we were moving and we were moving right out of the hospital door.

We pulled in front of AJ's at ten of four, which meant we supposedly had ten minutes to drink. I wasn't worried. Kelley went in first, followed by Al and myself. The Foursome were all still there and they were in rare form.

"Ladies and gentlemen, the superhero trio—the Mick, the Mick-Polack, and the world's bravest canine!" Rocco announced. He then led the Foursome in a standing, albeit wobbly, ovation.

"AJ, set them up on me," TC shouted, raising his B&B to our presence.

"Nah, TC, this one's on me," AJ said.

"Holy shit—this must be an occasion," Jerry Number One said. "AJ's buying!"

"Fuck you." AJ poured shots of Jameson for everyone. "Here's to 'em. I'm proud to be your friend," AJ toasted.

They all yelled "hear, hear" and threw the shots back. Unfortunately, TC tipped over with the motion of throwing the shot down. He was down on all fours when Al ran over and licked him on the lips.

"Ahhh..." TC screamed. "I'm goin' to get AIDS."

Rocco helped TC to his feet and steadied him on his barstool.

"That dog's a hero. Don't be saying anything bad about him," Jerry Number Two said.

"That's right," Rocco said. "Let me buy that bastard a cheeseburger."

It went on like that for a few hours. By six in the morning, everyone was filing out, shading their eyes from the sun's light. Kelley drove me to the Moody Blue and made sure Al and I were going to be all right. I figured I'd sleep for a week.

"You guys goin' to be okay?" Kelley asked at the door.

"Yeah, until Monday."

"What happens on Monday?"

"I just remembered, I get fired. Monday is a month since my extra-special written warning, and they're charging me with looking at porn on my computer."

"Aw man, Duff. You and Rudy losing your jobs, and on the same day, no less."

"What are you talking about? Did Rudy hear something?"

"I'm sorry, Duff. I thought you knew. According to Rocco, he was in AJ's yesterday afternoon, bombed out of his mind, saying he had to go in front of the administrator and the board on Monday."

"Shit, that ain't right."

"Duff, I heard it was awful. Rudy was carrying on, they had to get him a cab and help him in it. He was crying so hard, it was pitiful."

"We're going to have to do something," I said.

"Duff, you've done enough saving for a while. You need to rest and let some things go."

"Not this, Kel. Not Rudy."

I said good night to Kelley and Al and I got into bed. I was exhausted and everything hurt. Tomorrow was Sunday and I had a day to help Rudy out before I got my ass fired on Monday.

39

I got up around noon and, walking through the Blue, I found new parts of my body that ached. Al opened his eyes just enough to see me and then went right back to sleep. I looked at the paper and the only thing that made it from last night was an arrest of a Lawrence Espidera for promoting prostitution and for kidnapping, and several arrests of the women for soliciting. There was also a mention of the parties resisting arrest and assaulting an officer. Seemed to me that they were missing a whole bunch of minor details, like the deployment of a radioactive bomb in the Bronx and the local connections to an international terrorist organization by a prominent area oncologist. Thank God, I didn't make the news.

I poured myself some coffee and flipped on the TV. I forgot about Duffy's cable world of "All Lifetime, All the Time," but I didn't have the energy or motivation to get up and do anything about it.

It was early afternoon on Sunday, which meant there wasn't a whole hell of a lot of programming on Lifetime except for infomercials. The one on in front of me was from Crawford Medical Center,

and it was advertising their new state-of-the-art Incontinence Treatment Center. I didn't really want to form any visuals about the state of the art of incontinence care, so, despite my fatigue and pain, I started to get up to change the channel. No amount of pain would be worse than a half hour of incontinence treatment.

I got up and was at the TV when the hospital administrator, Dr. Broseph, came on. He was at his desk with his white lab coat on, talking about the pain and suffering that comes with incontinence. This was the asshole that was getting Rudy fired, and I felt my hand ball up in a fist as I listened to his saccharin-laced speech about person-centered patient care.

"At Crawford, our mission is caring for the body and the spirit," Broseph said. "It's what makes the difference at Crawford. We care about you."

I looked at his white coat and thought about the expression, "body and the spirit."

I had an idea.

I threw on some clothes, took half a dozen Advil, woke up Al, and headed to AJ's. The NFL season had started, and the Foursome would be there—they'd be hungover and miserable—but they'd be there.

I got there at halftime of the first game, which was good because I had a chance of getting some of their attention. They kept quiet during the game, but at the half they usually got right back into it.

"It fucks up the entire water supply for weeks," Rocco said. He was clearly angry that Jerry Number One seemed to be doubting him. "Everyone is flushing at the same time during the commercials and the water pressure gets dangerously low."

"I've taken a shit during a commercial on Super Bowl Sunday and everything went down okay," Jerry Number Two said.

"It's not that it won't go down—" Rocco didn't have time to finish before TC interrupted.

"You know, in South America the water swirls down the toilet the opposite way," TC said.

"The opposite of what?" Jerry Number One said.

I decided it was as good a time as any to break in.

"Uh, fellas, I need some help," I said. The Foursome stopped and looked at me.

"Rudy's going to lose his job tomorrow unless we do something," I said.

"Look, Duff, I like Rudy as much as the next guy, but what can we do to save a doctor from the hospital bigwig that has it in for him?" Rocco asked.

I had the Foursome huddle up and let them in on my plan. To a man they were all in. Rocco went home to get his hunting fatigues, portable generator, and high intensity lamp. TC went to get his boom box and the Boston Pops Fourth of July CD. Jerry Number One went to his son-in-law's to borrow the deejay's PA system, and Jerry Number Two went to get some of his high-end computer stuff. We were to meet back at AJ's at 7:30 for a pre-game meal, actually several pre-game shots, with a plan of attack for 8:45.

I had a few phone calls to make and went back to the Blue to make them. The first was to Rudy, and I got his machine. I kept shouting into the receiver for him to pick up, but he was either out or too depressed to deal with me. I tried one last time, and after yelling "hey, pick up!" a few times, I just said, "Rudy, don't worry about your job. We're about to take care of things." And I hung up.

The next call was to set things up. I made the call to my contact discreetly and agreed on a code phrase to let everyone know when to get things started. I wasn't sure if this was going to work, but it was going to be fun trying. It was the least I could do for Rudy.

I got to AJ's half an hour early and with the pain I was in, I had doctor AJ write me a prescription for a couple of Jim Beams. Within minutes, the Foursome were in and they were ready to go to work. We all got into the Eldorado, and although Rocco wasn't pleased to have Al step on his balls, he was happy when Al decided to sit on TC's lap.

We parked a half-mile away from where things were going to happen because I didn't want the headlights to alert anyone ahead of time or scare anyone away. Rocco was in charge of reconnaissance and he went on ahead, walking the first quarter-mile and then crawling commando-style on his belly to get in position just ten feet from the spot. Through the darkness, I could see him set up the generator and have the lights in position.

TC gave me the thumbs-up with the boom box cued to the right track. Jerry Number One saluted me, letting me know the PA was ready and Jerry Number Two, at my right flank, said the battery was charged and everything was a go.

We waited in silence as I kept my eyes on my watch and counted down the time. The only sound in the pitch-black park was the tapping of Al's tail on the grass.

We listened and waited. There was a stirring and a rustle in the bushes. I looked at my watch, and it was right on schedule. The Foursome were quiet and I could feel the intensity of the anticipation. Then the call came, albeit in a slightly lisped voice.

"The doctor is in!" Froggy yelled.

Rocco hit the switch and flooded the bushes with light. TC hit the boom box and John Williams led the most resounding version of "The Stars and Stripes Forever" that you ever wanted to hear. Jerry Number Two quietly but officially said, "Rolling tape."

Right on cue, Jerry Number One began announcing.

"Ladies and gentleman, I present to you the administrator of Crawford Medical Center, the one, the only...Doctor Albert Broseph...uh, and his friend Froggy! Hey, Doc, it really sucks to be you tonight!"

There in the bushes, on his knees, doing unmentionables to a very happy Froggy, was Rudy's arch nemesis. He was frozen and looked like he was going to choke, but not for the reasons you might think. I guess after tonight, no one could ever accuse him of not giving person-centered service to the Medicaid population. Jerry handed me the mic.

"Hey, Doc, you may be wondering what we're all doing here tonight." TC turned down the music slightly, and Jerry Number

Two moved in for a close-up of the administrator on his knees in front of a naked-from-the-waist-down Frogman. "It's very simple. We're friends of Doctor Rudy and we don't want to see him lose his job. We have all of tonight's activities on DVD and would be happy to upload all of it to the Crawford Medical Center website. Of course, we won't do that as long as Rudy has his job. Understand?" I said.

Broseph nodded.

"Are you sure?"

"Yes!" Broseph yelled through his tears. He looked more angry than shocked.

"Good, now get the fuck out of here!"

Broseph hurried to his feet, already running in the direction of the parking lot before he got his knickers all the way up and his shirt tucked in. As he ran off into the horizon, a spontaneous cheer went up from the Foursome with Al adding a baritone harmony.

"Nice work, gentlemen," I yelled in my best George C. Scott as General George Patton voice. "Tonight, I'm buying!" I looked over to the Frogster and we exchanged the thumbs-up signal.

Cheers went up even louder. I had Rocco call Kelley on the cell and told him to do whatever he had to do to get Rudy to AJ's. We exchanged handshakes and slaps on the backs and poured into the Eldorado for our victory ride back to our headquarters. It was a hell of a fun ride.

We all piled out, AJ poured five shots, and we toasted each other on a night well done. We were repeating the shot and carrying on with tonight's war stories when Kelley walked in with Rudy behind him. It got really quiet as everyone looked at Rudy. His head was down, he hadn't shaved in a couple of days, and he even looked like he had lost weight.

"Duffy, what the fuck are you up to? I'm in no mood for your bullshit tonight," Rudy said.

"Is that any way to talk to the man who just saved your

career?" AJ said from behind the bar.

"What? My career? My career is fucked as of tomorrow."

A giggle came up from the Foursome and they could barely contain themselves.

"Aw shit, Jerry, let's stop the suspense. Show Rudy how we spent our night," I said.

Rudy was confused and sort of stumbled over to Jerry Number Two, who hit a button on the back of his space-age gadget. Rudy reluctantly watched the two-by-two screen like a guy who was being forced to hear a joke. Then he got a puzzled look on his face.

"What the?...that's Broseph...sonofabitch..." Rudy looked up at me. "You...holy shit." Rudy was stammering.

"Shhh, Rudy. Listen to Duffy's speech," Rocco said.

Rudy looked at the recording in disbelief. His eyes welled and he started to chuckle, at first almost silently and then louder. Before long he was bent over with his hands on his knees, laughing so hard I thought he would hurt himself.

"You crazy Irish-Polack bastard. C'mere," Rudy said.

He gave me a bear hug that hurt my ribs and sent shivers of pain through my body. Rudy had tears on his cheeks and was laughing as he hugged every single one of the Foursome. Then he picked up Al and pirouetted around with him until the hound howled.

"You fuckin' guys..." Rudy said, shaking his head.

"I'm guessin' you got ol' Broseph by the balls for as long as you want him," TC said.

"That asshole blows anyways," Jerry Number One said.

"Poor guy has had a frog in his throat for a long time," Jerry Number Two added.

"Yeah, a long time ago, Froggy told me about some big-deal doc giving as much as getting in the park. He said something about him being on TV and talking about 'body and spirit,'" I said. "It wasn't hard to get the Frogster on board."

"Looked pretty hard to me," Rocco said.

Rudy looked me in the eyes and I saw him start to well up again. I raised my Schlitz to him and he toasted me back with his cognac. Mission accomplished.

We drank for a few hours and laughed until it hurt. It was a Sunday night, so the guys were starting to look at their watches and think about the workweek. Kelley came over with his Coors Light to say good night.

"There's no doubt about it, man—you're nuts," he said, cracking a smile. "Shouldn't a hard-working social worker type like you be heading home to meditate and get ready for a Monday in the business of saving lives?"

"Geez, Kel, I almost forgot. Tomorrow I'm getting fired. It's the sixteenth."

"I'm sorry, Duff, I forgot," Kelley said.

"After this weekend, Kel, I'm not sure I care."

Kel slapped me on the back and I headed out to the Eldorado with Al at my side. I thought about getting fired, and I had lied to Kelley. I did care, not because I was worried about Claudia or getting in trouble, but because sometimes, though I don't like to admit it even to myself, I like helping people no one else wants to help.

40

On Monday morning I dragged myself out of bed and got ready to go get fired. I thought about just not showing up and not giving the Michelin Woman the pleasure of doing it, but I didn't want to be a coward. I'd live without the job, though it might not be real easy to get another one in human services after getting canned here.

Before I headed to the clinic, I took a ride past McDonough High. It was just after eight and the kids were gathered outside delaying going into school until the last possible minute. I let the Eldorado idle and listened as Elvis sang "If I Can Dream." I spotted the girls I had met a week or so ago on my visit and they were snapping gum and all talking at once. I looked closer and saw Shony in the circle with the other girls. She was part of the circle, but she was quiet and not taking part in all the gabbing.

I tooted my horn and all the girls looked up, stopping their activity just for an instant before going back into it. Shony strained to see who I was, and when she recognized me, she smiled and came to my window.

"Mr. Duffy, what are you doing here?" she said.

"Just driving by," I said.

"Thank you for all you did for me." Shony looked down.

"Shony, do me a favor?"

"Sure, Mr. Duffy."

"When you think of your stepmom, please remember how

much she loved you. And do your best to remember that's what counts."

A tear ran down Shony's face, and she nodded without saying anything.

"Thanks, Shony, I got to go," I said.

Before I could get the car in gear, Shony dropped her books and hugged me awkwardly around the neck and head and kissed me. Just as quickly, she picked up her books, turned away, and ran into school.

Elvis was finishing up the song. He was giving it all he had and was letting me know that as long as I'm standing, as long as I am alive, I can continue to dream.

He was right, of course.

Elvis was always right.

I couldn't put it off any longer; it was time to face Claudia and get it over with. I tried to slip into the office inconspicuously, but there's something about having your face black and blue and having four sets of stitches across your mug that seems to draw people's attention.

Monique winced when she saw me.

"You okay?"

"I think so," I said. "There's a note on my desk from Claudia to be in her office at nine thirty and to bring my keys. I'm guessing I'm not getting a promotion."

"Duff, you'll always be all right by me," Monique said and lightly touched my shoulder.

I went out to see Trina. She couldn't look at me and welled up. It was awkward for a second, so I left her alone. I didn't want to make the situation worse.

At exactly nine thirty I went in to see Claudia for my execution. I could tell she was just thrilled, having outlasted me and won our little conflict. Today's process was her reward. She was going to draw this out and make it as painful as possible.

"Please, sit down, Duffy," she said.

She closed the door and returned to her seat behind her desk.

"One of the hardest things I have to do is to tell people that their performance is not measuring up. I feel in your case, I have made my position well known about how you did your job. I also feel that your latest behavior has left me no choice in the matter."

"Oh for Christ's sake, get on with it." I rolled my eyes.

"That's your problem, Duffy, you don't take criticism well. There are several things I need to go over procedurally," she said.

"Gee whiz," I said.

She ignored me and started to read off a prepared statement.

"Four weeks ago you were warned about the inadequate state of your medical records. A thorough audit of those records Friday indicated very little improvement," she paused to clear her throat.

"There have also been incidents of inappropriate use of the clinic's resources. This includes viewing pornographic material on the Internet." She briefly looked up to check my reaction. I did my best to look indifferent.

"There also have been several situations in which your judgment involving over-involvement with the clients has been documented. Despite warnings in all of these incidents, there has been very little improvement in your performance, conduct, or attitude," she paused to look at me.

"Do you understand each of these concerns as they have been stated, Duffy?"

"Yes."

"Therefore, effective immediately, I am officially term—"

Someone was yelling outside the door. There was a disturbance coming from the lobby, and it was getting louder. Claudia buzzed Trina.

She said a few words and quickly hung up and went and opened her office door.

"Where is he? Where is that crazy man?" It was Hymie and he was being uncharacteristically loud. I dreaded facing him and dealing with the shame of letting him down.

"Where is he? He's like some sort of superman, this Duffy!" Hymie was outside Claudia's doorway. He walked right past Claudia, ignoring her greeting.

"You crazy goy bastard!" Hymie yelled with his arms wide. Then he reached up and pinched me hard on the cheek. Behind him, just outside the doorway, was Kelley in full uniform, and next to him was Crawford's mayor, Jerry Jenkins. I hadn't a clue what was going on.

"Mayor, Officer Kelley, come in here," Hymie said.

Claudia was frozen.

"Claudia, c'mon and join us, we got big news today," Hymie said.

Claudia walked like a zombie into her office.

"This guy Duffy, do you have any idea the heroics he pulled this weekend? He's a superhero."

"Well, Mr. Zuckerman, actually—" He didn't let me finish. "Never mind! Mayor, excuse me for talking over you, I'm just so excited!" Hymie said. "Please, Mayor, go ahead."

Mayor Jenkins was a stately, handsomely tan man, and he was dressed in a perfectly tailored midnight-blue suit.

"Duffy, Officer Kelley has brought to our attention what you did over the weekend. You put yourself in harm's way for the sake of one of your clients. You saved countless children from horrific trauma, and it is clear that you are a committed human service worker," Jenkins said.

I still had no idea what was going on.

"Therefore, on behalf of the city and upon the recommendation of Officer Kelley, Mr. Zuckerman, and the city of Crawford, we would like to honor you with a special ceremony this week at city hall. You, Duffy Dombrowski, will be our very first 'Human Service Worker of the Year.'"

"You hear that, son?" Hymie said, shaking my hand. "You made me very proud."

Claudia's jaw hung open and she went pale.

"So, Duffy, you haven't answered us," Mayor Jenkins said.

"Can we honor you with a ceremony at city hall this Friday?"

"Of course, Mr. Mayor, I'd be honored."

"Now, I'll be there and Mr. Zuckerman will be there. We'd like someone else in your life to present you with the award and say a few things about your dedication. Is there someone who comes to mind, Duff?"

"Yes, sir, there is." I smiled from ear to ear.

"Who would that be, Duffy?" the mayor asked.

"I can't think of anyone who I'd like to give me that award more than my boss, Claudia Michelin."

I thought Claudia was going to collapse. Hymie and the mayor looked at Claudia. Through gritted teeth and a face that showed more tension than a bungee cord, Claudia managed the most painful smile I'd ever seen.

"I'd love to," she said.

It was the second best time I ever had in this office.

TOM SCHRECK is the author of Amazon's #1 hard-boiled mystery, THE VEGAS KNOCKOUT. He counts Robert B. Parker, John D. MacDonald, JA Konrath, Reed Farrel Coleman, Ken Bruen and Michael Connelly among his favorite crime fiction authors and his Duffy Dombrowski series has been referred to as "As good or better as the early Spenser." He is a columnist with Westchester Magazine and a frequent contributor to Crimespree Magazine, Referee, and other publications.

On the following pages are a few
more great titles from the
Down & Out Books publishing family.

For a complete list of books and to
sign up for our newsletter,
go to DownAndOutBooks.com.

Holland Bay
Jim Winter

Down & Out Books
November 2021
978-1-64396-237-5

A young gang banger and a disgraced detective find a chance at redemption on opposite sides of the law.

In the city's worst winter storm in years, two related murders put them on a collision course.

Gang member Armand Cole aims to make his mark. Jessica Branson attempts to revive her police career.

It will come to a head on the city's infamous Pier 9.

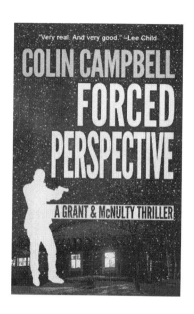

Forced Perspective
A Grant & McNulty Thriller
Colin Campbell

Down & Out Books
December 2021
978-1-64396-241-2

Jim Grant enlists Vince McNulty's help to invite criminals to audition as movie extras. The plan is almost derailed when McNulty and Grant protect a girl from an angry biker but the plan is successful. Mostly.

Except the sting is a dry run for the main person Grant wants to arrest; a crime lord movie buff in Loveland, Colorado. A sting that won't be nearly as successful.

NEW YORK TIMES BESTSELLING AUTHOR

Moonlight Kills
A Dick Moonlight PI Thriller
Vincent Zandri

Down & Out Books
January 2022
978-1-64396-244-3

When Dick Moonlight PI and his professional impersonator sidekick, Fat Elvis, uncover the head of a decapitated, long blond-haired woman under the floorboards of an under-construction luxury home, they come into contact with a husband-and-wife construction team who also fancy themselves Hollywood filmmakers. Only, it turns out that the filmmakers aren't interested in making romcoms, but instead, snuff films.

With Fat Elvis the perfect candidate for a starring role in their new film, Moonlight is hired by the police to go undercover and expose the operation.

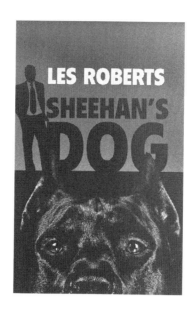

Sheehan's Dog
Les Roberts

Down & Out Books
February 2022
978-1-64396-247-4

Former Irish mafia hitman Brock Sheehan lives quietly on a boat fifty miles from Cleveland. When his long-lost nephew, Linus Callahan, tracks him down and asks him for assistance, he agrees to help. A few days earlier, the nephew got into a bar argument with a multimillion-dollar basketball player just released from prison for running a high-level dog-fighting ring. Then the athlete is murdered, and Linus becomes the Cleveland police department's "person of interest."

Investigating the athlete's former dogfight ring, Brock winds up with a pit bull of his own, which he names Conor. And eventually, with Conor's instincts, he discovers and turns over to the police the real killer of the dog-killer turned sports legend.

Made in the USA
Middletown, DE
27 May 2023

31540223R00179